The Revolution in German Theatre 1900–1933

Michael Patterson

Routledge & Kegan Paul

Boston, London and Henley

First published in 1981
by Routledge & Kegan Paul Ltd
39 Store Street,
London WC1E 7DD,
9 Park Street,
Boston, Mass. 02108, USA and
Broadway House,
Newtown Road,
Henley-on-Thames,
Oxon RG9 1EN

Set in 11/12 Plantin by
Computacomp (UK) Ltd
Fort William, Scotland
and printed in the United States of America by
Vail-Ballou Press, Inc.,
Binghampton, New York

British Library Cataloguing in Publication Data
Patterson, Michael
The revolution in German theatre 1900–1933. –
(Theatre production studies).
1. Theater – Germany – History
I. Title   II. Series
792'.0943   PN2189   80–41730

ISBN 0–7100–0659–4

Contents

Illustrations

Figures

All figures and plates were supplied by the Akademie der Künste in West Berlin, with the exception of Plates 17, 18, 19 and 26, which are taken from *Continental Stagecraft* by Kenneth MacGowan and Robert Edmond Jones, Harcourt, Brace & Company, New York, 1922.

To my mother

Acknowledgments

Grateful acknowledgment is due to the following for permission to use copyright material: Akademie der Künste, West Berlin; Arche Verlag, Zürich; Avon Books, New York; Ernest Benn, London; Bertolt-Brecht-Archive, East Berlin; Bibliographisches Institut, Mannheim; Calder & Boyars, London; Friedenauer Presse, West Berlin; Gehlen Verlag, Bad Homburg; Harcourt, Brace & Co, New York; Henschelverlag, East Berlin; Eyre Methuen, London; Oxford University Press; Rowohlt Verlag, Reinbek bei Hamburg; Rütten & Loening, East Berlin; Secker & Warburg, London; Stanford University Press; Bertolt Brecht, *Schriften zum Theater*, © Suhrkamp Verlag, Frankfurt a.M. 1963.

Every effort has been made to trace the holders of copyright material. Will those whom I have failed to contact please accept my acknowledgment.

I should also like to thank: John Russell Brown for his patience and encouragement; Professor J. M. Ritchie for his support and for pointing out a number of errors in the manuscript; the staff of the Brotherton Library, University of Leeds, for their untiring search for obscure works; Leeds University, whose generous travel grants allowed me to conduct research in Germany; Professor Walther Huder and the staff of the Akademie der Künste in West Berlin for access to the Georg Kaiser, Ernst Toller and Erwin Piscator Archives; the staff of the Bertolt-Brecht-Archive and the Berliner Ensemble Archive, East Berlin; Michael Huxley for information about dance in this period; Phil Young, whose direction of Kaiser's *Gas I* in 1976 taught me an enormous amount about Expressionist theatre; the staff and students of the Workshop Theatre, University of Leeds, and of Bretton Hall College, whose committed exploration of the theatrical possibilities of a whole range of Expressionist texts helped me to new insights; finally, the Shepherd Construction Company, whose building operations in the University of Leeds provided me with a constant reminder of the discomfort with which the Expressionist intellectual responded to modern technology.

All translations, unless otherwise indicated, are my own, although I have used the standard English translation of play-titles even where I regard these as inelegant or inaccurate.

Acknowledgments

Introduction

A good play can only in part be committed to paper.
                                   Goethe: *Preface to Theory of Colour*

When in Max Reinhardt's production of *A Midsummer Night's Dream* in 1905 the lights went up on a slowly revolving woodland scene, the audience witnessed more than the revolutions of a stage set; they were seeing the beginnings of a revolution in theatre itself.

That this revolution should occur in Germany is in part explained by the lack of any strong national dramatic tradition in that country. In the seventeenth century there had been the religious drama of the Baroque period, much of which was originally composed in Latin, and in the early eighteenth century the misguided attempts of Gottsched and his followers to transplant French theatre onto German soil. But it was not until the latter half of the eighteenth century that a theatre that was both native and literary became established in Germany, two centuries later than England's Elizabethan flowering and over a century after France's classical renaissance.

When German drama did finally emerge with Lessing, Goethe, Schiller and Kleist, it created the best poetry in the theatre since Racine and, in works like *Faust*, introduced to the stage a depth of philosophical thought of a kind unparalleled in modern times. What it did not do was discover a new theatrical style. Having rejected the severe and inappropriate constraints of French neo-classicism, the young German theatre willingly embraced its new mentor, Shakespeare – with abandon as in the case of the young Goethe and Storm and Stress playwrights or with more restraint in the older Goethe, Schiller and Kleist. Indeed, the achievement of these later playwrights was to have discovered a synthesis between Shakespeare's historic breadth and the formal discipline of the neo-classical style; but this was a drawing together of former styles rather than the basis for renewal.

With the exception of Büchner, who was to remain unperformed for some seventy years, there were hardly any stylistic developments in nineteenth-century German theatre, its greatest exponents, Grillparzer and Hebbel, continuing to write predominantly historical and mythical five-act tragedies in blank verse (Hebbel's one contemporary social drama in prose, *Maria Magdalene*, looked back to Lessing's bourgeois tragedies rather than forward to anything new).

Renewal finally came from Scandinavia and Russia. Germany, like France and England, drew inspiration from the new realistic theatre, but Germany's leading Naturalist, Gerhart Hauptmann, was a minor talent compared with Ibsen, Chekhov or Shaw.

Then, in the first third of this century, Germany's lack of a strong national dramatic tradition at last stood it in good stead. For it was here, as in Russia, amidst the social, political and cultural turmoil of those years of peace and war and revolution, of disintegrating monarchy and teetering republic and incipient dictatorship, that the theatrical styles that dislodged realism were born. In this plethora of experimentation in the German theatre one can discover, if not the absolute origins, at least a major stage in the development of all the following theatre styles: abstract theatre, the Theatre of Cruelty, absurdist theatre, happenings, satirical cabarets, agitprop theatre, documentary theatre and environmental stagings.

For the first time, Germany had a major contribution to make in terms of theatre style. Whereas the period of German classicism (Goethe and Schiller) excelled in its poetry and thought but had little to offer in terms of staging, the new German theatre hardly distinguished itself in either its writing or its content. The intoxication with language of the Expressionists and the prosaic idiom of the early socialist theatre did not make for great poetry; the ecstatic utterances of the former and the trite exhortations of the latter could hardly be regarded as philosophical thought. Only Brecht, still a long way off the achievements of his later works, showed a capacity for either.

The inadequacies of the written texts help to explain the prevailing ignorance about German theatre of this period. Enid Starkie, writing in 1960 about the influence of France on English literature, asserted that 'the most advanced and stimulating theatre in Europe'[1] between the wars was to be found in Paris.

This ignorance of the achievements of the German theatre of the period is commonplace and easily explained. When the curtain falls after a theatre performance, the text of the play is the only substantial record that remains. For the rest, the style of the performance has to be deduced from various fragments of information, each of which suffers from certain inadequacies:

1 *The playwright's stage-directions*: While these are a good guide to the intentions of the author with regard to the staging of his play, they do not necessarily coincide with the actual execution of the piece. Moreover, a writer may himself be hardly conversant with the theatre practice of the day and so may entrust the realization of his text to the director and designer.

2 *Manifestos and theoretical writings by writers and theatre practitioners*: While these again reveal demands and intentions about the theatre, and are obviously of particular importance in the case of Brecht, they do not necessarily reflect what was actually achieved on stage.

3 *Prompt-books*: These are a valuable source of information regarding the staging of a play, although here moves, light-changes, etc. are usually recorded without any analysis of the reasons why they were done in this way. Regrettably, too, no prompt-books of any major Expressionist productions are extant. The only important source of this kind I have discovered for this period is Piscator's detailed prompt-book for Toller's *Hoppla, wir leben!*, lodged in the Piscator Archive in Berlin.

4 *Set and costume designs*: Once more these express well the intention of the designer, but it is clear that the theatrical realization often resulted in a compromise due to the lack of resources and conservatism of the theatre management. A comparison between designs and photographs of the same production will frequently bear this out.

5 *Photographs*: While these should supposedly offer an authentic record of the visual quality of the staging, their value is severely restricted by the technical limitations of the photography of the period, not least in that they could not record colour. Until 1926 it was not possible to photograph during a performance: all pictures were taken with the actors posed under full lighting (one of the special exhibits at the Magdeburg Theatre Exhibition of 1927 was 'Photographs taken during performance' with the new Ermanox camera).[2] Under these conditions it is not surprising that photographs were taken of scenes that did not even exist in the play: an example is Plate 20, where three actors are shown who never appear together in the action.

6 *Sketches made during performance*: Although a rapid and subjective impression by one artist, these provide probably the most reliable record of the visual impact of a production. Compared with Strohbach's impressionistic design for a scene in Toller's *Masse Mensch* (Plate 24) and the banal photograph of the same scene (Plate 25), Robert Edmond Jones's excellent sketch (Plate 26) would seem to capture best the quality of the original.

7 *Programmes*: While recording the names of the performers and resolving questions about the doubling of roles, these are usually of little value.

8 *Contemporary reviews*: These are obviously a major source of information. They suffer, however, from the journalistic pressure of providing a response to a new theatrical event: the work itself will usually be discussed in some detail, the reaction of the audience will be

recorded, and usually little space remains for any analysis of the theatrical style of the performance. Moreover, the contemporary reviewer may lack perspective: a set design may appear startlingly innovative when in fact, in the light of later developments, it may be more properly regarded as a minor modification to an existing style.

9 *Critical works*: Here the critic possesses the perspective lacked by the journalistic reviewer, and works like Felix Emmel's *Das ekstatische Theater* (1924) and Bernhard Diebold's *Anarchie im Drama* (1921) provide invaluable insights into the theatre of the period. However, the tendency in critical works is to remain on the sure ground of textual criticism, and theatrical style is therefore seldom discussed.

10 *Personal reminiscences*: Occasionally these will also provide useful records of early productions, but all too often the analytical is replaced by the anecdotal.

11 *Films*: There are no extant recordings on film of any stage productions of this period, but the cinematic treatment of a play text, as in Karl Heinz Martin's 1920 film of Kaiser's *Von morgens bis mitternachts* or G. W. Pabst's 1931 film version of Brecht's *Die Dreigroschenoper* may at least give an impression of the acting style of the period.

In addition to the fragmentary and inconclusive nature of these sources there are further reasons why the theatre practice of this period in Germany is so neglected. The names of the major theatre innovators of the twentieth century that spring to mind, Stanislavsky, Appia, Craig, Meyerhold, Piscator, Brecht, Artaud, Grotowski, Brook, are significantly those who have set down their ideas about theatre on paper and have left a substantial body of writing to posterity. But, uncharacteristically for the Germans, until Piscator and Brecht, most of this brilliant generation of directors, designers and actors were too involved in the process of experimentation to step back and theorize about their work. After a lifetime in the theatre Max Reinhardt left behind little more than an unfinished, unpublished autobiography and some interviews and prompt-books, and Leopold Jessner's scattered comments on the theatre would hardly fill a thin pamphlet.

Another reason is that the caesura of Nazi barbarism halted the normal spread of influence and ideas from the German theatre. By the time the Nazi regime had collapsed, the exciting theatrical developments of the first third of this century had passed into history.

Finally, there is the problem of language. While there was strong cross-fertilization between England and France, the hitherto supreme theatre nations of Europe, the German language erected a barrier around German theatre. Schönberg in music, and the artists of Der blaue Reiter and Die Brücke and later of the Bauhaus, could easily exert an international influence. But with rare exceptions, like Auden and Isherwood, the English, and to a lesser degree the French, remained unaware of the revolution taking place in the German theatre.

Nevertheless, something filtered through. O'Neill in America (*The Great God Brown*) and O'Casey in Ireland (*The Silver Tassie*) began to find the Expressionist path out of debilitating realism; and if T. S. Eliot had developed his Expressionistic style seen in *Sweeney Agonistes*, and James Joyce had exploited the theatrical possibilities of the Night-Town sequence in *Ulysses*, they might have discovered a more vital form of theatre than that represented in *The Cocktail Party* or *Exiles*.

This present study is an attempt to rescue the German theatre of the first third of this century from its undeserved neglect. It has long been acknowledged that the strength of this theatre lay in its bold stylistic experimentation rather than in its writing. In his book on German Expressionist drama, J. M. Ritchie re-asserts Hans Schwerte's view that 'Expressionist drama was at its best when at its most theatrical and at its least literary',[3] and yet no attempt, in German or English, has hitherto been made to provide a comprehensive account of its theatrical strengths.[4]

Moreover, the Expressionist revolution in the theatre was not only of significance in itself, it was the prerequisite for the political theatre that was to supersede it. And while excellent accounts of Piscator's and Brecht's theatre have appeared in English, notably by Christopher Innes and John Willett, it is important to see the political theatre of the 1920s in the context of the Expressionist legacy. This book will attempt to show where the theatrical strengths of Expressionism lay and how Piscator and Brecht transformed them to their own ends.

Note on Tables 2–5 (pp. 50, 56, 116, 154)

In order to provide a point of reference for the more discursive arguments in the body of the text, I have included four tables which juxtapose different types of theatre: Naturalism/Expressionism; Abstractionism/Primitivism; Expressionist theatre/Political theatre of the 1920s; Piscator's theatre/ Brecht's theatre. Such tables, while being in the best tradition of German dialectics, in their very simplicity have a tendency to over-simplify. The reader is asked to treat them merely as a clear, and, one hopes, stimulating complement to the more specific ideas discussed in the text.

Part One

The Expressionist revolution in the German theatre

The uniformity and stupidity of mankind are so outrageous that only through outrages can they be dealt with. Let the new drama be outrageous.

Ivan Goll: 'The super-drama'

1 · **Origins of the revolution**

Political and social background

> With the help of your Emperor and of Richard Wagner you have made of the 'German virtues' an operatic display which no one in the world took seriously but yourselves. And behind this pretty humbug of operatic splendour you allowed your dark instincts, your servility and your swagger to proliferate.
>
> Hermann Hesse (1919)

One evening in the spring of 1914 a young writer 'with lean face and burning eyes'[1] rose to his feet in Kurt Hiller's literary cabaret Das Gnu to give a reading of his first play, *Der Sohn* (*The Son*). Listening to this remarkable new piece by the twenty-three-year-old Walter Hasenclever, the audience could hardly have imagined that the revolution it foretold would be achieved within five years. The play describes the grotesque situation of a twenty-year-old youth who is kept prisoner by his whip-wielding father for failing to pass his school examinations. Eventually the Son rebels, and pulls a revolver on his father. The father drops dead from a heart-attack, and the Son steps over his father's corpse into freedom.

Like the Son, Hasenclever's generation felt itself imprisoned by the bourgeois society of Wilhelminian Germany; and four and a half years later the Father of the German People, Kaiser Wilhelm II, abdicated and fled into exile without a shot being fired at him. It was, to say the least, an unpredictable development. In the spring of 1914 the German Empire seemed to be built on rock-firm foundations. The Second Empire had been in existence for over forty years, still proud of the glorious victory over the French which had brought it into being. The nationalists' dream of creating a united German nation (admittedly with the exclusion of Austria) had at last been realized, and the Reich now commanded almost universal allegiance. True, the liberal middle classes were critical of the authoritarian structure of the state, the socialists objected to its exploitative capitalism, and the Catholic

9

Church was still nursing its wounds from Bismarck's 'Kulturkampf'. But the basis of the Imperial State remained virtually unchallenged. Even the Social Democratic Party (SPD), which was theoretically committed to the revolutionary ideology of Marx, had in practice become distinctly revisionist, allowing a gradualist policy of reform to weaken the will of the proletariat, a development later to be evidenced by the Party's wholehearted support for the war. Thus the German bourgeois could sleep sound in his bed at night, secure in the knowledge that his Emperor was loved and respected and that, if the call came, even the grumbling workers would rise up in his defence.

Germany's standing in the world seemed also assured. A century earlier it had been a jigsaw of 360 states and principalities, each with its own currency, its own system of weights and measures, and its own laws. Now in 1914 united Germany was a world power with its own colonies and a colossal navy second only to Britain's. In sixty-five years the population had doubled: from 35 million in 1849 to 70 million in 1914. In response to rapid industrialization most of this increase had been in the cities, whose population had risen from 10 million to 40 million, with the capital Berlin expanding from 400,000 to 2 million inhabitants.

The extraordinary growth in the industrial sector had increased the productive capacity of Germany eightfold in the first forty years of the Empire. By comparison, Britain's capacity had merely doubled during the same period and France's had trebled. Only the USA could boast a faster growth-rate. Germany's steel industry was the most powerful in Europe, and its chemical and electrical industries dominated the world markets; for example, 85 per cent of the world's requirements of synthetic dyes were supplied by German concerns.

Not only was this industrialization extremely rapid, but it was also highly centralized. The much more leisurely expansion of the British economy had produced 50,000 joint-stock companies by 1910, whereas German capital was concentrated in just 5,000. Within a single generation the Germans had seen the medieval one-man workshops and travelling journeymen eclipsed by huge concerns like Krupp's of Essen (70,000 employees) and AEG of Berlin (30,000 employees). To sustain their power, the industrial magnates formed 'cartels' or price-fixing agreements within an industry, often by cynical recourse to an appeal to 'Gemeinschaft' (community) instead of 'Gesellschaft' (society), or, to put it more bluntly, to co-operative capitalism in place of competitive capitalism.

Assured of internal security and ever-increasing prosperity, Germany now sought the missing components in its bid to become a world power: foreign markets for its products, and influence in international affairs. It seemed unfair: a nation of such economic and cultural wealth was excluded from the great movements of history and was being treated like some parvenu shut out from an aristocratic club reserved for Britain, France and Russia. It seemed unfair, and Germany was going to make a fuss; it demanded 'a place in the sun'. It was not that Germany was any more expansionist than the other European Great Powers; it was just that it was more aggressively so. It was a newcomer to the imperialist scene and so had been late in the grabbing of colonies; it had the geographical misfortune to be squeezed between France and Russia; its chief ally, Austria-Hungary, was crumbling from inner instability; and the potentially moderating influence of the liberal middle classes was confined to a virtually impotent Reichstag. Moreover, aggression towards foreign powers helped to cement unity at home, a case of 'exporting the social question', as one politician cynically observed.

But the more vociferously Germany asserted its strength, as in the two Moroccan crises of 1905 and 1911, the more it weakened its own position. By 1914 it had isolated itself completely, its displays of aggression having hastened the alliance of the other three great powers. Committed to an ever-expanding armaments programme, aggrieved by the unwillingness of the other imperialist powers to let it join in the expansionist game, convinced of its mission to bring civilization to the Slavic peoples to the East, Germany decided that war was inevitable. But it would not be Germany's fault; Germany had sought to promote its imperialist ambitions without open conflict; if war came, it would be because the other imperialist aggressors wished it. It would, in fact, be a defensive war which all right-minded Germans would support. So in 1911, when August Bebel, the ageing Social Democrat leader, prophesied to the Reichstag the mass destruction of war, most of his listeners jeered with derision:[2]

> Then there will be general mobilization in Europe and sixteen to eighteen million men, the flower of the manhood of different countries, will march against each other, armed with the finest weapons of destruction. How will it end? After this war there will be mass bankruptcy, mass poverty, mass unemployment, the great famine. ... (Disagreement from the right.) You don't believe me? (Shout from the right: Things get better after every war!)

While the stability of the Empire and its economic and military power made it easy to dismiss prophets of doom like Bebel, there were admittedly unfortunate incidents which only slightly tarnished the self-image of an otherwise healthy society. There was, for instance, the regrettable fact that so many young people opted out of this society by taking their own lives. Suicide for a time assumed, if not epidemic, at least alarming proportions: in Prussia alone 110 schoolboys committed suicide between 1883 and 1889 in response to the kind of conditions described in Wedekind's *Frühlings Erwachen* (*Spring Awakening*, 1891). Then there was the Zabern incident. In this small Alsatian town in 1913 the local military commander arbitrarily arrested twenty-eight civilians. Almost the whole of Germany united in its condemnation of the action, and the Reichstag passed by 293 votes to 54 a vote of no confidence in the Chancellor Bethmann for defending the conduct of the military. But Bethmann remained in office and the commander was acquitted at his court-martial. It was clear that civil government was powerless before the military, and the capital levy for army expenditure continued to increase.

But it did not do for the bourgeois to be too disturbed by such things. Surely the Jugendbewegung (Youth Movement), which had been founded in 1897, would give healthy ideals to the young and preserve them from the few morbid and perverse characters like that Moritz Stiefel in Wedekind's play. And even if the military were sometimes a little high-handed, well, a strong army was naturally indispensable to a strong state.

If the sleep of the bourgeois was, then, undisturbed, how did the young intellectual like Hasenclever respond to the world about him? In a word, he was alienated. Socially, he felt he did not belong to any particular class. For although his background was normally middle-class, he rejected its materialism and complacency, and yet his basic elitism, the value he placed on intellectual and aesthetic achievement, allowed him no more than a sentimental and unreal relationship with the proletariat.

Politically, too, he was homeless. As Roy Pascal points out:[3]

The theme of the famous publicist Werner Sombart's articles in the pre-war decade is that the intellectual, faced by a choice between conservative conformism and impotent opposition, can reasonably only decide to have nothing to do with politics.

If there was any attempt at involvement in politics, the resultant ideology was predictably high-flown and vague. Thus in 1911, when Franz Pfemfert founded his periodical *Die Aktion*, significantly subtitled *Wochenschrift für Politik, Literatur und Kunst* (*Weekly Journal for Politics, Literature and Art* – in that order), he justifiably castigated the SPD for its revisionist compromises with the state, but his paper hardly proposed alternative policies of any substance. Characteristic of the ill-defined political attitude of the intellectual who was to march under the banner of Expressionism, is the anarchic utterance by Erich Mühsam in the first issue of the periodical *Revolution* (1913):[4]

All Revolution is active, unique, sudden and uproots its causes. ...

Some forms of Revolution: tyrannicide, deposition of a ruler, establishment of a religion, smashing ancient tablets (in convention and art), creating a work of art, the sexual act.

Some synonyms for Revolution: God, Life, Passion, Delirium, Chaos.

Let us be chaotic!

The alienation of the creative intellectual was not, of course, confined to Germany. It is significant that the function of the playwright in the theatre of the past was to celebrate the society in which he lived. There were naturally, at least from Aristophanes onwards, satirical attacks on aspects of contemporary society, but these tended to reinforce traditional social norms rather than to challenge them. Yet since the advent of Naturalism it had become an almost unquestioned assumption in the western world that the stage would be used as a platform from which to launch criticism or even abuse at the society which supports both the theatre and its playwrights. Indeed, modern plays which lack any critical stance towards social conditions will now be condemned by a majority of intellectuals.

The explanation of this radical change in the theatre's conception of its own function must lie again in the sense of alienation experienced by those who work in it and write for it. With the decline of aristocratic patronage the artist discovered himself more and more at the mercy of market forces. While the artist of former times knew what would please his *polis*, his monarch, his church or his patron, the modern artist was selling his wares to an almost unknown customer, a formless middle-class mass, whose tastes, if one could grace them with that word, seemed to favour uncomplicated entertainment spiced with reassuring sentimentality. The artist faced a dilemma: he could either respond to the demands of the public and 'go commercial', or he could 'preserve his integrity' and work for the only person whose judgment he trusted totally — himself — in the hope that a like-minded minority would provide sufficient financial support and critical encouragement to permit him to survive. This minority, sharing the same sense of alienation as the artist, rallied to his support. Priding themselves on the 'higher values' instilled in them by their education and their own sensitivity, they could compensate for being economically at a disadvantage and socially uprooted by feeling superior to the bourgeoisie and joining with the artist in shocking and attacking them.

This analysis, simplified as it may be, is true for all western societies over the last hundred years. But in Germany the sense of alienation was even more acute. Because for centuries Germany had had no cultural capital like London or Paris, the German writer was isolated in his corner of the country and was hard put to find aristocratic patronage. (This perhaps explains the pre-eminence of Germany in that more accessible art, music.) On the other hand, there was no established cultural audience to allow works of art to be marketable commodities. Thus, while Walter Scott could not only live off his writing but become decidedly rich on it, Lessing had to work as a librarian, Goethe as a civil servant and Schiller as a professor of history.

The result was that the artist *qua* artist felt himself rejected by his society, a feeling embodied in Goethe's drama *Torquato Tasso* (1789), a classic study in the alienation of the artist. So the German writer turned inwards, away from society to the products of his own mind. As Michael Hamburger observes of German classicism: 'to a degree incomprehensible to non-Germans, culture and society tended to be regarded as separate, if not as mutually hostile, domains'.[5] And in the transcendent philosophy of Romanticism, which originated in Germany, we see alienation revealed in the yearning to go beyond this world in search of a higher reality, a search which was to be a major characteristic of Expressionism.

The sense of alienation of the young German intellectual in 1914 was therefore extreme. While the alienated artists in England and France could remain relatively playful, whether they called themselves Aesthetes or Bohemians, whether they walked round with green carnations in their buttonholes or with lobsters on the end of a string, their German counterparts were forced to take things more seriously. For them the glorious Empire of Kaiser Wilhelm was a 'swamp' and 'a heap of filth' (Kornfeld).

So it was small wonder that the war, when it came, was enthusiastically welcomed, not only by the conservative bourgeoisie in whose interests it was being fought, not only by the SPD who allowed themselves to believe that it was a necessary defensive war, but also by the alienated intellectuals who imagined that the mighty upheavals of war and its heroic idealism would usher in a new civilization. This was to be the great 'Kehraus', the sweeping clean of the materialism and complacency that had stifled the spirit of man. In the first year of the war one and a half million war poems were published, concluding with lines like 'Death or victory!' (Schickele) and 'We gladly bleed for the fatherland' (Dehmel), and even the sensitive and gentle Rilke was moved to say of the war: 'It was a purification – a liberation!'

Soon, however, the initial ecstasy evaporated in the face of reality. Letters from the front, then the wounded and the dead, gradually revealed to a generation for whom war had seemed a romantic affair exalting individual human courage that this war was an undignified exercise in maiming and slaughter. Of the 33,000 German officers on active service, more than half were killed in the first few months of hostilities. By the beginning of November 1914 five of Germany's leading poets and artists had already died on the battlefield. The following years were to see the deaths of Stramm, Franz Marc and Sorge, and the wounding or nervous collapse of Kokoschka, Kirchner, Beckmann, George Grosz and Toller.

Such sacrifices might have been bearable if the initial victorious advance of the German army through Belgium and France had continued. Instead, the war settled into the muddy nightmare of trench warfare with the occasional suicidal attempt to gain a few hundred metres of ground.

With growing awareness of the inhumanity and senselessness of the war, the Expressionist writers turned vehemently against it. Hasenclever, for one, declared himself a pacifist (cf. his version of *Antigone*), gaining a discharge from the army by simulating mental derangement, and encouraged Schickele to export his periodical *Die weissen Blätter* to Zurich, where it could conduct its opposition to the war free from German censorship.

This disillusionment which had begun amongst the intellectuals a few months after the outbreak of the war very gradually reached other sections of the German community. By the beginning of 1917 Kaiser and Reichstag

Table 1 *The cost of the First World War*

Nation	Mobilized	Killed	Wounded
Germany	13,250,000	1,885,291	4,248,158
Austro-Hungary	9,000,000	1,500,000	2,000,000
Russia	19,000,000	2,500,000	6,000,000
British Empire	9,496,370	946,023	2,121,906
France	8,194,500	1,358,872	2,560,000
Italy	5,615,000	496,921	949,576
United States	3,899,696	56,618	245,994
Others	5,500,000	1,600,000	1,200,000
Approx. totals	75,000,000	10,000,000	20,000,000

In 1924 there were 663,726 war-wounded in Germany. Of these 2,734 were blind, 4,990 mentally deranged, 44,109 without one leg, 20,640 without one arm, 1,250 without both legs, 131 without both arms.

In 1926 the state in Germany gave war pensions to 1,514,150 individuals: 370,981 widows, 917,890 orphans, 225,279 parents of war victims.

alike were powerless to control the course of the war, the military leaders Hindenburg and Ludendorff having achieved total command after pushing through their foolhardy decision to employ unrestricted submarine warfare against Allied shipping. The winters of 1916–17 and 1917–18 were bad ones with shortages amongst the civilian population verging on famine. The great Spring Offensive of 1918, which was Ludendorff's last desperate attempt to break the deadlock of the trench warfare, failed horribly. Owing to his deception the German public had no idea of this failure and continued to imagine that they were on the verge of total victory. From this arose the 'Dolchstosslegende', the fiction that the cowardly liberal politicians at home had stabbed the almost victorious army in the back, a fiction to be employed against the Weimar Republic and to pave the way for militaristic revival and the Nazi takeover.

Meanwhile at home conditions were worsening. The civilian population was starving. At a cabinet meeting of 17 October 1918, when Ludendorff insisted that it was the politicians' role to raise the nation's morale, the Social Democrat Scheidemann pointed out: 'The emergency is so pressing that one is confronted by a complete mystery when one wonders what keeps the poorer parts of Berlin alive. So long as we cannot solve this mystery, we cannot hope to boost morale.'[6] By the end of October 1918 the German populace was now simply awaiting the abdication of the Kaiser, one of the conditions President Wilson had insisted on before peace negotiations could commence.

Already in January 1918 there had been a spate of strikes by German industrial workers, but their effect was limited. Now on 29 October, as the admirals planned to steam the German navy into the North Sea as a last mad gesture of aggression, the stokers went on strike. This action led to a full-scale naval mutiny, and by 4 November red flags were flying from every ship. Revolutionary sailors joined with disillusioned and hungry workers in many cities. The Kaiser abdicated and the war ended with the signing of the Armistice on 11 November. At last, after four years of senseless conflict, the Revolution, even if not quite in the manner that Hasenclever had envisioned, seemed about to be achieved.

But it was not to be: political power fell into the hands of the revisionist Social Democrats, economic power remained in the hands of the capitalists, and military power remained in the hands of the army leaders that had plunged their nation into ruin. Although a Council of People's Representatives, modelled on the Russian Soviet system, governed Germany for three months after the end of the war, there was no handing over of power to the people, and when the leaders of the revolutionary Spartacus League, Karl Liebknecht and Rosa Luxemburg, were murdered on 16 January 1919, not a murmur of protest was heard from the Social Democrat government.

The establishment of the Weimar Republic, therefore, had meant a certain democratization and an end to the Prussian oligarchy, but it had not made any fundamental difference to the structure of the German state.

The even further disillusioned and alienated intellectual could now turn in one of three directions: to the past, in the conservative belief that ancient values must be restored to Europe (Stefan George, Hugo von Hofmannsthal); to the future, in the revolutionary belief that society can and must be changed by political action (Piscator, Brecht); or inwards, in the mystical belief that only through man's individual regeneration can the world be improved. It is this last, inward-turning belief that shaped the Expressionists' response to the age in which they lived.

Philosophical background

> The Germans have *thought* what others have done.
>
> Karl Marx: *Critique of Hegel's Philosophy of Right*

Kant's *Critique of Pure Reason* (1781) offered two basic insights: that the essential world of reality, the 'Ding-an-sich', was unknowable, and that human reason organized the chaotic sense-impressions of the perceivable world of phenomena into a logical and coherent structure. The human mind could not penetrate to the essence, but it could impose its own order on the observable world.

There were two basic reactions to these insights. Those who understood

Kant best, like Friedrich Schiller, celebrated the moral autonomy of human reason. By asserting that the Ding-an-sich was beyond our reach, Kant helped to establish, in E. A. Whitehead's phrase, 'a closed system' in the universe. Ultimate reality, if unknowable, could no longer be held to be relevant to the affairs of man. And just as Newton in the previous century had introduced the closed system into the natural sciences, whereby the laws of physics were derived entirely from observable phenomena, so too in much moral philosophy of the nineteenth century the transcendent was excluded. In the Positivism of Auguste Comte and Ludwig Feuerbach and in the Dialectical Materialism of Marx and Engels man's reason became the sole arbiter of truth. It is to this tradition that Piscator and Brecht belong.

On the other hand, there were those who viewed the Kantian limitations on human reason more pessimistically. For Heinrich von Kleist it was a source of extreme anguish and almost certainly contributed to his eventual suicide. Schopenhauer in *Die Welt als Wille und Vorstellung* (*The World as Will and Idea*, 1818) re-interprets the Ding-an-sich as the Will, a blind cosmic force holding the world in its thrall. Human unhappiness derives from our self-delusion in allowing the Idea, that is, the constructs of our intellect and so-called civilization, to obscure the Will. The recognition that we are deluding ourselves is in itself liberating. (Significantly, in an idealistic philosopher like Schopenhauer insight into the 'truth' alone is the beginning of salvation, whereas in Marx this can only be achieved through action.) If we were to recognize the Will in all things, that is to say, the essential identity of all things and persons, we should overcome the 'principle of individuation' and become free. Similarly, through art, especially music, we can penetrate the false structures of the Idea to arrive at a direct experience of the Will. In the aesthetic experience we no longer consider 'the where, the when, the why, and the whither of things' but look instead 'simply and solely at the *what*'.[7]

From Schopenhauer's exhortations the Expressionists derived two of their central ideas: first, the need to embrace the brotherhood of man (even if only as an act of recognition and not as a practical programme); second, the possibility of using art to go beyond the limits of human reason and so by non-rational means to attain to the essence. In this way Schopenhauer offered welcome reassurance to the confused subjectivity of the alienated artist: 'the subjective principle, one's own consciousness ... is and remains what is immediate; everything else, whatever it may be, is communicated through this alone and is conditioned by it'.[8]

The Expressionists could derive similar comfort from the other great philosopher of German nineteenth-century irrationalism, Friedrich Nietzsche, 'the earthquake of our epoch', as Gottfried Benn described him. Thanks to his sometimes apparently contradictory aphoristic pronouncements, it has been particularly easy to misunderstand Nietzsche, and the Expressionists were no better than most. As Sokel observes: 'By taking him literally and reading him partially, they misunderstood him totally.'[9] There were three strands of Nietzsche's thinking which proved particularly amenable to misunderstanding.

First, there was the moral aspect. In *Zur Genealogie der Moral* (*Towards a Genealogy of Morality*, 1887) Nietzsche argues that conventional western morality came into being as a code to protect the weak. In place of the 'aristocratic' values, according to which 'good = noble = mighty = beautiful = happy = beloved of the gods',[10] there arose the 'Sklavenmoral' (slave-morality) which was completely life-denying in its humble conformity and repression of the human spirit. Traditional Christianity, Nietzsche maintained, was characterized by this slave-morality, which determined too the bourgeois' cowardly view of life. The answer must be for the enlightened individual to restore the manly virtues of the aristocrat, even at the risk of overstepping the mark:[11]

> If the aristocratic way of evaluating conduct commits a transgression and sins against reality, then this will happen in the sphere which it does not sufficiently comprehend, indeed in the sphere which it must adamantly protect itself from comprehending, the sphere it despises, that of the inferior man, of the common people.

Such a dangerously elitist pronouncement could justify to the Expressionist playwrights the immoral and destructive behaviour of their protagonists, just as later it was exploited more terrifyingly to excuse Fascist atrocities.

Second, Nietzsche proposed an ethical response to the recognition that 'God is dead'. Now that 'the system is closed' and man can no longer find the meaning of existence by reference to some transcendent Being, he must create values for himself: 'See, I preach to you the Superman! The Superman is the meaning of this earth. Let your will declare: the Superman must be the meaning of this earth!'[12] Now Nietzsche intended this ideal of the 'Übermensch' to be recognized as a potential for regeneration within each individual, something to be achieved through an ethical decision. All too often, however, the Expressionists projected this ideal into the future and conceived of the Superman as a utopian figure, a special being who would one day be born to save mankind. Often, too, the Superman was thought of as the 'blond beast', a beautiful savage of unreflective innocence. While Nietzsche insisted that the type of the Superman was 'the Caesar of Rome with the soul of Christ',[13] the Expressionists frequently applauded only the physical strength and ruthlessness of the Caesar and overlooked the spiritual strength of the Christ.

Perhaps the most influential aspect of Nietzsche's thought originated in his essay on the birth of tragedy, *Die Geburt der Tragödie* (1872). Following Schopenhauer's duality of Will and Idea, Nietzsche argued that tragedy had come into being when Dionysian insights about the meaninglessness of existence had been given a positive shape by Apollonian form: the resulting synthesis gave birth to tragedy, the jubilant celebration of the destruction of the tragic hero, who was ultimately an embodiment of the god Dionysus. For Germans traditionally nurtured on Winckelmann's 'noble simplicity and tranquil greatness' formula about the Ancient Greeks, Nietzsche's discovery of the Dionysian origins of Greek tragedy came as a shock. The seemingly most serene creations of western civilization were inspired by the god of ecstasy ('Rausch'), the god of joyous self-destruction. Overlooking Nietzsche's acclaim of the genius of the Greeks in giving Apollonian form to deeply pessimistic Dionysian insights, the Expressionists yielded themselves willingly to this god of ecstasy.

Other philosophical currents, though less important, had some impact. Henri Bergson's emphasis on the importance of intuition, and Sigmund Freud's psychoanalytic revelations of the workings of the unconscious mind were pressed into service to support the anti-rational stance of Expressionism. Edmund Husserl's Phenomenology at the turn of the century concerned itself with the study of essences stripped of accidental appearance and so closely belongs to the noumenal search of the Expressionists.

But, apart from Schopenhauer and Nietzsche, the strongest influence on Expressionist philosophical attitudes came from the scientific thought of the age and its technological achievements.

Scientific and technological background

It was as though men only now deliberately worked together to make the star habitable on which they lived. ... With new eyes they saw all around them how materials they had seen but never used could be exploited for their comfort. Their environment changed more and more from decade to decade, then from year to year, then almost from day to day. ... I travel in new conveyances at a speed which my grandfather could not imagine; nothing travelled so fast then ... I spoke to my father from another continent, but it was only with my son that I saw the moving pictures of the explosion in Hiroshima.

Bertolt Brecht: *A Short Organum for the Theatre* (1948)

From the middle of the nineteenth century the extension of human knowledge in the natural sciences and its practical application in technological development proceeded at a staggering rate. In the case of Naturalism the single greatest inspiration for the movement had come from scientific thought, notably from the environmental theories formulated by Darwin in *The Origin of Species* (1859) and popularized in Germany by Haeckel in his *Natürliche Schöpfungsgeschichte* (*History of Natural Creation*, 1868). If the environment had such a determining effect on the development of animal species, then, the 'Social Darwinist' argued, it was almost certain that man too was a product of environmental conditioning. Add to this a crude understanding of the laws of heredity, and one arrived at the mechanistic formula of Naturalism, which treated man as a victim of his milieu and his genes, and which proved so unacceptable to the liberal humanist. Indeed, the anti-scientific reaction of Expressionism may be regarded as the last attempt by western man to assert the unassailable integrity of the individual.

The scientists themselves assisted the reaction against the mechanistic thinking of nineteenth-century science. Einstein's Theory of Relativity (1905) and Max Planck's Theory of Radiation (1906) spelt the end of Newtonian physics, something the Expressionists were quick to seize upon. As Gottfried Benn wrote in his introduction to an anthology of Expressionist poetry, all that remained of traditional science in 1910 were 'relationships and functions'.[14] Kandinsky, too, in his widely-read work which ran to three editions in its first year, Über das Geistige in der Kunst (On the Spiritual in Art), 1912, responded enthusiastically to the 'theory of electrons, i.e. of moving electricity which is to replace matter completely', praising those scientists 'who repeatedly examine matter, unafraid of any question, and who finally place in doubt the very existence of matter, on which only yesterday everything was founded and the whole universe reposed'.[15] The recognition that the universe was no longer created from stable matter but was in a state of constant flux accorded well with the political and philosophical perceptions of the Expressionists. As Sokel observes:[16]

Modernism is not ... opposed to the technological century, but on the contrary extremely consistent with it. The transformation of the ancient concept of substance into the modern concept of function is probably the single most important philosophical revolution wrought by modern physics, in which matter is defined as energy. In modern psychology behavior replaces character as the fundamental concept.

Significantly, however, most Expressionists recoiled from taking the final step and accepting that their own identity was a matter of relationships and functions. Clinging to the Schopenhauerian view that one's own subjectivity was the sole absolute, they adopted a virtually solipsistic viewpoint which was well suited to their sense of alienation. They looked out on a shifting, unreal world, certain only of their own identity.

While the Expressionists might, as far as they were able, reconcile themselves to the latest advances in scientific thinking, their relationship to technology was a different matter altogether. All the inventions of which their fathers and grandfathers had been so proud seemed to be the products of a conspiracy to crush man's humanity.

The rapid industrialization described above had led to the enslavement of millions to the machine, and when in 1913 Henry Ford introduced conveyor-belt production, the dehumanization of industrial technology seemed total.

The invention in Philadelphia in 1867 of a rotary printing press which could print from a continuous web of paper suddenly made possible the dissemination of printed matter to the masses. This led to the establishment of the popular press and 'pulp' literature, anathema, of course, to the elitist attitudes of the Expressionists.

Similarly, the introduction of the wireless telegraph represented a cheapening of human communication, as shown by the outburst of Hasenclever's Son:[17]

I find it outrageous that buildings are erected from which the air is ruined by means of electric waves. How I hate these messages from Kaiser to clerk! The devil has seen to it that everyone who dies and everyone who is married gets wired around the earth.

The invention of the internal combustion engine, and with it the speeding up of both public and private transport, must have had a profound effect on urban consciousness. In 1902 a Daimler reached the dizzy speed of 100 kilometres per hour, and a year later the first taxi was licensed in Berlin. By 1913 there were 1,300 taxis in the Prussian capital in addition to an efficient motorized bus service and a city rail network which had already been largely electrified by the turn of the century. Within a couple of decades the city-dwellers had moved from the speed of a trotting horse to that of motor-buses, taxis and electric trains, from the gentle rhythm of hooves to the roar of engines.

More disturbing still were the developments in the technology of warfare. The curious novelty of the heavier-than-air-machine, which managed in 1903 to remain aloft for all of 59 seconds, was to become the most effective weapon of destruction in the twentieth century until the invention of the rocket. This was also the period of the development of the submarine, of the tank and of chemical warfare, all of which, together with the general improvement in weapons and explosives, were to play a decisive role in the First World War.

It is small wonder, then, that most modernist writers responded negatively to technological developments. Until the Constructivist vogue in the 1920s, only the Futurists welcomed the technical achievements of the age. So Marinetti in his Futurist Manifesto of 1909, published in Germany in 1911, thrilled to the roar of the racing-car and the rattle of the machine-gun. Significantly, Futurism originated in Italy and spread primarily to Russia, both countries with a largely agrarian economy and little experience of advanced technology.

By contrast, in the process of rapid industrialization in his country, the German intellectual had witnessed the degradation of the workers by the machine, the despoliation of land and city by industrial pollution, and the obsessive concern with profits by the bourgeoisie. The reaction was violent:[18]

> The machine: how we hate this beast, this cold muzzle of murderous iron.
> Down with technology, down with the machine! ...
> A curse on you, you vain inventors, childish constructors in blood!

In Toller's *Die Wandlung* (*Transfiguration*, 1918) a factory is identified with a prison, and the manic figure of technology becomes a stock character of Expressionist drama: the Father in Sorge's *Der Bettler* (*The Beggar*, 1912), who draws plans with the blood of a small bird; Felix, 'the modern mathematical man', in Ivan Goll's post-Expressionist satire *Methusalem oder der ewige Bürger* (*Methusalem or the Eternal Bourgeois*, 1924); and above all the Engineer in Kaiser's *Gas I* (1918), a play in which Kaiser proposes the abandonment of technology and the return to subsistence farming as a solution to man's problems.

Despite the prevailing distrust and fear of the machine, which provided a further impetus to withdraw from a hostile environment into the human spirit, the Expressionists could not avoid adopting certain attitudes from the world of technology.

The invention of photography and later of the cinema may have been the work of the devil, as Peer Gynt learned from the Thin One, but it could neither be rejected nor ignored. As the ultimate achievement in pictorial mimesis, photography clearly had a profound effect on the realism of the Naturalist theatre; equally, it afforded a new awareness of light and so contributed to the chiaroscuro style of Expressionism. The film with its facility for instantaneous scene-changing also inspired similar multiplicity of settings in many Expressionist plays, e.g., Hasenclever's *Die Menschen* (*Humanity*, 1918). As Brecht commented on the 1921 Munich production of Kaiser's *Von morgens bis mitternachts* (*From Morning till Midnight*, published 1916): 'Kaiser has made a film!'[19]

The speed of representation made possible by the cinematic medium was one aspect of the speeding up of life as a whole: faster travel, more efficient means of production, immediate conveyance of news through the popular press, immediate communication of information by telephone or telegram, all this pressed modern urban man to search for novelty and to adapt himself to the increased pace of living. One does not need to be an expert philologist to recognize the more abrupt speech-patterns of the city-dweller compared with those of his country cousin. In the same way, the so-called telegram style of playwrights like Wedekind, Sternheim, Stramm and Kaiser consists of a concise and staccato language in response to the pace of contemporary life.

Not only in its language, but frequently in its images also does Expressionism reflect the pace of modern life. In his essay 'Der neue Standpunkt' ('The new point of view', 1916) Theodor Däubler compared the imagery of modernism to the old and presumably untested belief that a hanged man experiences his whole life again in the instant before he dies. Like the flashes of foreground seen from a railway-carriage window, like the ever changing frames of cinematic celluloid, instantaneous images will often be employed by the Expressionist writer and theatre-director in preference to extended debate or gradual movement towards a climax.

Clearly, however, the most important technological influences on the theatre came from innovations in stage machinery and lighting. Paradoxically, despite their distrust of the machine, the Expressionists did not anticipate the Poor Theatre of Grotowski. Even if their theatres dispensed with boxes and plush, most of them were technically very sophisticated, for it was only in these that the exciting imagery of many of their plays could be realized. When in 1914 the American H. K. Moderwell grew enthusiastic about recent technical developments in Germany, he expressed the widely held belief that 'technical progress does not mean the mechanization, but the humanization of the stage'.[20]

It was in the Residenztheater in Munich that the first revolving stage in Europe was installed by Karl Lautenschläger in 1896; but it was in the Deutsches Theater in Berlin in his 1905 production of *A Midsummer Night's Dream* that Reinhardt for the first time used the revolve as an integral part of the performance. The revolving stage and other contemporary improvements in sinking and sliding stages, as in Adolf Linnebach's advanced design for the Dresden Hoftheater of 1914, theoretically permitted the speeding up of scene changes. In practice, unimaginative scenic designers did not use these facilities very effectively, and Kenneth MacGowan recorded in 1922 seeing 150 technicians at work on scene changes for *Das Rheingold* despite the availability of a sliding stage.

Nevertheless, when properly used such equipment made possible the increased tempo sought by many Expressionist productions. Even if, as in the case of the first night of the Hofmannsthal/Strauss opera *Ariadne* (Stuttgart, 1912), court ceremonial did not extend each interval to some fifty minutes, it was quite normal for audiences to have to retire for supper while an elaborate scene-change could be effected. Such a leisurely approach to theatre performance was clearly irreconcilable with the frenzied pace of most Expressionist dramas, and here technology had come to their rescue.

Effective stage lighting also proved a valuable innovation. Electric arc lamps had already been in use at the Paris Opera for several years, and in 1881 Richard D'Oyly Carte's new Savoy Theatre in London became the first theatre to be lit entirely by electricity. The invention of the incandescent carbon filament lamp had made it possible to provide a steady light source which could be dimmed by means of simple resistances instantaneously and without flickering (gas lighting could also be dimmed by the simple expedient of turning down the taps at the gas plate, but the effect was not as rapid, steady or as controllable as with electric light). Initially the brightness of electric lighting was no greater than that of gas, and some traditionalists continued to use gas long after the introduction of electricity.

With the introduction in 1910 of the tungsten filament and in 1913 of gas-filled lamps, unprecedented illumination of the stage could be achieved, and by 1922 extremely powerful three-kilowatt bulbs had become quite common. With the ability to set light at any required level of intensity, to direct individual beams of light on to the set or the actor, whether moving or stationary, and to project colour on to the stage, the theatre designer now had at his command a whole new medium of stage decoration. This could provide the impetus to seek ever more convincing illusionistic effects of Naturalism or to experiment imaginatively with the psychological effects of light and colour in reinforcing the mood of the play.

As well as providing illumination, the lighting could also create the setting. With the adoption of the plain white cyclorama ('Rundhorizont'), invented in 1869, and the construction of Fortuny's sky-dome or 'Kuppelhorizont', first employed in Germany at the Krolloper in Berlin in 1907, it became possible to dispense with painted backdrops. Instead, striking lighting effects could give the impression of a sky, perhaps with rising sun or stars, or indeed create abstract patterns as a background to the action. There was also now available the possibility of projecting scenery by means of painted slides or diapositives, a technique perfected by Linnebach in Dresden and later frequently exploited by Piscator.

An enemy of technological advance, the Expressionist did not carry his fears and prejudices into the theatre. Rather, as Bernhard Diebold observed, 'Machinery for changing scenery, revolving-stages and cinematic rhythms became ... basic principles of drama'.[21]

Theatrical background: administration

> The whole world is astonished ... at the development of German theatre which has come closer to being genuinely national and to enjoying the support of the people than any other developments in modern times.
>
> Julius Bab: *Theatre in the Light of Sociology* (1931)

The Revolution of 1918 proved somewhat more effectual in the theatre than in political life. During the Empire there had been three types of serious theatre: the Hoftheater (court theatres), the Stadttheater (municipal theatres) and the privately owned commercial theatres.

The thirty-one Hoftheater were aristocratic foundations, created as a prestigious adornment of even quite modest courts. They were presided over by aristocratic directors, often appointed as a mark of favour rather than in recognition of any theatrical ability. Their audiences comprised the scanty resident nobility and the wealthier elements of the bourgeoisie. In these circumstances a visit to the theatre was regarded as a social rather than a cultural occasion, and productions tended to range from the incompetent to the tedious. With very few exceptions like the Weimar Hoftheater under Goethe or the famous Saxe-Meiningen troupe, the Hoftheater had become synonymous with conservative taste.

One of the better examples of Hoftheater, evidence of the inadequacy of the rest, was the Kaiser's own court-theatre, the Königliches Schauspielhaus in Berlin. After being offended in 1902 by one of its productions, the Kaiser replaced the director, Bolko Graf von Hochberg, by a less euphoniously titled but more able man, Georg von Hülsen-Haeseler. Despite Hülsen's desire to reform the theatre and to raise it to the standard of those directed by his Berlin rivals, Brahm and Reinhardt, he found himself constantly hampered by interference from the court. The Kaiser would not permit the performance of modern realist dramas in his theatre on the grounds that one does not 'plant potatoes in a vineyard'.[22] Instead he demanded that the productions should reflect the magnificence of his own court. So Hülsen found himself obliged repeatedly to perform historical pageants like the plays of Wildenbruch, and the actor Eduard von Winterstein, who was fortunate to have worked with Brahm and Reinhardt, recorded: 'Under his direction every artistic idea was stifled by overburdening external pomp and splendour'.[23]

Generally speaking, the quality of the Stadttheater was little better. Traditionally theatres were regarded by the authorities as places of entertainment rather than of culture and so were usually under the supervision of the 'Gewerbepolizei' (police administration concerned with trading) and not the ministry of culture. Actors were treated as any other public performers and were subject to the same legislation as that affecting jugglers, acrobats, tight-rope walkers and puppeteers. After the 1848 Revolution proposals had been made in the Prussian Ministry of Culture to reform the theatre, including plans to set up schools for the training of actors and directors. Within three years, however, a newly-appointed right-wing Minister considered these proposed reforms to be too progressive and put a stop to them.

As a result, as in Britain to this day, few cities showed any sense of responsibility towards their so-called municipal theatres. Normally they would be leased out to a manager, who thus found himself subject to the same pressures as the commercial theatres.

The commercial theatres themselves tended to fare best by offering a light diet of variety and operettas. Where they attempted 'Sprechtheater' (what the British call 'legitimate' theatre), they had to respond to the generally trivial taste of the bourgeoisie, whose sudden wealth had made them patrons of art without the critical education to distinguish the good from the bad. The result, predictably, was a plethora of light comedy and melodrama.

Given the conservatism of the Hoftheater, the precariousness of the Stadttheater and the triviality of the commercial theatres, the wonder of it is that any theatre of quality was performed in the Second Empire at all.

A major breakthrough occurred through the ingenuity of those attempting to circumvent the rigorous censorship of the age. When in 1886 the Duke of Saxe-Meiningen staged the German premiere of Ibsen's *Ghosts*, he outmanoeuvred the ban on its public performance be declaring his performance private. It appeared that if no money was taken at the door and the audience came by invitation, the censorship regulations no longer applied. The implications of this were sometimes exploited most imaginatively, as in the case of the society based on the periodical *Pan* (founded 1910), which charged its audience nothing for the seats but demanded excessive payment for hanging their coats in the wardrobe (a ruse that the authorities did not tolerate for long).

A more significant organization that was formed for the staging of prohibited works was the Freie Bühne (Free Theatre) of Berlin in 1889. Modelled on Antoine's Théâtre Libre in Paris, the Freie Bühne under the directorship of Otto Brahm hired theatres and actors for the occasional Sunday matinée. Through these occasions and the resultant reviews in the press the Berlin public became acquainted with a number of major works banned on the public stage, e.g., Ibsen's *Ghosts*, Tolstoy's *Power of Darkness*, Strindberg's *Miss Julie*, Hauptmann's *Vor Sonnenaufgang (Before Sunrise)* and *Die Weber (The Weavers)*.

Because of the spasmodic nature of these *ad hoc* performances and the limited number of the audience the Freie Bühne could hardly hope to have much influence on the theatre style of the period, but it helped to keep the public abreast of developments in modern dramatic writing and, most importantly for the Expressionists, it established a tradition of private performances, eagerly attended by a self-styled elite.

An even more significant organization, the Freie Volksbühne (Free Theatre of the People), similarly had little direct effect on artistic policy, but it helped to bring about major changes in social attitudes towards the theatre. Founded in Berlin in 1890, it was an effort by some members of the Freie Bühne to apply socialist principles to the theatre. In return for a small subscription the Volksbühne gave to the working classes the possibility of participating in a culture from which they had hitherto been excluded. Initially they were offered club performances of uncensored plays; later cheap tickets for existing theatres were negotiated in return for a guarantee to fill the auditorium with Volksbühne members. Despite early political differences between those who regarded the Volksbühne as a purely cultural institution and those who wished to use it as a means of specifically socialist education, the organization went from strength to strength. By 1913 it had 70,000

members, and in the following year its own theatre, the Neue Freie
Volksbühne, was opened on the Bülowplatz in Berlin. It was imitated in other
centres, until by 1930 there were 305 Volksbühne clubs totalling half a
million members, and it is still a significant force in German theatre.[24]

The Freie Volksbühne showed theatre managements that the working
classes were a potential audience for something more worth while than the
commercial pap of variety shows, a consideration to shape the thinking of
Reinhardt, the Expressionists and, most obviously, Piscator and Brecht.
Moreover, it helped to re-establish the social function of theatre, shaming the
authorities into supporting their theatres more generously.

In addition to the mobilization of audiences there were also encouraging
signs among theatre practitioners themselves. In 1908 in Berlin a playwrights' union, Der Verband deutscher Bühnenschriftsteller, was formed
to protect playwrights from unscrupulous theatre managements and to
negotiate fair royalties. They set up their own agency for stage-scripts and had
success with their campaign to prevent agencies acting on behalf of both
playwrights and actors, as this often led to a conflict of interests.[25] In Berlin
also in 1911 the Vereinigung künstlerischer Bühnenvorstände (Union of
Artistic Theatre Managers) was established with the intention of providing
mutual help to directors and Dramaturgs (artistic advisers). They issued the
journal *Die Szene* and founded an archive for production prompt-books from
which hard-pressed provincial directors might seek inspiration.

This more serious approach towards theatre and the shift towards an
understanding of its social role was eventually to bear fruit after the
establishment of the Weimar Republic. During the war the artistic standards
of German theatres had declined even further. The theatres, still unchallenged
by the film industry which had virtually ceased to function during the war,
became immensely popular as a form of escape from the horrors and
deprivations of the real world outside. As a result, audiences became less and
less critical, demanding light entertainment, jingoistic celebration or
reassuring sentimentality.

Working conditions in the theatres also deteriorated considerably. The war
effort led to the need to economize on materials, and actors who (unless they
were stars) had never been well treated, now found themselves obliged to
accept low wages and longer hours. Younger male actors were especially
vulnerable, because any complaints they made might lead to dismissal and so
to conscription. Censorship now became particularly stringent. It had been
severe enough before, whether administered by the Theatersicherheitspolizei
('Police responsible for theatre security' – a branch of the Sittenpolizei or
'moral police') or in the timid self-censorship of the court and municipal
theatres. But now censorship of plays was executed first by the regional
military governors and then, from 1917, directly by the army leadership, the
Oberkommando in den Marken. Any piece which could be held to undermine

the war effort or the morale of the public was certain to be banned from public performance. One solution was to resort to the old device of giving a private performance, although even then, as in the case of Reinhardt's production of Goering's *Seeschlacht* (*Naval Encounter*) on 3 March 1918, it was likely that the authorities would insist on censoring the reviews before they appeared. Another device was to slip plays past the censor by disguising their content in an acceptable form. So Hasenclever's *Antigone* (1917), with its pacifist message and containing actual quotations from the Kaiser's speeches in the lines given to Creon, nevertheless was passed for public performance because of its 'harmless' Greek dress and the veneration afforded to the Sophoclean original. Hasenclever later admitted that he had chosen the Greek setting 'to mislead the censor'.[26]

With the new democratic age supposedly introduced by the Weimar Republic, important changes took place. The thirty-one Hoftheater came under the control of the federal states, and many of the aristocratic appointments were replaced with new and often young directors better qualified to administer a theatre. The lease system on the civic theatres was ended and here too directors were often replaced. State and municipal theatres now became the norm and private theatres the exception, and the principle, if not initially the practice, of subsidies was established, so laying the foundations for the colossal public spending on German theatre which is the envy of theatre practitioners throughout the world.

The Republic also abolished censorship. Until 1919 many of the most important plays of contemporary German drama had not been publicly performed. Wedekind's *Frühlings Erwachen* had been allowed on the stage in 1906, fifteen years after its publication, and then only with cuts, but it was banned again during the war. The second part of his Lulu tragedy, *Die Büchse der Pandora* (*Pandora's Box*, 1902) had been seen only in private performances, as had his *Totentanz* (*Dance of Death*, 1906). Although, after a furore in the press, the original ban on Sternheim's *Die Hose* (*The Bloomers*, 1911) had been lifted, he had to wait until after the war to see *1913* (1914) performed in public. In addition, many Expressionist plays were restricted to private showings, amongst them Sorge's *Der Bettler*, Unruh's *Ein Geschlecht* (*One Family*, 1916) and Goering's *Seeschlacht*.

The abolition of censorship, however, did not mean total freedom of expression. Instead of dealing with the strict but predictable censors, theatre managements now had to pick their way through a mass of laws relating to obscenity, blasphemy and defamation of authority and institutions. A major scandal was caused by the attempt to ban the performance of Schnitzler's *Reigen* (*La Ronde*, published 1900) in 1920, the Prussian Minister of Culture even threatening to imprison any theatre manager who staged it. Meanwhile the commercial theatre exploited the new permissiveness without interference, the point being of course that trivial entertainment which was sexually titillating did not threaten the state, whereas a serious questioning of existing morality might have challenged the fabric of society. So while Schnitzler's play narrowly escaped prohibition, the erotic revues, like those sponsored by the appropriately named Rotter Brothers, flourished, and so contributed to the puritanical backlash of Nazism with its condemnation of 'Jewish decadence'.

Set against the improved administration and greater freedom of the post-war theatre was a deterioration in their financial situation. Subsidies as yet represented a victory of principle rather than a guarantee of financial security. Initially in Berlin, for example, only the former Hoftheater, now Staatstheater, was subsidized. Understandably in a nation impoverished by the war and now facing ruin with the demand for reparations, theatres could not yet be regarded as a major priority for public spending. In addition, the inflation which raged until Stresemann began to negotiate new terms for settling reparations in 1924, most seriously affected the middle classes who formed the majority of theatregoers. The theatre was therefore plunged into a period of austerity, some like the Schauspielhaus Düsseldorf eventually forced to close, some like the Schauspielhaus Frankfurt and the Krolloper in Berlin repeatedly threatened with closure, others dependent on grants like those administered by the Preussische Landesbühne (Prussian State Theatre). This organization, which was composed of representatives from the Prussian government and public organizations, considered requests for money and materials and distributed them to Prussian theatres according to need, rather on the lines of the Arts Council in Britain today. The economies thus forced on German theatres were reflected in the style of performance of the Expressionists, and there is some truth in the cynical assertion that Expressionist directors favoured abstract settings of black drapes with minimal scenery because they could not afford anything more elaborate.

Another artistic consequence of the economic situation was the frequency with which large-cast plays could be staged. Few theatres, unless subsidized at the level of opera, can today afford to mount a production with a cast of over twenty, and yet Reinhardt massed his stage with actors and, without doubling, all the following pieces performed between 1917 and 1922 prescribe a cast of at least forty: Rubiner: *Die Gewaltlosen* (*The Non-Violent*, 1918); Hasenclever: *Die Menschen* (*Humanity*, 1918); Kaiser: *Von morgens bis mitternachts* (*From Morning till Midnight*, published 1916) and *Gas I* and *II* (1918–19); Toller: *Die Wandlung* (*Transfiguration*, 1918), *Masse Mensch* (*Masses and Man*, 1920), and *Die Maschinenstürmer* (*The Machine-Wreckers*, 1921). This 'Massenregie' reached its extreme in Karl Heinz Martin's production of Schiller's *Die Räuber* (*The Robbers*, 1781) at the Grosses Schauspielhaus in 1921, when, according to Felix Emmel,[27] Martin used 800 actors to form his robber band. With unemployment rife, manpower was one of the cheaper commodities in the theatre of the 1920s. It was, after all, much pleasanter to earn even a few marks as an extra in a warm theatre than to go hungry in the cold.

The post-war resurgence of the film industry proved a mixed blessing. On the one hand, it indirectly subsidized theatres by providing a source of additional income to otherwise poorly paid actors, for it was possible to earn as much from one day's filming as from a whole month's work in the theatre. On the other hand, it seduced actors away from the stage. It was common practice, especially for the stars, to spend the day filming and to perform on stage in the evening. Apart from the inevitable strain on the actor, it became impossible for directors to rehearse a new piece during the run of a play, so forcing on theatres the need to present productions en suite rather than according to the traditional repertoire system, whereby a theatre staged a different production each night of the week, continuing to rotate them throughout the season. Where daytime rehearsals were attempted, the result was often disastrous: in 1923 Kurt Pinthus recorded that it was not unusual for a piece to be rehearsed for four weeks without once having all members of the cast present.[28]

This clearly had a destructive effect on the old ideal of ensemble playing, established by Saxe-Meiningen and continued by Brahm and Reinhardt. A leading actor would now be most reluctant to take a small part in a production, working for minimal wages only to be overlooked by the public and ignored by the critics when he could be earning thousands in the films. Even where a star was given a major role and so in 1921 might earn up to 3,000 Marks a night (= approx. 300 dollars), it was frequently the case that his other commitments permitted him to perform it only at the premiere and at one or two subsequent performances. As he moved on to a new film or another star role, perhaps in a different city, his understudy would be thrust on to the stage after a couple of inadequate rehearsals with the assistant director (the director himself no doubt having moved on to the next profitable venture).

So while gloomy predictions about the cinema's threat to theatregoing were not fulfilled, and, if anything, the effect of films was to make audiences more receptive to new theatre styles, the cinema industry clearly had a debilitating influence on theatre practitioners themselves. As Berthold Viertel, who forbade his actors to film while under contract to his Truppe theatre, commented: 'The theatre grows like a tangled weed in the distressing conditions of our age; and it grows with the film, ... which supports the theatre by raping and slaughtering it'.[29]

The traditional repertoire system was also threatened by financial pressures. The system was popular with both audience and actors for its variety and flexibility. But the daily changing of sets, resetting of lights, reorganization of the wardrobe, etc., was costly, and in the 1920s several theatres, like those of Reinhardt, found themselves forced to adopt en suite programming. The Berlin Volksbühne, for example, was playing each piece approximately forty-five times (i.e., some six to seven weeks including matinées) before changing its programme. Unpopular as it was, the en suite system had its advantages: the semi-permanent sets and lighting could be designed with more care, and actors had the opportunity of polishing their performances by daily repetition.

The effects of inflation on the dwindling middle-class audiences and the competition from the cinema also proved a spur to the theatres. Grown complacent from their easy wartime popularity, they now had to work hard to win their audiences. Some admittedly opted for easy commercialism, but others sought to produce work in tune with the age, an age that, for the liberals at least, rejected its imperialist past and looked forward optimistically to a new Germany. In like spirit, and impressed by the success of the Volksbühne organizations, theatre directors now sought to open their theatres to a wider cross-section of the public, notably in Reinhardt's so-called Theatre of the Five Thousand and in the proletarian theatre of the 1920s. With ticket prices held very low (from 6 Marks (= 2 cents) for a standing place to 120 Marks (= 40 cents) for the best seats at the Frankfurt Schauspielhaus in 1922), serious theatre was now no longer the preserve of the moneyed middle classes.

As so often in the history of art, it seemed that economic stringency might produce other riches of a more lasting kind.

Theatrical background: production styles

If God ever came to Berlin, he'd make sure he got tickets to see Reinhardt.
Arthur Schnitzler: The Big Scene (1915)

One of the more remarkable aspects of Expressionism is that for the last time in the western world, however briefly and variously, a single dominant theatrical style was subscribed to and explored by the majority of writers, actors and directors. Before Expressionism held sway on the German stage from 1919 to 1923 there had been the following wide variety of styles, all of which shaped Expressionist theory and practice, sometimes by exerting influence, sometimes by provoking antipathy: (1) conventional productions; (2) the Naturalism of Otto Brahm; (3) the stylized realism of Max Reinhardt; (4) the design work of Appia and Craig; (5) the staging of non-realistic works by the Neo-Romantics, and by Büchner, Strindberg, Wedekind and Sternheim; (6) the theatrical experiments of Kokoschka and Kandinsky.

The first type, the conventional productions, need not detain us long. All fields of artistic endeavour have always suffered from a deadweight of second-

or third-rate talents, and since popular taste generally prefers the mediocre and familiar to the innovative and challenging, it is obvious that, especially in as public a medium as the theatre, the tediously conventional will not only survive but thrive. With the exception of Reinhardt, who managed to combine popularity with a measure of artistic integrity, nearly all the significant productions between 1900 and 1918 were seen by a mere handful of people. For the majority of theatregoers, the standard of production was typified by the performances of the Düsseldorf Stadttheater. Recalling her significant venture in setting up the artistically important but commercially insecure Düsseldorf Schauspielhaus with Gustav Lindemann in 1905, Louise Dumont wrote of the theatre style of the Stadttheater: 'They were trying to create something new from the outmoded grand manner and superannuated Naturalism and stumbled around hopefully amongst the remains of both. Speech, facial expressions and design were in total confusion'.[30]

Even in 1905, then, Louise Dumont regarded Naturalism as passé, and the curious spectacle of the Expressionists vehemently attacking Naturalism is reminiscent of dogs savaging a dead sheep. Naturalism on the German stage began in the late 1880s, principally under the impetus of the Freie Bühne, and grew with increasing familiarity with the works of Ibsen, Zola, Strindberg, Chekhov, Gorky, Hauptmann and Schnitzler. The unquestioned leader of the movement was Otto Brahm, first as director of the Freie Bühne and Freie Volksbühne, then also of the Deutsches Theater, Berlin (1894–1904), finally of the Lessingtheater, Berlin (1904–12). Even before Brahm's death in 1912 Naturalism had lost its momentum. The decision in 1904 by Adolph L'Arronge, the owner of the Deutsches Theater, to hand over the lease to Reinhardt was a clear indication that Brahm's Naturalist style was going out of fashion. After 1905, apart from Hauptmann's occasional return to Naturalism, e.g., *Die Ratten* (*The Rats*, 1911), *Vor Sonnenuntergang* (*Before Sunset*, 1932), little of significance was being written for the illusionist theatre: Zola and Chekhov were dead, Ibsen and Strindberg, like Hauptmann in most of his works, had progressed into a symbolist style, and only at the extremes of Europe, in Russia (Gorky) and in the British Isles (Shaw, Galsworthy, Granville-Barker, Barrie, Synge, O'Casey) was the death of Naturalism a well-kept secret.

The most striking aspect of Naturalist theatre was its anti-theatrical character. When, as one of its earliest productions, the Freie Bühne staged *Die Familie Selicke* (*The Selicke Family*, 1890), a domestic tragedy by Holz and Schlaf, the critic and director Paul Schlenther explained that the intention of the authors was 'to put a piece of real life on stage without any consideration of what the stage appears to demand, but considering only what sharp and assured powers of observation discover in life'.[31] This was mimesis taken to its extreme: accurate representation was regarded as more important than aesthetic shaping. Considerable accuracy of detail was applied to costumes, properties and sets, leading to the clutter characteristic of the illusionist stage. As Karl Frenzel, the critic, ironically complained about the notorious premiere of Hauptmann's *Vor Sonnenaufgang* (*Before Sunrise*, 1889) which provoked one of the early theatre riots of Naturalism: 'What a pity that [the director] forgot the main item from the second act set — the dung-fork with the crowing cock on it.'[32]

In Otto Brahm's theatres furniture and props would be available from the first rehearsal, and he would work with his actors on every detail of their use, as well as directing intonation, phrasing and gesture. He seemed less concerned with the set itself and would often use what happened to be available in the store. This included the painted backdrops for outdoor scenes which rendered so much Naturalist staging crudely artificial. Only the lighting, which was used atmospherically, seemed to represent progress in terms of stage design.

The most significant contribution by Naturalism was to acting style. Here, too, the blatantly theatrical delivery of the traditional actor was replaced by anti-theatrical realism. The plays no longer told of heroic events in ringing blank verse but described ordinary lives in ordinary prose. There were no longer any star performers; the emphasis, as at the Moscow Art Theatre, was on ensemble playing, and for this reason Brahm would never allow his actors to take a curtain-call.

The actor was called upon to be as true to life as possible: for Brahm 'the ideal actor is one who totally forgets that he is acting on the stage and who thinks he is surrounded by life when he is surrounded by the play'.[33] Without the high degree of articulation offered by poetry the Naturalist actor had to find other means of revealing his inner state to the audience, of communicating the sub-text, as Stanislavsky called it. This he achieved by the realistic means of introducing psychologically motivated pauses and by the expressiveness of his face, gesture, posture or handling of props (all of which could be better lit than ever before).

Thus, although a great deal of Naturalist theory and practice was anathema to the Expressionists, they equally contained much that made Expressionism possible in the theatre. It was Naturalism that established the need for a director to co-ordinate all the elements of production and to create a unified vision, so removing from the actor the responsibility for the artistic quality of the whole. It was also Naturalism that rejected the false pathos of the nineteenth-century declamatory style in acting and so cleared the ground for the genuine intensity of Expressionism. By showing the importance of gesture and movement in underlining the text, the Naturalist actor revealed how the visual elements of performance could go beyond the spoken word. By abandoning the conceit of the star performer, he also prepared the way for the Expressionist actor who had to accept the humble role of being the functionary of the author's vision.

In more general terms, Naturalism also passed on to Expressionism basic attitudes about the role of the theatre. Both movements subscribed to the following assertions: that truth is more important than beauty; that the theatre must be concerned with contemporary society; and that the individual must be examined in relationship to his environment.

Paradoxically, it is these assertions concerning the social relevance of the theatre which separate the Expressionists from the work of Max Reinhardt, who in terms of style formed a transition between Naturalism and Expressionism.

Max Reinhardt, born Goldmann, described by Ihering as 'the most colourful theatre talent of all time',[34] was certainly one of the most prolific directors of the twentieth century, who nevertheless managed to maintain an impressive standard in all his work, whether he was directing plays, opera, ballet or films. By 1930 he had been responsible for about 170 productions, an average of some six new stagings for each year of his career in Germany.

Originally working as an actor at the Deutsches Theater under Otto Brahm, he soon discovered that with few exceptions, like that of his own mentor, the German theatre was in a parlous state. As he recorded in his notes towards his (unpublished) autobiography: 'True, Brahm sat in the stalls and made infallible critical remarks, but on the stage there were only technicians who never made any artistic suggestions. The actors had to do everything themselves.'[35] In place of Brahm's easy-going attitude towards stage décor, Reinhardt worked with set-designers with strong creative imagination: Karl Walser, Gustav Knina, Alfred Roller, Emil Orlik, Ludwig von Hoffmann, and, most successfully, Ernst Stern. For his production of Ibsen's *Ghosts*, with which he opened the Kammerspiele at the Deutsches Theater in 1906, he even called upon a leading contemporary painter, Edvard Munch, to design the sets, so initiating a tradition much exploited by the Expressionists.

The result of Reinhardt's concern with the total stage picture has been described as 'stylized realism' or 'impressionism', and as such is a step on the way from the photographic reproduction of Naturalism towards the abstract and symbolic sets of Expressionism. Reinhardt's visual style sought to be aesthetically pleasing by careful selection within the elements of production: set, lighting, costume, etc. As Reinhardt stated in his autobiographical notes: 'Introduce furniture, tables, chairs, walls as means of expression. Nothing arbitrary. No furniture that does not play a part, that is only used as decoration.'[36] Apart from this basic principle of selectivity, which cleared his stage of Naturalist clutter, there seemed to be no uniformity of style in his productions. They ranged from the realistic décor of Roller and Orlik to the more impressionistic style of Stern and to the Expressionistic designs of Munch for *Ghosts* (a black armchair and walls 'the colour of decaying gums'[37]).

In fact Reinhardt's eclecticism was one of his more notable features. As Ihering observed: 'Every work was performed from within itself. With each new production the art of the theatre was begun anew. ... Classical tragedies and comedies were looked at with young eyes, as though they had never been performed before.'[38] Certainly, he attempted a wide range of styles. On the one hand, he approached the Oriental theatre with his direction of Friedrich Freska's mime/ballet *Sumurûn* (1908), introducing into the auditorium the 'Flowery Way' or catwalk along which the actors made their entrances and exits. On the other, he had considerable success with the realism of his production of *A Midsummer Night's Dream* in 1905. On the newly installed revolving stage at the Neues Theater in Berlin he had invited his designer Gustav Knina to construct a 'real' forest with three-dimensional trees and authentic grass (in fact, it was green raffia). As the forest began slowly to turn, ever new perspectives were revealed – of trees, hillocks and a little lake – and leaping through the forest were green-clad elves and sprites, no longer actors set before a backcloth but an integral part of a complete stage picture. For a public used to the heavy-handed and static presentation of the classics, this was a revelation: a 'real' world of beauty was laid before them in place of tawdry backdrops.

Moreover, Reinhardt's use of stage machinery in this production introduced a revolutionary concept into the theatre. Machinery had been used in the theatre for centuries but nearly always to create spectacular illusory effects, remarkable imitations of real events. But a real forest does not turn; by placing his set on a revolve, Reinhardt drew attention to its artificiality. Thus, although part of the delighted response of the spectator was to the realistic illusion of a forest, at the same time the audience derived pleasure from seeing this 'real' forest put on display as a work of art. So, despite the realism of the woodland scene, the aesthetic enjoyment of it as an autonomous artefact in fact anticipated the imaginative use of stage machinery in abstractionist theatre.

Karl Kraus, for one, was unimpressed by this 'epoch-making humbug', which had 'genuine grass but cardboard actors'.[39] It was in response to the need for a stronger ensemble of actors that Reinhardt set up his acting school at the Deutsches Theater in 1905, the same year that similar institutions were founded in Cologne and Düsseldorf. Until then there had been virtually no training available for the acting profession, and a casual attitude towards the basic skills of the actor prevailed for some while, as evidenced by Reinhardt's preparedness to give Sorge, a writer with no theatre experience whatsoever, the main part in his own play *Der Bettler*, or the ease with which Hasenclever obtained a role in productions of *Der Sohn*.

As a former actor himself, Reinhardt was also of considerable help to established actors. He would 'play hunches' and cast actors in seemingly unsuitable parts which stretched their resources and added variety to their experience. His casting of the young Alexander Moissi in leading classical roles was a daring gamble: at first the public jeered at his 'outlandish' southern accent and effeminate manners but were soon won over by the extreme sensitivity of his playing. Although Reinhardt would arrive at his first rehearsal with every detail of the production noted down in advance, including the actors' gestures and intonation, he remained extremely flexible, often accepting an actor's proposed change and allowing him the freedom to develop the part as he conceived it. Moreover, unlike Brahm, whose comments called out from the stalls often had the effect of demoralizing his actors, Reinhardt would get up on stage to demonstrate a gesture or a move. This willingness to share the difficulty with the actor and the balance he maintained between directorial firmness and encouraging receptivity to an actor's own contribution made Reinhardt the best loved director of his day. Despite the comparatively poor rates of pay he offered, actors struggled to be associated with him, and there was not a leading actor or actress up to the early 1920s who had not worked with him and so could lay claim to the honoured title of 'Reinhardtschauspieler'.

Apart from this decisive contribution to the arts of stage design and acting, Reinhardt's greatest stylistic gift to the modern theatre was his iconoclasm. There was hardly a theatrical convention he was not prepared to breach in his search for fresh modes of expression. In 1906 he introduced a new concept into theatre when he opened the Kammerspiele at the Deutsches Theater and so realized Strindberg's demand in his *Preface to Miss Julie* (1888) for an intimate theatre in place of the large public playhouses which were so difficult to fill by presenting serious drama (Strindberg's own Intima Teatern opened in Stockholm a year later). As Reinhardt explained to his biographer Gusti Adler: 'Since I've been in the theatre I've been haunted and finally obsessed by a certain idea: to bring together actors and audience – squeezed together as tight as possible.'[40] The Kammerspiele, a name coined by Reinhardt on an analogy with 'Kammermusik' (chamber music), had an auditorium seating 292 which was not much bigger than the stage. The décor was simple and functional, and the closeness of the stage was reinforced by dispensing with footlights and having steps from the auditorium on to the stage. Not only did other centres, like Munich and Hamburg, found their own Kammerspiele, but Reinhardt also gave to theatre architecture the new concept of including a small studio theatre within a larger theatre building, a practice common to many European theatres today.

The one drawback of this innovation was the need to charge very high prices for the few seats in the theatre. Initially all tickets cost 20 Marks each (= 5 dollars), and Reinhardt was only too well aware of the exclusive nature of the Kammerspiele. Moreover, it was for him the worst section of the public who could afford to come: 'The so-called "good" public is in reality the worst. Dull sophisticates. Unattentive, blasé, used to being the centre of attention themselves. ... Only the gallery is worth anything.'[41]

The first attempt by Reinhardt to restore the popularity of serious drama was, significantly enough, with a Greek tragedy. For Hofmannstal's version of Sophocles' *King Oedipus* he hired first the Munich Exhibition Hall, then the Zirkus Rienz in Vienna and finally the Zirkus Schumann in Berlin. It was also at the Zirkus Schumann the following year that he staged Hofmannsthal's adaptation of the medieval morality play *Everyman* (*Jedermann*). In the course of his career Reinhardt staged productions in exhibition halls, on the steps of churches and cathedrals, in a ballroom and in a riding-school. Shortly after the war, in 1919, he realized his dream of a purpose-built arena theatre when Hans Poelzig converted the Zirkus Schumann into the Grosses Schauspielhaus, the so-called Theatre of Five Thousand. In fact, it seated 3,200, arranged in horseshoe rows around an arena, behind which lay the proscenium stage. This democratic seating arrangement gave the audience the sense of surrounding the action and so of sharing in a communal experience. On occasions this experience was reinforced by having actors, as in the 1920 production of Romain Rolland's *Danton*, shout their lines from seats in the auditorium, so inviting the audience to identify with the Parisian populace of the Revolution. Siegfried Jacobsohn was clearly elated by his experience of the production:[42]

> In the list of the dramatis personae after the name of Madame Duplay comes the last actor: the People. ... Reinhardt loves them. ... We are crushed in with the people – in front and behind, above and below and on every side. To my right, almost by my elbow, sits the President of the revolutionary tribunal. It is not always possible to distinguish the audience in the boxes from the extras. Everywhere, scattered on the balconies or in the stalls, the mob is shouting, and you cannot tell whether it is the old Parisians or the new Berliners.

The cost of staging spectacular productions to justify the arena stage was very high, and the theatre could hardly have opened during a worse time – the period of inflation. To save money, more and more conventional proscenium productions were staged and the arena was filled with seats, with the result that the audience at the sides had to endure very bad sight-lines. In fact, it has been calculated that, because of the horseshoe arrangement of seating and the high dome over the auditorium, only two-thirds of the audience could see and hear action behind the proscenium arch.[43] Eventually, by the middle of 1923, no more plays were performed there, and the magnificent dream of the Grosses Schauspielhaus became the home of operettas and revues. A failure though this enterprise proved to be, it reminded the European theatre, for centuries restricted to the peepshow stage, of its many possibilities: the arena, the thrust, playing in traverse or in the round.

One of the most exciting elements of Reinhardt's arena staging was his handling of crowds. With the exception of the work of the Duke of Saxe-

Meiningen, extras had traditionally been treated as a necessary evil, bodies often enough drafted in from the local barracks to compose an ungainly crowd, and the director was happy enough if they got on and off stage at the right moments without drawing too much attention to themselves. Here again Reinhardt's work was of major importance. Production pictures reveal how dynamically he used his crowds: Thebans strain their upraised arms towards Oedipus, or the band of the Robber-Baron in Vollmoeller's mime-piece *Das Mirakel* (*The Miracle*, 1911), some lying, some crouching, reach threateningly towards the Nun.

An anecdote told by the actor Fritz Kortner shows how much care Reinhardt gave to his extras. Directing *King Oedipus* for a performance in Moscow, Reinhardt was working with the ten servants of Jocasta. After four hours the servant who had to bring the news of Oedipus' blinding collapsed from fatigue. Nothing daunted, Reinhardt took a short break, divided the speech between all ten actresses and continued working for a further two hours. The perseverance of the director, the loyalty of the actors, and, by all accounts the result, were exemplary.

In addition to the inspiration Reinhardt gave as a director, he also brought to public attention work which might otherwise have been neglected. First and foremost, he restored to the German theatre a love of the classics, which (again with the exception of the Meininger) if they had been produced at all, had been usually performed perfunctorily and without understanding. After Reinhardt the Greek tragedies, Shakespeare, Schiller and Goethe's *Faust* became standard in theatre repertoires. He had shown the viability of poetic drama in the modern theatre and so provided an important encouragement to Expressionist playwrights. Furthermore, a classic like *Jedermann*, as with the Greek tragedies, restored the possibility of portraying generalized human struggle, of depicting universal beings in conflict with cosmic forces in place of the petty domesticity of Naturalism. Reinhardt's production of Schiller's *Die Räuber* in 1908 and his season of Storm and Stress plays in 1916 also revealed to the Expressionists the potency of declamatory political drama and the effectiveness of episodic construction.

As well as reviving the classics, Reinhardt was also responsible for putting on stage virtually all modern playwrights of importance. He produced the Neo-Romantics and Symbolists: Wilde's *Salome* in 1902, Hofmannsthal's *Elektra* in 1903, Maeterlinck's *Pelleas and Melisande* in 1903 and *The Blue Bird* in 1912. In the face of harsh censorship he boldly performed Wedekind's *Frühlings Erwachen* in 1906 and Strindberg's *Dance of Death* in 1912. He was the first to direct Sternheim (*Die Hose* in 1911, *Bürger Schippel* in 1913 and *Der Snob* in 1914); and right up to the 1920s he was still occasionally among the first to tackle new experimental pieces (e.g., Pirandello's *Six Characters in Search of an Author* in 1924).

Significantly, too, he initiated 'Das junge Deutschland' ('Young

Germany') experimental season of new works in 1917. He himself directed Sorge's *Der Bettler* two days before Christmas 1917 to begin the series, and in the next year Goering's *Seeschlacht*. He left the rest of the plays to Heinz Herald, Felix Hollaender and, in the case of the author's own plays, Kokoschka. Reinhardt's reluctance to direct more of these plays stemmed from a lack of sympathy with what was happening in the theatre. His staging of Sorge's *Der Bettler* was reasonably successful with its use of spotlights to define areas of action, but then Sorge had laid this down already in his stage-directions. His set, designed by Stern, for Goering's *Seeschlacht*, which consisted of a massive but entirely realistic ship's gun, showed how he avoided the frenzied overstatement of extreme Expressionist style. Perhaps the most telling observation on Reinhardt's direction of Expressionist pieces was made by Alfred Kerr with reference to the production of Stramm's *Kräfte* (*Forces*, 1914) in 1921: reacting against the 'impressionistic shading' of this elemental piece, Kerr said that 'Reinhardt produced flesh – where Stramm would have wanted lines'.[44]

It is clear in fact that Reinhardt had outlived the developments and changes in the modern theatre. When he left Berlin in 1920 it was not entirely for economic reasons; he recognized that his reign had ended just as surely as he had seen Brahm deposed by himself in 1904–5. Jürgen Rühle speaks of 'the titanic struggle of an artistic genius with the recalcitrant spirit of the time which he wished in vain to bend to his will. And yet the revolutionary theatre of Germany is unthinkable without Reinhardt – just as the Russian is without Stanislavsky – for he ploughed the soil in which the seed could take root, he set the high artistic standards and awoke the many talents without which the age would have brought forth only barren fruit.'[45]

Without Reinhardt neither the Expressionist theatre nor the political theatre of Piscator and Brecht would have been possible. This was the man who anticipated the famous steps of Leopold Jessner by over a decade (*Lysistrata* and *King Lear* in 1908) and Piscator's simultaneous staging techniques by almost the same length of time (*Ghost Sonata* in 1916, *Der Bettler* in 1917). Though essentially apolitical, he introduced innovatory democratic thinking into the theatre and was accordingly appointed Director of the Berlin Volksbühne for three seasons during the war. Above all, he restored to the theatre a respect for quality in design, acting and writing which has laid the foundations for all that is best in European theatre today. Herbert Ihering defined Reinhardt's contribution to the revolution in the German theatre as follows: 'The revolution in the theatre was no other than this: that for the first time theatre sought to be an art. Art, measured not against life, but according to its own laws, like painting, music or poetry.'[46]

Two men who helped to raise twentieth-century theatre to an art-form and who had a special influence in Germany were the designers Appia and Craig. Significantly, it was in Germany that the major theoretical work of Adolphe

Appia, a French-Swiss, was first published in 1899 under the title *Die Musik und die Inscenierung* (*Music and the Art of Production*). Appia was inspired by Richard Wagner's demand for a 'Gesamtkunstwerk', a total work of art that would embrace all art-forms in harmony: music, language and visual elements of movement and décor. Unfortunately, the theatre of Wagner's day was ill-equipped to realize his vision. A contemporary English reviewer who witnessed the staging of *The Ring of the Nibelungen* at Her Majesty's with the properties and scenery from the original Bayreuth production of 1876 was singularly unimpressed:[47]

> So far as concerns the scenery, dresses, decorations, armour and c., lent by the King of Bavaria, we must say that the scenery was of the poorest kind – such as would probably be jeered at if exhibited at one of our minor theatres. The dresses were appropriate, but the steam apparatus was not well arranged, and the clouds of steam which should have hidden per- sonages and scenery during changes of scene, frequently failed to realise this design.

Seeking a means to find a more meaningful response to the challenge of Wagner's conception, Appia sought to reproduce the rhythms of the music drama in the stage décor. This he achieved by two principal means: the insistence on three-dimensional, geometrically rhythmic scenery, and the use of light not merely to illuminate the stage but as an aesthetic component of the design. In place of the crudely representational backdrops of conventional Wagnerian productions Appia offered in his concept of 'rhythmic space' monumental designs of walls and steps sculptured in light and shadow, and so prepared the way for the abstract settings of Expressionism.

In 1912 Appia went to Hellerau near Dresden to join forces with the modern dance teacher Jaques Dalcroze at his Institute and initiated with him the influential Hellerau Festivals. In 1913 they collaborated on a production of part of Gluck's opera *Orpheus and Eurydice*, and Appia caused a sensation with his abstract set and use of directional lighting (see Plate 2). It was another decisive landmark in the revolution of the German theatre, and one may forgive Nicholas Hern his exaggeration when he says: 'It is no exaggeration to say that this was the birth of the modern stage.'[48]

As in the case of Appia, the work of the Englishman Edward Gordon Craig was most eagerly seized upon by the Germans. *The Art of the Theatre* was immediately translated into German in 1905, in the same year that Craig had a public row with Otto Brahm over his designs for Otway's *Venice Preserv'd*. Paul Fechter recognized in these designs a major impulse towards Expressionism:[49]

> Craig dispensed with objects. He painted neither backdrops nor wings. Though a painter himself, he dispensed with the actual qualities of paint, just as Expressionism was soon to do, and worked instead from the space of the stage and its magical atmosphere. By means of huge curtains floating

downwards in different planes he constructed images instead of painting them. By means of passages, surprising glimpses into the depths of space, effects achieved by changing the dimensions of the human appearance, through the emphasis of height and depth, the parallel lines of spears, banners and upright and diagonal lances he made the space resound in a way that had never been experienced on stage before. He was almost more an architect than a painter; he pointed forwards to future developments with such power that he helped to destroy those techniques whose demise was already long overdue.

Characteristically, Brahm complained of the lack of realistic detail in the designs, and Craig's response was predictably withering. The year 1905 also saw exhibitions of Craig's work in five German cities and brought an invitation from Reinhardt to work with him. The invitation was repeated in 1908, and although the collaboration came to nothing, the sketches submitted by Craig appear to have had some influence on the sets of *King Lear* in 1908, *King Oedipus* in 1910 and *The Oresteia* in 1911.

In his theoretical writing Craig in many respects lays down a blueprint for Expressionism. He insists on the autonomy of the theatre as an art-form; theatres should not be mere houses for the performance of dramatic literature but places of artistic creativity. Indeed, he provocatively argued that Shakespeare's plays were unfit for the stage since they were better when read than when performed: 'Of course, it all depends whether you come to theatre for drama or literature. .... If you come for a literary treat — best catch the first train home and own up to having made a blunder.'[50] There was a need therefore for works which were incomplete when read, which only achieved completion in being performed on stage. Since we go to the theatre to see and not hear, asserted Craig, productions must no longer be the vehicles of the written word but above all must stimulate the visual imagination: 'To be theatrical — that should be the highest aim of the Theatre of today and of to-morrow. To chant — to strike attitudes — to sweep on and off the stage — to mouth — to glare — to whisper with baited breath ... to become more, not less theatrical.'[51]

From this it is clear that he was violently opposed to Naturalism, 'the vulgar means of expression bestowed upon the blind'.[52] For him theatre had to be revelation not representation, and to this end he, like Appia, designed his monumental sets with soaring vertical lines and was well aware of the atmospheric quality of light and colour. Already in 1903 at the Imperial Theatre, London, he created the church scene in *Much Ado About Nothing* by causing a pattern of coloured light to fall obliquely on to the empty stage. He went further still in his design of elaborate props, costumes and masks. The symbolism he applied to these and the abstract nature of his stage sets provided further assistance in dismantling Naturalistic style, and Craig's productions of Strindberg in the late 1900s exactly anticipate the

Expressionist manner of staging Sorge's *Der Bettler* in 1916 and of the Mannheim production of Hasenclever's *Der Sohn* in 1918:[53]

> The spotlight fell into the scanty scenery while pouring a sharp bright beam of light on the face of the speaker. Black velvet curtains that absorbed the light enclosed the bare stage. The objects on the stage lay like white streaks, before which the actors stood without make-up in their timeless costumes, like chalk ghosts. Like a remonstrating solitary figure or one in impassioned despair, the actor stepped with primitive, abrupt gesture into the midst of the spectators.

Despite his work on the stylized gesture of the actor and his encouragement to him to be ecstatically theatrical, again anticipating Expressionist methods, Craig believed ultimately that the actor was incapable of being an artist in the same way that a musician, a designer or indeed a director was one: 'That ... which the actor gives us, is not a work of art; it is a series of accidental confessions.'[54] Because his skill lies in imitation, the actor is 'the means by which a debased stage-realism is produced and flourishes',[55] and so:[56]

> The Theatre will continue its growth and actors will continue for some years to hinder its development. But I see a loop-hole by which in time the actors can escape from the bondage they are in. They must create for themselves a new form of acting, consisting for the main part of symbolic gesture. To-day they *impersonate* and interpret; to-morrow they must *represent* and interpret; and the third day they must create. By this means style may return.

Clearly, however, Craig did not have much faith in the actor's ability to advance beyond mimicry and so he progressed to his extravagant demand that the 'Über-marionette' should replace the actor. It is significant that Craig should have chosen a German term to describe his super-puppet, because his thinking recalls Heinrich von Kleist's seminal essay 'Über das Marionettentheater' ('On the Puppet-Theatre', 1810), which argued that the unreflective grace of the puppet was greater than that of the human dancer. This serene and innocent moving effigy, the Über-marionette, 'will not compete with life – rather will it go beyond it. His ideal will not be the flesh and blood but rather the body in trance – it will aim to clothe itself with a death-like beauty while exhaling a living spirit.'[57]

Impracticable, even ludicrous as Craig's proposal for the Über-marionette may have been, it had a profound influence on the Expressionist search for an acting style that went beyond imitative realism, and anticipated one of the major difficulties that was to confront the Expressionist theatre – the presence of a real actor in an abstract setting.

A further influence on Expressionism was the growing number of non-realistic works that were being staged. The Neo-Romantic or Symbolist productions by Reinhardt of Wilde's *Salome*, Hofmannsthal's *Elektra*, and Maeterlinck's *Pelleas and Melisande* and *The Blue Bird* have already been referred to. Although their mythical and legendary sources and the powerlessness of their protagonists before their own passions gave these works a timeless mystical character far removed from the contemporary social preoccupations of Expressionism, their declared attempt to reveal 'the invisible through the senses' corresponds exactly to the Expressionist aesthetic, and the obsessive and perverse conduct of Elektra and Salome anticipates the ecstatic 'Schrei-dramas' that were to follow.

The staging of these pieces was appropriately anti-realistic. Hermann Bahr wrote of the Reinhardt production of *Pelleas and Melisande* in the Kleines Theater Berlin, 1903:[58]

> Impekoven, the scene-painter, clearly aims not at illusion but at sugges-
> tion, not at the mirroring of 'reality' but at the translation of the tone of the
> scene into colour. . . . He also tries . . . to fill the stage with his set, so
> confining the actor and forcing him to restrict himself to essential gestures.

More immediately significant to Expressionism, however, were productions of non-realistic pieces with political or social content. Despite the enthusiasm of Gerhart Hauptmann, the plays of Georg Büchner, in every sense the most revolutionary playwright of nineteenth-century Germany, had remained unperformed until 1900, with the exception of his comedy *Leonce und Lena*. After the discovery of this neglected genius following the premieres of *Dantons Tod* (*Danton's Death*, 1835) in 1902 and *Woyzeck* (1836) in 1913, Büchner became one of the favourite authors of the Expressionists. In *Woyzeck*, especially, they found the poetic treatment of a social problem, abrupt linguistic expression and a plot constructed on brief episodic scenes.

Even more popular became the work of Strindberg. Between 1913 and 1915 in Germany there were 1,035 performances of twenty-four of his plays, and before this he had already been widely read and performed. By 1906 some thirty of his works had been translated into German, and Reinhardt alone produced seventeen of his plays. The anonymous protagonist of *To Damascus* (1898–1901), the Stranger, and his spiritual progress through a series of stations, in which he encounters unnamed characters, were to become a model for Expressionist playwriting, just as the author's note to *A Dream Play* (1901) might have been a manifesto written by a young German playwright during the war:[59]

> In this dream play the author has . . . attempted to imitate the inconsequent
> yet transparently logical shape of a dream. Everything can happen, every-
> thing is possible and probable. Time and place do not exist; on an insig-
> nificant basis of reality the imagination spins, weaving new patterns; a
> mixture of memories, experiences, incongruities and improvisations. The
> characters split, double, multiply, evaporate, condense, disperse, assem-
> ble. But one consciousness rules them all, that of the dreamer; for him
> there are no secrets, no illogicalities, no scruples, no laws.

While René Schickele proclaimed in *Die Aktion*: 'Strindberg is our password,'[60] Rudolf Kayser, writing in *Das junge Deutschland*, insisted: 'In the beginning was Wedekind. He is the first Expressionist.'[61] Certainly, *Frühlings Erwachen* (*Spring Awakening*, 1891) was both popular and influential. In the twenty years following its premiere in Reinhardt's Kammerspiele at the Deutsches Theater in 1906 it was performed 661 times. Almost everything about it prefigured Expressionism: the theme of youth in revolt against a repressive older generation; its optimistic conclusion in Melchior's decision to choose life instead of suicide; the economy of language; the episodic structure; the grotesque caricatures, especially of figures of authority; and, finally, the symbolic figure of the Man-in-the-Mask in the last scene (see Plate 1). What separates Wedekind from Expressionism is the ironical distance he preserves from the situation. However disturbing the theme, whether here or in the notorious Lulu tragedies, *Erdgeist* (*Earth-Spirit*, 1895) and *Die Büchse der Pandora* (*Pandora's Box*, 1904), Wedekind never became as impassioned as the 'ecstatic' writers of Expressionism.

It is this same feature of mocking irony that characterizes the comedies of Sternheim, who in his series of plays *Aus dem bürgerlichen Heldenleben* (*From the Heroic Life of the Middle Classes*) pours scorn on the self-satisfied bourgeoisie. Nevertheless, his polemical viewpoint, terse style and generalized characterization show him clearly to be another forerunner of Expressionism.

From 1905 onwards Wedekind began to tour his own plays around Germany, usually directing and starring in them himself. Although it would appear that his productions were reasonably conventional affairs with the main emphasis on clear delivery of the text, his own acting was by all accounts extraordinary. Kasimir Edschmid considered Wedekind his greatest 'acting-experience',[62] and Hugo Ball, later a prominent member of the German Dada group in Berlin, spoke of the convulsions that shook Wedekind's body on stage and described his acting as 'flagellant', 'hypnotic' and as 'gruesome as hara-kiri'.[63]

The last major influence of the 1900s on Expressionist theatre were the experiments by two painters Oskar Kokoschka and Wassily Kandinsky. In his book on Expressionist theatre Lothar Schreyer, who staged Kokoschka and Stramm on the Sturmbühne in Berlin, recalls a further debt of his generation to a pictorial artist: to Paul Scheerbart's *Kometentanz* (*Dance of the Comets*, 1903). This 'astral mime', which has never been performed, is an impressionistic piece in a fairy-tale setting with balletic figures representing comets and stars, who dance as a background to the action. Clearly, something of the abstract and ethereal quality of this mime anticipates Expressionism, but there is otherwise no evidence to support Schreyer's description of Scheerbart as the 'uncle of the Expressionists'.[64]

Kokoschka too has been one of the many to be declared the founder of the modern theatre. In 1916 Albert Ehrenstein declared: 'In the beginning was

Oskar Kokoschka. It was as though the painter had to teach them how to write.'[65] This accolade refers primarily to Kokoschka's extraordinary little verse play *Mörder Hoffnung der Frauen* (*Murderer Hope of Womankind*, 1907–9), although his *Sphinx und Strohmann* (*Sphinx and Strawman*, 1907) had been performed earlier.

In the early summer of 1909 Kokoschka, already something of an *enfant terrible* in Viennese artistic circles, approached the committee of the Vienna Kunstschau (Art Gallery) and asked permission to use their open-air stage to perform his piece *Mörder Hoffnung der Frauen*. After a couple of postponements and a single night-time rehearsal the play was presented in the 'Garden Theatre' on a beautiful summer's night, 4 July 1909. The set, illuminated by flaming torches, consisted of a large tower with a cage door and a black ramp leading up to it, against which the figures stood out in relief. The actors,[66]

> most of them drama students, hurled themselves into their parts, as if act-
> ing for dear life. . . . As there was no money, I dressed them in makeshift
> costumes of rags and scraps of cloth and . . . decorated the actors' arms and
> legs with nerve lines, muscles and tendons, just as they can be seen in my
> old drawings. The actors entered into the spirit of the play body and soul,
> without a trace of false pride or false emotion. In the end some emerged
> bloodied and bruised.

Unfortunately, the audience did not share this enthusiasm for the play and were outraged by the portrayal of an elemental conflict between ancient warriors and Amazonian women. From the beginning the actors could hardly be heard over the jeers and laughter of the audience, and when the chief warrior branded the Woman, a group of Bosnian soldiers who had wandered over from a near-by barracks decided that as experts in violence they might as well join in the fun. A brawl started, the police had to be sent for, and Kokoschka was hustled away.

Although this occasion caused a furore and so got the play talked about, it was not until its publication the following year in *Der Sturm* that German intellectuals could respond to its innovatory quality. The high-pitched shriek of its dialogue and its violently erotic action caused many subscriptions to *Der Sturm* to be cancelled, but while it may have been more shocking than *Salome* or *Elektra*, it clearly belonged to the same Neo-Romantic school. What was particularly innovatory about *Mörder Hoffnung der Frauen* was the way it was to be staged. Remarkably, here was a piece which was unintelligible without the stage-directions, where indeed the stage-directions contained the meaning, and where the dialogue was merely word-music which amplified the visual elements. Here in fact was a play which fulfilled Craig's demand for a piece that was 'incomplete anywhere except on the boards of a theatre'.[67]

As in Kokoschka's original production, part of the play's effect is achieved by the white mask-like faces emerging from gloom hardly penetrated by the flickering torchlight, and again by the choreography of the warriors and maidens. What could not be achieved in Kokoschka's premiere and perhaps never can be in the theatre is the final typically Expressionistic image of apocalypse and a new dawn, which he added in his second version of the play (1917): 'The flame jumps over to the tower and rips it open from top to bottom. Through the path between the flames the man fast departs. Far, far away, cock crows.'[68]

Similar difficulties are thrown up by the published text of another excitingly experimental theatre piece, Kandinsky's *Der gelbe Klang* (*The Yellow Sound* or *Chord*, 1909–10). This 'Stage Composition', which was published in *Der Blaue Reiter* almanac of 1912, drew, as its title suggests, on a theory of synaesthesia which Kandinsky expounded in *Über das Geistige in der Kunst* (*On the Spiritual in Art*, 1900–10, published 1912) and now hoped to see realized on stage. Like Rimbaud in his poem 'Vowels' and Scriabin in his table of equivalent musical and colour tones before him, Kandinsky asserted the relationship of sound and movement to colours, and of all three to mental associations: thus yellow is high-pitched and 'earthy', green has a dull tone and is 'passive'. This assertion lent a new dimension to Wagner's conception of the 'Gesamtkunstwerk', for which Kandinsky had due praise but which he argued could not be achieved as long as the solution was sought in the external bringing together of the disparate arts of drama, opera and ballet. What was needed was a totally new form, not a piecing together of different styles. This new form would not develop from past tradition nor, needless to say, be discovered in the imitation of reality, but would proceed from 'inner necessity': 'The inner necessity becomes the only source.'[69]

This concept of inner necessity, which clearly stands in the idealistic tradition of Kant and Schopenhauer, insists on the autonomy of the work of art and depends on the subjective associations of the artist, even though these may be shaped by the age and country he lives in and the 'eternal quality of art'.[70] So there is no guarantee that the spectator will understand the signals the artist is attempting to transmit. Kandinsky may think that yellow is an earthy colour; Van Gogh, on the other hand, referred to it as the colour of love. What is called 'inner necessity' may equally be subjective arbitrariness, and to this possibility Kandinsky could only respond with an optimistic declaration of faith:[71]

> There is no man who does not respond to art. Each work and each method of work causes in every man without exception a vibration fundamentally identical to that felt by the artist. ... Therefore each work is correctly 'understood' in the course of time.

This crisis of the modern artist, which derived from his sense of alienation from his own society, was central to the experience of Expressionist theatre, both in the writing and in the staging of plays. The very name of the movement   suggested   that   expression   was   more   important   than communication, that, having rejected realism, artistic creation could have its source only in the subjective personality of the artist; and yet, especially in a public medium like the theatre, the artist's desire to communicate remained intense. As we shall see, this tension between expression and communication was to be decisive in the development of Expressionism.

Der gelbe Klang, then, in its bold attempt to create a new theatre faced the dual problems of intelligibility and technical feasibility. Often its meaning is obscure; at other times it resorts to conventional symbolism, as in the final image of regeneration – a giant raising both arms and growing taller until 'his figure resembles a cross'.[72]

With giants that grow taller and 'vague red creatures, *somewhat* suggesting birds',[73] that quickly fly across the stage and a backdrop that changes from bright purple to brown and a green hill upon which a yellow flower remotely resembling a large crooked cucumber appears, Kandinsky was issuing a colossal challenge to the technical resources of the theatre of his day, and it is little wonder that the piece has been so seldom performed.[74] In the British premiere at the Workshop Theatre of Leeds University in May 1977[75] the director John Davies found an ingenious solution to the technical problems of representing the green hill and the chapel in Picture Four by using cartoon films, employing a technique unknown to Kandinsky at the time but whose potential for abstraction would surely have delighted him; for as Béla Balázs says of the cartoon in one of the earliest works to appear on the cinema:[76]

In this world only sketched beings exist. Yet their lines are not only representations of their appearance but also their real substance. ... Here there is no difference at all between appearance and reality. If the tail of Felix [the Cat] curls and looks like a wheel, he can immediately use it as a bicycle. Why should it first have to become reality?

While the cartoon cat could instantaneously transform its tail into a bicycle wheel, the theatre with its conventional solutions, limited techniques and real actors found it a good deal harder to respond to the imaginative challenge of Appia, Craig, Kandinsky and the new writing. Nevertheless it too would try to spin off into a world of abstraction.

2 · The theory of Expressionist theatre

Philosophical viewpoint

> Eucharistic and Thomistic,
> And besides a bit Marxistic,
> Theosophistic, Communistic,
> Gothic-cathedral-religionistic,
> Activistic, Arch-buddhistic,
> Super-eastern Taostic,
> Saving-all-from-the-mess-we're-instic,
> Seeking truth in negro aesthetic,
> Constructing barricades and phrases,
> Combining God with foxtrot paces ...
>
> Franz Werfel: *Mirror-Man* (1920)

Already by 1920 Werfel had gained sufficient distance from the confusions of Expressionist philosophical theory to be able to ridicule it. Indeed, it is remarkable how so many writers of such differing philosophical positions could be regarded as belonging to the same movement, from the Catholic mystic Sorge to the left-wing activist Toller. The lack of a coherent ideology is revealed by their later political alignments: thus Benn and Johst became Fascists, while Becher and Bronnen joined the Communist Party. Nevertheless, there are certain basic ideas which unite the Expressionists and which therefore inform the theatre for which many of them wrote.

By this assertion I am adopting a narrow use of the word Expressionism to describe a specifically German phenomenon and not a general aesthetic term, a phenomenon which in terms of playwriting begins with Sorge's *Der Bettler* in 1912 and ends by 1921 with the publication of Toller's *Die Maschinenstürmer*, the last consistently Expressionist play of any significance, and in terms of theatrical style begins with the premiere of Hasenclever's *Der Sohn* in 1916 and is largely exhausted by 1923.

Such precise dating appears arbitrary but is based on the description of

Expressionism that follows. To extend the time limits of Expressionism in the theatre would be to broaden its definition.

The unifying force behind Expressionism was not a positive ideology but a negative reaction. In the earlier discussion of the social and political background we observed how, faced with the effects of technology, the war and the failed Revolution of 1918, the intellectual's sense of alienation grew ever more acute. He might have responded by withdrawing into the world of history and myth like Rilke, George and Hofmannsthal. Instead, he continued to concern himself with the society of his day; and this is the first major characteristic of Expressionist drama, that almost all the plays treat of the contemporary social situation (even if in disguise, as in Hasenclever's *Antigone*).

In reacting against social conditions the Expressionist did not seek solutions in political change. Understandably disillusioned by political life, he sought renewal not in mass movements but within the individual. Even the self-styled Socialist Ernst Toller showed in his play *Masse Mensch* (*Masses and Man*, 1919), which he wrote in prison after taking part in the attempt to set up a Soviet Republic in Munich, that he considered individual regeneration the major hope for social change, however hotly he was later to deny this interpretation of the play. It is this passionate search for individual regeneration, whether achieved or not, that is the second major feature of Expressionist drama, and it is the characteristic which most obviously distinguishes it from the post-Expressionist playwriting of the later Bronnen, Hans Henny Jahnn and Alfred Brust, where only the horror and suffering of Expressionism remains, with none of its earlier light and optimism.

Unlike the Neo-Romantics, then, the Expressionist boldly confronted contemporary reality; unlike the Naturalists and the political playwrights of the 1920s, having faced reality he sought refuge in the human spirit. We have already observed how this subjectivism derives from the idealistic tradition of Kant and Schopenhauer and was reinforced by the aggressive individualism of Nietzsche. A more immediate influence was provided by Wilhelm Worringer, whose *Abstraktion und Einfühlung* (*Abstraction and Empathy*, 1906) was first published in 1908 and had run to seven editions by 1919. Worringer's central thesis is that civilizations which have felt at home in the world have produced 'empathetic' art, that is to say, a realistic art which celebrates the world about them. A prime example is classical Greece. On the other hand, civilizations which have regarded existence as a terrible burden, like the Ancient Egyptians, have turned to abstract art to express their response to the world:[1]

> While the impulse towards empathy depends on a happy pantheistic relationship of trust between man and the world of external appearances, the impulse towards abstraction is the consequence of a great inward disturbance in man through the same world of appearances. ... We should like to call this state a colossal spiritual agoraphobia.

Table 2 *Naturalism/Expressionism*

Naturalism	Expressionism
Positivism	Idealism
Phenomenal	Noumenal
Classical	Romantic
Scientific	Supra-rational
Fact	Truth
Determinism	Assertion of moral freedom
Objective	Subjective
Representational	Visionary
Reproduces superficial detail	Seeks essential
Environment conditions the individual	Environment an extension of the individual

Worringer puts the mimetic tradition of western art into perspective and clearly regards the tendency to abstraction as a higher form of aesthetic response:[2]

> The impulse to abstraction therefore stands at the beginning of all art and remains dominant in certain peoples that achieve a high standard of civilization, while for example with the Greeks and other Western peoples it slowly fades to make way for the impulse to empathy.

For the alienated artist who was suffering extreme 'spiritual agoraphobia' in the first two decades of this century, the message was clear. So Paul Klee, after personal experience of the horrors of war, noted in his diary in 1915: 'The more terrible this world (as it is today), the more abstract our art, while a happy world produces art of the here-and-now.'[3]

The impulse to abstraction was followed by many modern artists, notably by painters (Picasso's revolutionary *Demoiselles d'Avignon* predated the publication of *Abstraktion und Einfühlung* by one year). But abstraction was a cool, 'non-empathetic', cerebral response to the world. It was, according to Klee, 'cool Romanticism without pathos',[4] or, as Franz Marc said, 'Our European will towards abstract form is nothing other than our highly conscious, violently active response to and conquest of the reflective spirit (des sentimentalen Geistes). Early man, however, had not encountered reflection when he loved the abstract.'[5]

But in their intense and involved agonizing the Expressionists were loath to give up pathos, and in Worringer, as in the words of Marc, they learned that the impulse to abstraction was a primitive response to reality, an impulse which had been perverted by the sophisticated complacency of western civilizations. For many Expressionists it became more immediately exciting, as in the misunderstanding of the Nietzschean concepts of the Apollonian and

Dionysian, to reject the impulse to abstraction and to plunge romantically into a totally primitive response to the world — to replace the geometry of the abstract line with the intensity of the primeval cry.

The Expressionist rejection of realism therefore carried within it two strains. 'Abstractionism' sought to replace mimesis by the autonomous constructs of the human mind. It was an attempt to establish the primacy of form. By contrast, 'primitivism' in its revolt against civilization distrusted all form and sought to replace it by primitive, visceral expression. As Herwarth Walden said in 1913: 'Every conventional form is a scaffolding for a collapsing building or a corset for a decaying body.'[6] On the one hand, there were the Kantian autonomy of the work of art, the geometrical aesthetics of Cubism, the concentrated language of the 'Telegrammstil' ('telegraphese') and the generalization of human types into two-dimensional figures; on the other, there were the Nietzschean 'Rausch' (delirium, rapture), the total expression of the 'Schrei' (scream, shriek), the unrestrained outpourings of ecstatic lyricism and the assertive individuality of the protagonists of the 'Ich-Drama' (a drama having the author's personality as its focus). The two tendencies usually subsisted side by side and often caused confusions in the theatrical style of Expressionism, as they have done subsequently in critical discussion. And it was when the two strands parted, when abstractionism led to Constructivism and Ivan Goll's 'Überdramen' ('super-dramas'), and primitivism dominated the savage pieces of Bronnen, Jahnn and Brust that Expressionism went into decline.

Abstractionism

The Expressionist does not see, he beholds. He does not describe, he experiences. He does not reproduce, he creates. He does not accept, he seeks. There is no longer the chain of facts: factories, houses, disease, whores, screams and hunger. Now there is the *vision* of these things. Facts have importance only because the artist reaches through them to what is beyond. He recognizes what is divine in factories, what is human in whores. He incorporates the accident of individuality into the totality that constitutes the world.

Kasimir Edschmid: 'Expressionism in literature' (1917)

In order that Naturalism might pursue its scientific investigation into cause and effect, the plots of Naturalist plays developed principally by means of exposition. Typically, a stranger from afar appeared in a household and so helped to reveal some decisive event or events from the past, usually with disastrous results. It was the leading German Naturalist, Gerhart Hauptmann, who asserted that the best drama was exposition from beginning to end. But Expressionism was not interested in causality but in essence, not in how things came to be as they are, but in the underlying reality behind their outward appearance.

In terms of dramatic structure this often led them to take up once more an ancient mode of dramatic story-telling, the episodic 'Stationendrama', probably named after the stations of the cross; that is, a series of tableaux used as a means of narration. In place of the analytic structure of the typical Naturalist play, the Stationendrama portrays events synthetically, the progression dictated not by the inner necessity of any plot but only by the writer/protagonist's search for self-realization. Thus in Kaiser's *Von morgens bis mitternachts* (*From Morning till Midnight*, written 1912) the central figure of the Cashier is initially released from his humdrum existence, then passes through a number of 'stations', each bringing its own disillusionment, until he reaches the final nihilistic recognition of the last scene. The careful symmetry of this structure is not intended as a record of a series of real events but as an abstract distillation of essential truth. In practical stage terms it represents a sequence of totally different locations each requiring its own set of actors.

Similarly, in terms of characterization, the past is seldom relevant to the abstractionist playwright. 'Psychology', Kornfeld states, 'tells us as little about the essence of man as anatomy.'[7] It is not psychological, any more than specific social or geographical origins, which are held to determine behaviour. So the Expressionist creates abstracted two-dimensional figures, nameless and often identical with others of their type: Newspaper-readers, Airmen (Sorge: *Der Bettler*); Gentlemen in Black, Blue and Yellow Figures (Kaiser: *Gas I* and *II*). As Brecht said, Expressionist plays made 'proclamations of humanity without human beings'.[8] Clearly such characters, devoid of what Arthur Miller called 'the gift of surprise', required a completely different approach to acting from the psychological introspection of the Stanislavskian method.

Just as characters become functionaries of the ideas of the drama, so too dialogue serves to present viewpoints in a debate conducted by the playwright. While linguistic differences in a Naturalist piece are used to determine social and geographical background, in the abstractionist play they merely reflect attitudes; for whereas environment had been a determining factor in Naturalist characterization, in Expressionism it is the character that creates the environment.

This treatment of the environment by the Expressionist playwright impelled the stage designer to seek abstract settings that did not suggest reality but were clearly constructs of the protagonist's mind. As in Edvard Munch's lithograph *The Scream* (1895) the whole landscape reverberates with the agony of the central figure. Given this, it is surprising how seldom Expressionist playwrights theorized about the kind of stage they were writing for. One of the few examples, which is a strong plea for an abstract theatre, is Hasenclever's article of 1916, 'The theatre of tomorrow':[9]

The theatre must become expression, not play! ... Let us get out of the habit of saying the forest must rustle and lightning must thunder. What good is a theatre that does not demand: Change the world about us! Let us, friends, believe that the russet dawn of the poet may no longer be spoilt by a stage set, however good it may be. Since we are unable to represent the impossible with the possible, let us at least forgo every possibility. If something fails to satisfy one of our senses, then replace it with its complement. Don't erect any more trees: use lights and shadows; don't bring on ghosts: turn to music. Concentrate the action into the smallest space and use the least number of actors; if you lack perspectives, learn to dance.

Disregarding the charged and exclamatory style which was *de rigueur* for the Expressionist, Hasenclever here proposes a serious programme for the staging of modern plays. It rejects the petty realism of Reinhardt (the rustling forest and the ghosts perhaps being direct references to Reinhardt's Shakespeare productions) and seems to draw instead on the abstractionist theories of Kandinsky, with its suggestion for the use of music and dance to replace action and to create space.

Most proposals concerning the staging of Expressionist plays are confined to stage-directions, and here again one notes the modesty – or perhaps unwisdom – of the playwright in not insisting on a particular style of presentation. Indeed, the writer normally defines the setting in terms that might have come straight out of a Naturalist play. The following opening stage-direction is not untypical:[10]

The Son's room in the parental home. In the central wall a large window with a view on to the park, in the distance the silhouette of the town: houses, a factory chimney.
In the room the moderate elegance of a respected middle-class household. Oakwood furniture: a study with book-cases, desk, chairs, map. Doors to the right and left. An hour before dusk.

This does not come from a play by Ibsen or Hauptmann, but from that arch-Expressionist piece, Hasenclever's *Der Sohn*.

Only occasionally do we encounter the following kind of prescription: 'Otherwise nothing which recalls the uniqueness of a definite room',[11] with which Anton Wildgans concludes the opening stage-directions to his tragedy *Liebe* (*Love*, 1916). A patently abstract setting is rarer still, like that proposed by Kaiser in his 'Sketch drama', *Die Erneuerung* (*Regeneration*, 1917): 'The scene throughout is a landscape. Stony plain. Low ridges mark the outlines of streets, squares and rooms. Enclosure within limited space is removed: all the action communicates with the cosmic whole.'[12]

The most striking exception, however, to this apparent lack of concern with theatrical style is provided by the stage-directions to the first truly

Expressionist play, Sorge's *Der Bettler*. This is all the more remarkable because this twenty-year-old youth, who had been to school in Berlin but now lived in the provinces (in Jena), can hardly have been familiar with advanced stage techniques. Perhaps this very lack of knowledge is the key to his inventiveness, and yet his suggestions are infinitely more practicable than the proposals of Kandinsky's *Der gelbe Klang*, which appeared in the same year as *Der Bettler*.

The play opens with an ingenious inversion worthy of Peter Handke: the Poet and the Friend converse in front of the closed curtain, behind which voices can be heard. It appears that we, the real audience, are backstage and the voices are those of the imagined audience out front. It is a simple but disorienting trick of stagecraft, whose imaginative spatial reversal is self-consciously theatrical. So the audience is alerted to the fact that they are about to see a play and not a 'slice of life'.

When the curtain then draws back, we see a scene reminiscent of the simultaneous staging of the medieval theatre, but with the introduction of a modern dimension – directional spotlighting. The scene is a coffee-house with a raised level to the rear up to which a central flight of steps leads. On the lower level to the right are customers at their tables, who speak quietly since they are, according to the stage-directions, merely 'decoration'. To their left is a more open area, occupied in turn by Newspaper-readers, Critics, Coquettes and Airmen. On the upper level appear the Poet with his Friend and his Patron, and to their right in an alcove sit the Girl and her Nurse. Each of these acting areas is picked out in turn by a spotlight, not merely as a theatrical device, but, as Sokel says, as a means of suggesting the mental processes in the mind of the Poet: [13]

> The lighting apparatus behaves like the mind. It drowns in darkness what it wishes to forget and bathes in light what it wishes to recall. Thus the en-tire stage becomes a universe of mind, and the individual scenes are not replicas of three-dimensional physical reality, but visualized stages of thought.

Moreover, the very quality of lighting is expressive. The alcove in which the Girl sits is lit from a hidden source (Sorge repeats this requirement twice) and the window behind her looks on to a night sky with a shining star and scudding clouds; by contrast, the Coquettes are lit by the single beam of a spotlight falling diagonally across the stage, and 'their voices contribute to the harsh effect of the naked spotlight'. [14]

Lighting here is no longer merely a method of illuminating the stage but is an expressive device to communicate meaning. In other words, it has become an art-form, judged not by verisimilitude but by effectiveness.

Sorge's understanding of abstract setting is also impressive. The Poet, by adhering firmly to his principles, has to part with both Patron and Friend, and, speaking of the burdens fate has cast upon him, slowly descends the central staircase to the now deserted lower level. It is a powerful visual image of the artist turning from the exploitation of his art to descend wearily into the wilderness; it is also the first of many Expressionistic uses of a flight of steps on stage.

The genius of the twenty-year-old Sorge already showed the possibilities of abstract staging, and Reinhardt in 1917, simply by following Sorge's stage-directions, was to become the first director to present a play in a wholly Expressionist style:[15]

> *Der Bettler* is performed on an empty stage. There is no pretence, no construction to reduce the space. The light tears out a piece of the great black space, which, untouched and limitless, seems to be waiting to be filled: the action takes place here. Or a man stands alone, as a patch of light in front of a black surface. In this darkened space a room is defined by a few pieces of furniture, window and door-frames and free-hanging pictures; a birch in blue light represents a garden. One is a long way from reality. ... At every moment reality is sacrificed for inner truth, most boldly and most successfully, I feel, when a starry sky appears over the heads of the lovers in their room without walls or ceiling.

That abstractionism was not more radically pursued in the mainstream of theatre lies in the nature of the medium itself, not least, as we shall see, because of the physicality of the actor; but the 'impulse towards abstraction' of the Expressionists nevertheless laid important foundations for the modern theatre. Oskar Schlemmer at the Bauhaus continued to explore abstraction in his ballets (see Figure 1), and in the hands of a major poet it has subsequently become the most significant development of the theatre since the Second World War; for Beckett, who like Sorge uses the spotlight as an inquisitor in his *Play*, has built magnificent edifices on the clumsy blocks placed by the German theatre half a century ago.

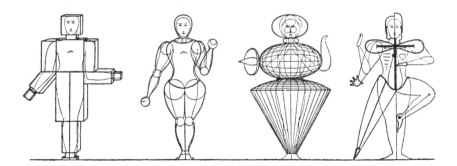

Figure 1   Four designs for costumes by Oskar Schlemmer

Table 3 *Abstractionism/Primitivism*

Abstractionism	Primitivism
Kantian autonomy of work of art	Nietzschean 'Rausch'
Voice	'Schrei'
Cool	Hot
Distance	Immediacy
Cubism	Primitive art: 'fauvisme'
Form	Expression
Symmetry	Distortion
Geometry	Chaos
Clarity	Intensity
Confrontation	Ritual
Debate	Ecstatic lyricism
Colour symbolism	Colour energy
Architectural sets	Painted sets
Lighting to define space	Lighting to produce atmosphere
→Beckett	→Artaud

Primitivism

To return to the beast through art is our commitment to Expressionism.
Theodor Däubler: 'The new standpoint' (1919)

In opposition to the essentially classical and formal tendencies of abstractionism stood the romantic formlessness of the primeval scream. For the Expressionists realism was a product of a society that was bourgeois, western and Christian (these adjectives were frequently treated as though they were synonymous). In their rejection of realism, therefore, many Expressionists turned back to primitive art and culture, giving to the twentieth century an awareness of the aesthetic achievements of peoples outside Europe, and they rescued from neglect painters like Cézanne and Van Gogh and writers like Büchner and Rimbaud, whose challenges to conventional form had condemned them to obscurity.

Clearly the theatre, which is especially bound by its conventions because its dependence on public acceptance allows it to change only very slowly, was not the most suitable art-form to express this primitivistic streak. But the Expressionists loved the stage, because their desire to communicate, and to do so loudly, was as strong as their need for fundamental expression.

Primitivism is obviously much more iconoclastic than abstractionism, because it is a challenge to rather than a distillation of form. In terms of dramatic structure, we find in place of the symmetry of the Stationendrama the apparent formlessness of kaleidoscopic images, in place of a clear progression an often reversible series of moments, as in a piece like Hasenclever's *Die Menschen (Humanity*, 1918). The complete text of Act 5, Scene 2 (the division into acts and scenes is a curiously formal gesture) reads as follows:[16]

Madhouse.
Men in the shape of animals. Assistant in the middle.
THE PATIENTS (*crawl*).
ASSISTANT (*mounts the throne*).
VOICE (*from outside*): Number 20.
ALEXANDER (*enters*).
ASSISTANT (*puts on the crown*).
ALEXANDER (*falls down, crawls on all fours*).

One of the most notable elements here is the way the images have almost totally replaced language. It is a predictable characteristic of primitivism that the writer becomes sceptical of words, because these are the constructs of civilization. Language is therefore used expressively, if at all, but neither expressing character as in Naturalism nor the idea as in abstractionism, but, quite simply, raw emotion. And because intense emotion is almost inarticulate, its linguistic expression becomes abrupt and exclamatory. As Bernhard Diebold wrote in 1921, 'The word in modern writing almost always tends to be a proclamation or a cry',[17] and, referring to the 'screaming images' of Kokoschka's *Mörder Hoffnung der Frauen*, he says, 'There is so much bestial howling and action without the contrast of any purer voices, that the muse of such a sexual orgy can only be called Vagina.'[18]

The abstractionist Kaiser was particularly aware of the need to moderate the primitive 'Schrei' in order to give it form:[19]

Fearful is this struggle between cry [Schrei] and voice. It bursts from the mouth as a shriek [Schrei] – a scream [Aufschrei] of horror and anger. It must become a voice again in order to be effective. Cool speech rolls towards passionate agitation – the molten must become rigid in form – and the harder and colder the language, the more turbulent and moving the emotion will be.

By failing to find the voice to shape the scream, the primitivist writer renders himself extremely vulnerable. The intense expression contained in the following extract from Stramm's *Geschehen (Happening*, written 1915) would require a very accomplished scenic realization to prevent its being merely laughable:[20]

SHE (*comes thoughtfully, stands, looks around her, walks, thinks, listens*).
SCREAM (*rustlingly fades*).

HE (*steps forward, commandingly*): Who? (*Seizes her by the hand*).

SHE (*calmly*): Man?

HE (*threateningly*): Woman?

SHOUT (*from the bushes*): Sweetheart? (*Closer caressingly*): Sweetheart?

SHE (*calmly*): Shout.

HE (*frightened*): I?

PROSTITUTE (*leaps out of the dark, stops, looks her in the face, insolently claps her hands*): You.

SHE (*lets go his hand and slowly leaves*).

PROSTITUTE (*mockingly*): Her?! (*Shakes him, laughing cheekily*): You! (*Tears and thrusts, kisses and rolls with him into the bushes*).

Clearly the writer is at best providing a scenario for the stage; it will be entirely in the hands of the director, designer and actors whether this scene can be made to work or not. In a theatrical tradition, so strongly attacked by Craig, in which the writer does not produce his own plays, the minimal dialogue and unhelpful stage-directions represent an abdication by the writer, an abdication urged at its most extreme by Waldemar Müller-Eberhart in an article published in *Die deutsche Bühne* in 1910. Here Müller-Eberhart proposes that all plays should henceforth be written as a bare text without stage-directions, division into scenes, etc., so leaving the director complete freedom in staging the play.

Exaggerated as this proposal may sound, it is preferable to the frequently unrealizable stage-directions in imagistic Expressionism. In Toller's *Masse Mensch*, for example, a number of pauses are indicated as follows: 'Silence flickers',[21] 'Silence is about to settle heavily in the hall',[22] 'Silence staggers',[23] 'Silence of impending death',[24] and 'Silence swings aloft'.[25] Obviously such stage-directions bear little relationship to the realities of stage technique, of what the actor can actually communicate to the audience. In this respect, they are little more than a self-indulgence on the part of the writer.

The final major difference between the abstractionist strain and the primitivistic is the one which has the greatest influence on acting styles. In the abstract mode, as we have seen, dramatic characters become two-dimensional. In the intense and immediate expression of primitivism the protagonist becomes a central figure of suffering and possible regeneration. He is not real, to be sure, but because we are invited to see the world through his eyes, he becomes more real than the phantasmagoria which pass by him. As Weichert said of Hasenclever's *Der Sohn*: 'All the characters that the Son struggles with lack objective reality, are only the extensions of his own inner being'.[26] While other characters usually remain on the level of sub-human automata, the Expressionist 'hero' is constantly straining towards superhuman ecstasy. So in *Die Wandlung* Toller requires that Friedrich 'walks ecstatically out of the door',[27] and in Hanns Johst's *Der junge Mensch* (*The Young Man*, written 1916), which is subtitled 'An ecstatic scenario', the Young Man 'having in ecstatic distraction silently formed words with his mouth, now suddenly cries out'.[28]

Such intensity and spontaneity make quite different demands on the actor from the realization of the two-dimensional figures of abstractionism. And just as the tendency towards abstraction bore fruit in the work of Beckett, we find the legacy of primitivism in the explorations of Artaud and Grotowski.

3 · Abstractionist theatre: the distillation of reality

Kaiser's *Von morgens bis mitternachts* (*From Morning till Midnight*) in performance (1917 onwards)

The play and its presentation

> In the morning at his counter
> Checking on the banker's gain,
> Then at midnight with the pistol
> Blowing out his muddled brain –
> And the author uninspiring,
> In his frenzy he's perspiring.
>   Alfred Kerr: 'From Morn till Midnight' (1919)

Written in 1912 and first performed in 1917, Georg Kaiser's *Von morgens bis mitternachts* proved one of the most popular works of Expressionist theatre, enjoying at least ten major productions on German-language stages between 1917 and 1925.

The premiere of the play was to have taken place in Berlin and, had this happened, it would undoubtedly have caused a much greater stir than the premiere of *Die Bürger von Calais* (*The Burghers of Calais*) in Frankfurt on 29 January 1917. But the Prussian censor refused permission for *Von morgens bis mitternachts* to be performed in Berlin, probably because of the attack on the (unnamed) monarch in the cycle race scene. Thanks to the intervention of playwright Gerhart Hauptmann and Munich Dramaturg Otto Zoff, Otto Falckenberg was persuaded to perform it at the Kammerspiele in Munich. It opened there on 28 April 1917 with designs by Leo Pasetti and with Erwin Kalser in the lead role (see Figure 2).

As it was, it became the second play of Kaiser's to be performed in Berlin (at the Deutsches Theater in 1919; Felix Hollaender had directed *Die*

MUNCHENER KAMMERSPIELE
Augustenstrasse 89. – Strassenbahnhaltestelle 2. 7. 17. Telephon 508 35.
Direktion: Dr. HERM. SINSHEIMER und BENNO BING.

Von morgens bis mitternachts
Ein Stück in zwei Teilen von Georg Kaiser

Spielleitung: Otto Falckenberg

Kassierer . . . . Erwin Kaiser		. Hanns Merck	Kellner . . . . . Wolf Benekendorfi
Mutter . . . . A. Prasch-Grevenberg		{ . Emil Reiter	Mädchen d. Heilsarmee . Erika Unruh
Frau . . . . . Claire Eckhoff	Herren als	{ . Egon Clauder	Offizier d. Heilsarmee . Else Ehser
Erste Tochter . . . Annaliese Funk	Kampfrichter	{ . Erwin Faber	1. Soldat d. Heilsarmee . Emilia Herdmenger
Zweite Tochter . . . Erika Unruh		{ . Wolf Benekendorff	2. Soldat d. Heilsarmee . Erwin Faber
Direktor . . . . Josef Karma		. Anders Wikmann	3. Soldat d. Heilsarmee . Richard Kellerhals
Gehilfe . . . . Richard Kellerhals		. Heddy Stauffer	4. Soldat d. Heilsarmee . Hanns Merck
Laufjunge . . . . Heddy Stauffer		{ . Lilly Freud	Besucher d. Heilsarmee { Otto Framer
Der dicke Herr . . . Ferdinand Martini	Masken {	{ . Mily Nenninger	versammlung { Ernst Martens
Dienstmädchen . Melanie Webelhorst		{ . Valeska Gert	{ Lotte Stein
Dame . . . . . Hany Speidel		{ . Egon Clauder	Schutzmann . . . . Emil Reiter
Sohn . . . . . Hans Carl Müller.	Herren in Frack {	. Erwin Faber	Portier, Herren, Publikum einer
Hotelkellner . . . Erwin Faber		. Hanns Merck	Versammlung der Heilsarmee,

1. Bild: Bankkassenraum 2. Bild: Hotelschreibzimmer 3. Bild: Schneefeld vor der Stadt 4. Bild: Stube bei Kassierer
5. Bild: Sportpalast (Sechstagerennen) 6. Bild: Ballhaus 7. Bild: Lokal der Heilsarmee

Orchester: Kapelle des Ersatz-Bataillons K. B. 2. Inf. Regts. „Kronprinz"

Die Dekorationen sind nach Entwürfen von Leo Pasetti in den Werkstätten
der Münchener Kammerspiele hergestellt. Ausführung: Peter Rochelsberg.

Pause nach dem 4. Bild   Bücher zu Mk. 2,50 an der Kasse erhältlich   Ende 6 Uhr

Figure 2   Programme of premiere, Munich, 28 April 1917

Koralle (*The Coral*) there the previous year). Of all Expressionist playwriting
it has stood the test of time better than any other piece (with the exception of
the contemporary – but not strictly Expressionist – work of Sternheim). One
reason for its popularity and its enduring quality is that it is not totally
representative of Expressionist writing. For one thing, it contains a fair
amount of gentle humour; for another, it contains no universal vision for the
solution of man's problems. The central figure, the Cashier, does indeed
discover personal regeneration; but, unlike Hasenclever's Son, Sorge's
Beggar or Kaiser's own Millionaire's Son (*Gas I*), he makes only the slightest
attempt to communicate this to those about him, and he finally arrives at a
position of nihilism and suicidal despair. So while this play is entirely serious,
it is not solemn; though often 'ecstatic', it never preaches.

We first encounter the Cashier at his place of work, wordlessly dealing with
the customers of a small provincial bank. His life is suddenly transformed by
the appearance of a beautiful lady who attempts to withdraw money without
the requisite documents. Overwhelmed by her sexual attractions and
convinced of her criminal intentions, the Cashier makes off with 60,000
Marks of the bank's money. Meanwhile the Lady has returned to her hotel
where her son is impatiently awaiting the arrival of their money to enable him
to buy a rare picture. The Cashier appears in her room, imagining that he can
win her with the stolen cash. She rejects his advances, and he suffers his first
disillusionment.

In a snow-covered field the Cashier now contemplates his new-found
wealth and freedom and seeks for experiences commensurate with the
enormity of his crime. A tree that changes into a skeleton beckons him

towards death, but the Cashier for the time being rejects this invitation.

He now begins 'the journey of his soul' by returning to his family: a petit-bourgeois household of wife, grandmother and two daughters. While conscious of the cosy surroundings of his own home, he rejects the narrowness of his former life in favour of new adventures. The Bank Manager comes to warn the family of the warrant for the Cashier's arrest.

The Cashier has gone to the big city of B, where he attends a six-day cycle race, kitted out in tails, cloak and top-hat. Discovering the power of money to buy the frenzied excitement of the spectators, the Cashier offers ever larger sums as prize money, until the crowd falls silent on the arrival of the 'Royal Highness'. Disgusted to find that the subservience of the people can so easily quench the flame of their excitement, the Cashier suffers his second disillusionment and moves on.

He now arrives at a night club, where he tries to buy the ultimate erotic experience. But the first girl he tries to seduce falls drunkenly asleep, the next two prove hideous when they remove their masks, and to his horror he discovers that the fourth has a wooden leg, another link in the chain of disillusionment.

In both the cycle race and night club scenes he has been approached by a Salvation Army Girl selling the *War Cry*. She now accompanies him to the final station, a Salvation Army meeting. One by one, penitents come forward to tell of their former lives, each one providing a striking parallel with the Cashier's own experience, until finally the Cashier offers his own confession. He tells of the stolen money and its worthlessness, and in an ecstatic gesture flings it into the crowd. Congregation and Salvation Army members alike pounce on the money and pour fighting out of the doors. This disillusionment is mitigated by the fact that the Salvation Army Girl has remained behind. But she too betrays him: she calls in a passing policeman in order to be able to claim the reward for apprehending the Cashier. Broken by this final disillusionment, the Cashier shoots himself.

The play therefore possesses a characteristically Expressionist structure, consisting of seven scenes or stations, each in an entirely independent locality. The order of the scenes, apart from the first and last, is not determined by the narrative but by the Cashier's development. The changing situation of the central figure alone determines the action.

Similarly the scenes do not develop from each other in a traditional manner; rather they give the effect of a montage. Apart from the Cashier, the Bank Manager, the Lady and the Salvation Army Girl, no character appears in more than one scene. Even with the Cashier's arrival in the Salvation Army Hall, which is prepared for by the two entries of the Girl, Kaiser does not attempt to show how the Cashier is induced into coming or the motives that have prompted him to do so. His progress is not linear, but proceeds by leaps.

One curious feature of the structure is that Kaiser calls the piece 'Play in

Two Parts'. Since the second part opens with the scene in the Cashier's home, the division is presumably intended to mark the point where the Cashier resolves to enter a new life. But this seems a primarily literary preoccupation and in the theatre the division falls more naturally at a point nearer half-way through the play, when the Cashier moves from his provincial home to the big city. In fact, this is where the interval has traditionally been placed in performance.

Since the localities exist only by virtue of their significance in the development of the central figure, the designer is impelled towards a certain level of abstraction − not that this impulse was always responded to in contemporary stagings of the play. A further pressure on seeking an abstract style of staging might have arisen from the need for rapid scene changes, without which the pace of the play would suffer. However, with the common use of revolving stages, most early productions of the play did not have to surmount this practical problem.

Compared with the abstraction implicit in the structure and in the unnamed characters of the play, Kaiser's own stage-directions are quite realistic. The setting for the first scene is described in concrete if minimal terms:[1]

Interior of small bank. Left, cashier's counter and door marked 'Manager'. In the centre, door marked 'To the Strong Room'. Exit (right), behind the barrier. Beside it a cane sofa and table with water-jug and glass. Behind the grille, cashier, and at the desk, assistant, writing.
The fat gentleman seated on the cane sofa snorts. Somebody goes off right.
Messenger boy at the counter stares after him.

Although there is some detail in this description, nothing in this scene is superfluous, nothing is included simply to 'dress' the stage. Even the water-jug becomes an essential property to provide the Cashier with the excuse to get rid of the Assistant and Commissionaire and so facilitate his theft from the bank. While the setting is austere (and therefore already closer to the clinical stage-directions of Dürrenmatt, for example, than to the clutter of the Naturalist stage), it is not necessarily abstract.

By the time *Von morgens bis mitternachts* received its premiere at the Kammerspiele, Munich, in 1917, the theatre generally had already moved from excessive Naturalist detail in its scenic design towards much simpler sets. As the critic Siegfried Jacobsohn observed:[2]

It was obvious that you could do away with all that stage-clutter, even at its simplest. Dispensing with sets is the ideal production style for an age which has no money, and which partly for this reason and partly from deeper causes is forced to appeal to our imagination.

This appeal to the imagination could take several forms: it might consist of the stylized realism or impressionism of Reinhardt and his chief designer, Ernst Stern; or it might follow the impulse towards abstraction; or again it might tend towards the distortions of primitive Expressionism.

The difference between these styles can be exemplified in three designs for
Fritz von Unruh's poetic war piece *Ein Geschlecht* (*One Family*) (see Plates
8–10). The design by August Babberger for the 1918 premiere at the
Schauspielhaus Frankfurt reveals a primitivist tendency. While the cemetery
walls and gates seem realistic enough, the crosses in the background reel
in horrifying confusion. When the play transferred in the same year to
Reinhardt's Deutsches Theater in Berlin, the designer Ernst Stern provided a
pleasing if barren landscape as a setting. Agonized distortion has here made
way for a feeling of serenity. By contrast, the stark symmetry of Walter von
Wecus's design for the Düsseldorf production is coolly abstract.

Of the three styles it is this last that is most appropriate to the staging of
Kaiser's dramas; for his plays lack the warmth implicit in Stern's gentle
conception, and only in part do they reveal the ecstatic vision characteristic of
primitive Expressionism. Kaiser once stated: 'to write a drama is to think an
idea through to the end',[3] and it is this hardness of abstract thought that he
reveals in both the content and structure of his plays. Bernhard Diebold, who
called Kaiser 'der Denkspieler' ('the thought-player'), observed of him:
'symmetry became the highest law of his dramatic architecture of glass and
iron'.[4]

Symmetry is a major element in the structure of *Von morgens bis
mitternachts*. The formal austerity of the bank in the first scene is balanced by
the noisy vitality of the Salvation Army hall at the end, and the silent
oppressed Cashier of the opening gives vent at the end to a voluble confession.
Similarly, the celebration of naive eroticism in the painting by Cranach and
the Lady's modest rejection of the Cashier's advances (Scene 2) contrast with
the commercial sexuality of the night club scene (Scene 6).

Within scenes, too, this architectural symmetry is maintained: in the bank
scene the garrulous intimacy of the Manager and his fat customer balances the
silent industry of the Cashier and the Assistant; and, most obviously, the
confessions in the Salvation Army hall follow a very formal pattern. Almost
exactly in reverse, the confessions, first by an officer then by a member of the
public, retrace the 'stations' through which the Cashier has passed: the cycle
race, the night club, the home and the bank.

This formal symmetry in the writing requires an appropriate style in the
staging of the piece. The bank is dominated by its three symmetrically placed
doors: to the Manager's office, to the safe and to the street. On the left are the
counter and desk, the areas of work; on the right is the cane sofa where the fat
capitalist sprawls. Nothing should be added merely to dress the stage; rather
the contrast between the industry of the employees and the indolence of its
richest customer should be accentuated in the setting. This was emphasized in
the film version of *Von morgens bis mitternachts*, directed by Karl Heinz
Martin in 1920, which offers fascinating insights into the visual style of
Expressionist staging. Here, in Robert Neppach's design, the Cashier was

framed by a construction of luminescent chicken-wire: he was literally cooped up at his counter (see Plate 14).

The hotel scene, which in terms of writing is the most realistic, still possesses an essential symmetry: a single door at the back; to the left a desk and telephone (again the area of activity); to the right an armchair and couch (on which the Lady sits to receive the Cashier). As with the couch and table in the previous scene, the furniture here poses a problem, threatening to dissipate the abstract quality of the setting. It is easy enough to present doorways in an abstract manner: a free-standing rectangle, perhaps surrounded by black drapes, is visually satisfying as a geometric abstraction, serving to define space and to focus entrances and exits. This was the manner in which the designer Ludwig Sievert presented the room for the first public performance of Hasenclever's *Der Sohn* at the Nationaltheater Mannheim in 1918, exciting Stefan Grossmann to call it 'the only Expressionist production based on a new idea' (see Plate 6).[5]

When it comes to furniture and properties, however, the tendency has always been to use real objects. This is partly a question of expense: the 1920 film version stylized all the properties – a trapezium-shaped suitcase, crudely marked outsize banknotes, a newspaper covered with blotchy hieroglyphs, an octagonal watch – but the cinema even then worked to a much larger budget than the theatre, and time and money will often preclude such consistent pursuit of abstraction on stage.

Furthermore, the presence of a living actor will jar with objects that are too far removed from reality. For the Lady to speak into a two-dimensional 'abstract' telephone would be merely distracting. On film the actor himself becomes two-dimensional and can more acceptably use stylized objects. On the stage such practice becomes too easily associated with the cartoon style of pantomime and comic revue – a possibility in Absurdist Theatre and its forerunners like Goll, but normally too frivolous for the serious themes of Kaiser. It is for this reason that Kaiser's other most successful play, *Gas I* (1918), can maintain its abstract setting more consistently: in the futurist world of the piece, stylized objects become much more readily acceptable. Where such a shift in time is not available to allow the imagination freer range, the solution would seem to lie in the course finally adopted by Brecht: the background which is an illusion must declare itself as such, while the objects used by the actors should be real.

This creates a further problem in the hotel scene of *Von morgens bis mitternachts*. The Son displays his artistic find, a picture by Cranach. The picture as described does not in fact exist, so there is no possibility here of using a 'real' property, although an artist might be called upon to paint a pastiche of Cranach, following the guidelines given in Kaiser's text. Almost certainly the way in which this problem was usually overcome was to stand the picture facing away from the audience while the Son described it. This was probably Kaiser's intention, as the Son enters with the picture covered in a cloth, and it also offers the enticing possibility of displaying a grotesque face on the reverse, since the Son mentions that the vendor 'had stuck his own photograph on the back'.[6] Perhaps even more appropriate, however, would be to display an entirely blank canvas, a technique used for the portraits in Leopold Jessner's staging of Wedekind's *Der Marquis von Keith* (Berlin, 1920). This would help to maintain the focus on the painting, while allowing the Son's words to create the picture in the imagination of the audience.

Scene 3 brings with it the most technically challenging demand of the play. Here the Cashier encounters a snow-laden tree which transforms itself into a skeleton. To fulfil the requirements of the stage-directions the tree has to be solid: the Cashier sits in a fork in the branches and the tree whisks the hat off his head. Moreover, the tree turns into a skeleton as the wind blows the snow off its branches, only to resume its former harmless appearance at the end of the scene. While back-projections could cope easily with the transformation, this would exclude the possibility of physical contact between the Cashier and the tree. It is highly unlikely that Kaiser himself had any conception of how this scene might be staged. As he once admitted: 'I never write plays with a view to their performance. It is mere chance that my ideological compositions meet the demands of the theatre.'[7]

It is characteristic of Expressionist playwrights that they refused to allow themselves to be limited by practical considerations – one recalls Kandinsky's *Der gelbe Klang* – and one wonders initially why such works were written for the theatre if the stage seems unable to realize them in performance. Yet on reflection it is this infuriating obstinacy of the Expressionist playwright to compose within acknowledged limits that makes the theatre of this period such an exciting and revolutionary medium. Kaiser's challenge to accepted theatre practice, while apparently irresponsible, was a spur to new creativity.

From the evidence available it seems unlikely that this challenge was effectively met in contemporary productions. It appears that directors and designers opted either for a physical tree/skeleton which made possible the business with the hat but made the transformation unconvincing; or they used a painted or projected image which may have had a more threatening aspect but which excluded contact between the Cashier and the tree. In the first Berlin production on 2 February 1919, directed by Felix Hollaender at the Deutsches Theater, the literal-minded Ernst Stern tried to create the skeleton by mechanical means. One critic dismissed it as 'a wholly dispensable Romantic property'[8] and another objected: 'Totally misconceived was the anatomical realization of the skeleton whose appearance in the original text already creates misgivings.'[9] Later the same year in F. R. Werkhäufer's production in Cologne a back-projection was used to create the tree/skeleton, but this was rejected by a critic as being 'too reminiscent of a child's magic lantern'.[10]

More acceptable, though not wholly appropriate to the abstractionist style of the play, was the decision to present the tree as a painted backdrop. In the second Berlin production, directed by Victor Barnowsky at the Lessingtheater on 14 April 1921, a production which was the most consistently Expressionist of any staging of the play, the designer César Klein created a primitive and threatening image which was at once a tree and a skeleton: the actor is dwarfed by the violent presence towering over him (see Plate 12).

By contrast, Fritz Schäfler's design for his own production of the play at the Neue Bühne, Munich, in June 1921, seems rooted in the grotesque rather than the threateningly primitive (see Plate 11). Compared with Klein's horrifying skeleton, Schäfler's tree is an amiable freak, like something out of a child's fairy tale. For the reappearance of the skeleton at the end, this time in the chandelier of the Salvation Army hall, Schäfler resorted to a mechanical device, and its rattling presence seemed closer to an effect from a puppet play than to ecstatic Expressionism.

By 1930, when Leopold Jessner directed the play at the Stadttheater Altona, the anti-Expressionistic style of 'Neue Sachlichkeit' (New Objectivity) had reintroduced a more realistic approach to design. So we see in Karl Gröning's proposal for the skeleton in this production a real skeleton in a real tree (see Plate 13).

Curiously, the 1920 film version of the play, which might most easily have realized Kaiser's conception, did not attempt it at all. The reason for this no doubt lay in the fact that this third scene relies heavily on its verbal content and would therefore have been meaningless in a silent film, which dispensed even with the standard practice of inserting written captions. Instead, the film's director Karl Heinz Martin made frequent use of the dissolve to suggest the omnipresence of death: each time the Cashier meets a woman – a maidservant, a beggar-woman, his daughter, the fourth girl in the night club, the Salvation Army Girl (all played by Martin's wife Roma Bahn) – her face dissolves into a skull (see Plate 15). In this way Martin imaginatively generalizes Kaiser's specific image, pursuing the subjective tendency of Expressionist style: the nightmarishly morbid projection of the Cashier becomes physical reality.

Such a response to the spirit rather than the letter of Kaiser's stage-directions suggests possibilities for the problematic presentation of the tree. It would be conceivable to construct an object which, lit normally, would appear convincingly as a snow-laden tree. Certain branches could be picked out in fluorescent paint, which then, under ultra-violet light, would suddenly become a skeleton (ultra-violet light was in use on the German stage from at least the early 1920s). Alternatively, the tree could be created from actors, perhaps draped in white cloth. The actors' arms would thus represent the branches, changing from a graceful to an angular, skeletal pose, and offering the intriguing possibility of allowing one of their wrists to bear the diamond bracelet worn by the Lady in the first scene, so giving a focus to the Cashier's apostrophe to the Lady in this scene. The appearance of the skeleton could be reinforced by illuminating the 'tree' from within, revealing the silhouette of a skull under the white cloth draped over the actors.

An even freer realization of the image, but very much in the spirit of the original, might be achieved by having the tree represented in a suitable framework by a single actress – perhaps the same actress who plays the Salvation Army Girl. Her tambourine could suggest the rustle of the leaves, and she or the tambourine might bear the image of a skull which leered over the Cashier's shoulder at the appropriate point.

Clearly, such imaginative responses could be extended endlessly. What is important, however, is not the particular solution to this difficult technical problem, but the incitement Kaiser provides to move away from a too literal realization of the image to an imaginatively theatrical moment.

The next scene, the Cashier's home, is again a sparsely furnished interior with two doors and a window at the back, table, chairs and piano. The only decoration prescribed by Kaiser is a window-box with faded geraniums, doubtless symbolizing the Cashier's disillusionment with his bourgeois existence. Again the protagonist's attitude transforms reality; the individual conditions his environment rather than the reverse.

The cycle race scene offers the most exciting opportunity for abstract Expressionism, and even Ernst Stern's set for the 1919 Berlin production is less realistic than one might have expected from this designer. The cycle race itself is never seen; instead there is simply an arched wooden bridge, presumably spanning the track, from which the officials and Cashier view the event. This siting of the scene has the advantage of allowing the characters to see both the competitors (the focus for the officials) and the public (the focus for the Cashier), thus providing the contrast of interest which is central to this episode.

The stage-directions for the night club scene are even more minimal: 'Night club. Chambre séparée'.[11] The scene requires a table and a couch, and the same observations made about the hotel scene would apply here.

The final scene is set in a long Salvation Army hall, enclosed at the back by a yellow curtain carrying a large black cross, in front of which stands a rostrum bearing the penitents' form and musical instruments. Before this are rows of benches. This arrangement means that the congregation is seated with their backs to the audience and that the speakers are very far upstage, a position having obvious disadvantages for a realistic staging. In Expressionist theatre, however, this is exactly what is wanted: the congregation becomes literally a faceless mass, and the speakers, signalling from the rear of the stage, are dwarfed by the space and require bold gestures to communicate with the theatre audience, which forms a continuum with the audience on stage. In his Expressionist staging of *Othello* (Berlin, 1921) Leopold Jessner adopted a similar arrangement for the scene in the Venetian Council Chamber, in which the senators sat facing upstage towards the speakers, thus concentrating all the attention on them.

Regrettably, the abstraction appropriate to *Von morgens bis mitternachts* was seldom achieved in early productions. Falckenberg's premiere apparently preserved a stylized realism such as Reinhardt might have employed, and when the play was performed at Reinhardt's own theatre, the Deutsches Theater in Berlin, this style was predictably maintained. One reviewer pointed to the clash between the stylized presentation of the home and cycle race scenes and the realistic settings of the rest,[12] and Ihering wrote of Hollaender's direction: 'Despite all his twitching and bouncing his conception is always somehow softened by Naturalism – or rather dulled and turned grey by it.'[13]

The 1920 film version achieved a more unreal quality, its sets, jagged and angular, heightened by broadly drawn luminescent white lines. As Scheffauer wrote:[14]

Space does not obtrude; the world becomes a background, vague, incho-ate, nebulous. Against this obliterating firmament, this sponge of darkness, the players move, merge into it, emerge out of it. In order that they may not be visually lost, their hands, faces and the outlines of their clothing are relieved by means of high lights carefully applied.

However, the primitive quality of Neppach's designs was more appropriate to the agonized cry of a writer like Toller than to the cool vision of Georg Kaiser.

It was César Klein's designs for the Berlin Lessingtheater production in 1921 that, despite a similar tendency towards primitivism, most successfully reproduced the spirit of the original. Already the previous year, again under Barnowsky's direction, he had impressed critics with his sets for the Berlin premiere of Kaiser's *Hölle Weg Erde (Hell Way Earth)*. As Ihering commented: 'César Klein's stage sets were illustrations to the text; they did not focus on the actor but on the visual tone of the scene. One did not so much hear as read the play with their help'.[15]

In the abstractionist style of design the set itself makes a statement. It is no longer a Naturalistic environment for the actor to move about in nor a painted backdrop for him to perform in front of; it becomes a visual symbol of which the actor is a component.

Similarly, lighting is now employed not merely to illuminate the set and actors but as a further means of artistic communication. The first reference to light is in the snowfield scene, where Kaiser prescribes 'Sun casting blue shadows',[16] reinforcing not only the physical coldness of the scene but also suggesting the barren landscape of the Cashier's soul, the *tabula rasa* before he begins his spiritual journey. This requirement could be fulfilled by back-lighting the upstage area with a blue 'wash' and projecting strong 'sunlight' from a source at the front. On the appearance of the skeleton, the sun is obscured by clouds, to break through again at the end of the scene as the tree resumes its former shape, an obvious use of atmospheric lighting.

By contrast with the warm interior lighting of the hotel and home scenes, the cycle race is lit by the harsh glare of an arc-light. Although it is not prescribed by Kaiser, it would be appropriate here to use a spotlight to isolate the Cashier in his ecstatic monologues, just as the Lady's appearance in the bank might be accentuated by the use of a follow-spot. Such devices deliberately flout realism and serve to provide a focus.

The night club scene begins in darkness. Music is allowed to establish a mood, until the waiter enters and turns on a red light. While wholly acceptable on a realistic level, the red light in which the scene is played clearly reinforces the erotic ambience.

Such colour symbolism was common practice in Expressionist theatre. Already in the stage-directions for *Der brennende Dornbusch* (*The Burning Thornbush*), written in 1911, Kokoschka required a white light while the male figure spoke, interrupted by red light while the woman replied,[17] and red light was used again by Weichert in his 1918 production of *Der Sohn* for the appearance of the prostitute.

The most startling lighting effects occur at the end of the play, although here again they are acceptable on a realistic level. Following the Policeman's instructions to switch off the light, all the lights on the chandelier go out except one, which lights up the bright wires above the stage in such a way as to create the image of a skeleton. When the lights are turned on again, all the bulbs explode, leaving the dying Cashier in darkness (although presumably a glimmer of light must illuminate him outstretched against the cross). The final stage-direction summarizes the despairing mood of the ending: 'It is quite dark'.[18]

Music and sound effects too, while always realistically justified, add an atmospheric dimension to the piece. Music, especially, plays an important role. The cosiness of the Cashier's home is established by his daughter's practising the Overture to *Tannhäuser*, a bourgeois favourite, on the piano. There are bands playing in the cycle race scene (at the Munich premiere music was provided by the band of the Bavarian Second Infantry Regiment). Throughout the night club scene muted dance rhythms from the orchestra are heard, and in the Salvation Army hall the band is seen on stage, striking up every time a soul is saved. Such musical colouring is vital and atmospheric, and it was not the least of the achievements of Expressionist theatre that it restored to music a place in plays dealing with contemporary social issues.

Music is used with particular effect to heighten the final ecstatic declarations of the Cashier. His triumphant address to the Salvation Army Girl is accompanied by beats and rolls on a drum that he has seized from the abandoned instruments. Not only do the sounds of the drum set up an insistent rhythm in themselves, they also echo the rhythm of the repeated phrase, 'Mädchen und Mann' ('Maiden and man'), with its two stresses separated by two unstressed syllables, reminiscent of the grand and ominous opening of Beethoven's Fifth Symphony.

The final speech of the Cashier is interspersed with blasts on a trumpet, at once an apocalyptic reference and a gesture of defiance against the meaninglessness of life. The last strangled note (demanding great competence on the part of the actor to avoid the bathetic) suggests his life ebbing away, an aural image that goes beyond language in its abstract coincidence of form and content.

Another effective use of sound is employed in the cycle race scene. Here there is a veritable cacophony: the rumble of bicycles over wooden boards, whistles, shouts, cat-calls, music, and the report of a starting-pistol. The volume of noise grows with the increasing excitement of the races until the stage-direction: 'Sudden dead silence',[19] followed by the playing of the national anthem for the royal visitor. The sudden silence (not wholly realistic, since the sound of the bicycles would in fact continue) is an effective and eerie moment: all activity is suspended at the appearance of 'His Royal Highness', and so with one decisive and simply executed device the swelling ecstasy of the Cashier is destroyed.

Already we have noted the problem of maintaining a consistently abstract style with regard to furniture and properties. This extends also to the costumes and make-up of the actors. As Bernhard Diebold observed:[20]

> The new representatives of total spirituality called themselves Cubists, for they found in the geometry of cubes and spheres the laws of form which were not conditioned by the senses and which could gain mastery over the natural matter they despised. Writers of this type let their words be petrified into the abbreviations of telegrams, their characters became nameless types. The 'father', the 'millionaire', the 'gentlemen-in-black' or 'yellow' presented the constructivist formula for every possible individual under this sign. They now all had to look as mathematically identical as numbers. ... Only the actors disturbed the 'transcendental' style with inappropriate physicality; with noses, eyes, ears and limbs all in the right place of their anatomy. With them neither cubes nor spheres are any help.

Costume could at best only help in the process of abstraction. It could never achieve it entirely.

Some directors in their pursuit of abstraction attempted to use costume to eliminate the human form. For Ivan Goll's *Methusalem* in 1924 George Grosz designed a jokey set of costumes for the surrealistic characters of the play. The central figure, Methusalem, was conceived of as having planks nailed over his head to represent his wooden, schematic manner of thinking. Rather than actual costumes, these were intended as constructions behind which the actor would stand to deliver his lines. Thus the son Felix has a gramophone loudspeaker in place of a mouth. For the rest, 'shining machine-parts − movable − perhaps transparent. ... The right hand blue, plastic, constructed with mathematical exactitude. ... Backside black, like a locomotive'.[21] Such unreal geometric creations point forward to the total abstractionism of Oskar Schlemmer's work at the Bauhaus, as in his four basic designs for dancers (see Figure 1).

In 1926 Schlemmer simplified this tendency to abstraction with his famous 'Stick dance'. Long thin white sticks were tied to the dancer's body: to the calves, thighs, forearms, upper arms, across the shoulders, and to either side of the trunk. As the performer 'danced', each move was extended into space and emphasized by the angular relationship of the sticks.

Such solutions would be far too extreme, however, for the admittedly abstract but nonetheless representative figures of Kaiser. The 1920 film version attempted a kind of abstraction by carrying the luminescence of the set over to the costumes, with strange white streaks round lapels and pockets. A striking and unifying idea though this was, its crude effect lent considerable scruffiness to the costumes. This was appropriate enough in the case of the Cashier, but not for the Lady's Son, who must come from a world of riches seemingly beyond the Cashier's reach. As it was, the Son seemed like an eccentric tramp.

More appropriate would be the type of costuming adopted by Leopold Jessner for his staging of *Der Marquis von Keith* in Berlin in 1920. Here all the actors wore exaggeratedly long tails, cut like figures from a cartoon, and, as splashes of colour, extravagant wigs ranging from bright green to flaming red. This style would be particularly appropriate for the Bank Manager and the Fat Man and the identically dressed Jewish Officials of the cycle race and the Gentlemen in the night club; and it would help to reinforce the superficiality of the Cashier's wealth when he decks himself out in similar garb after his entrance into the big world of the city. The Lady in her furs and silk would also present a picture of exaggerated elegance, in contrast with the dowdiness of the Cashier of the opening scenes.

A similar move towards abstraction can be achieved by treatment of the actor's face. As Ivan Goll said: 'We have quite forgotten that the first symbol of theatre is the mask. The mask is unchanging, unique and penetrating. It is immutable, inescapable Fate'.[22] But while theoretical writing from Craig to Goll recommended the use of masks, and Emil Pirchan designed some extremely striking examples,[23] they appeared only rarely on the Expressionist stage. The probable reason is that the set image of the mask militated against facial expressiveness, which was such an important feature of Expressionist acting style. As far as I have been able to discover, no leading director used masks in any of his major productions, unless it was specifically called for in the text, as for the Man-in-the-Mask of the final scene of Wedekind's

Frühlings Erwachen. Significantly, Reinhardt's German premiere of Pirandello's *Six Characters in Search of an Author* in 1924 was performed without masks.

Nevertheless, certain figures like the cycle race Officials would best achieve their identical anonymity by being masked, and a case could be made out for having all the characters masked except for the Cashier, so that they all appear as unreal projections of his mind.

What was common in Expressionist style was the use of a mask-like make-up. As in the early cinema, pallid faces with darkened eye sockets gave a certain bloodless uniformity to the appearance of actors and assisted in the creation of the anguished types beloved of Expressionism (see Plate 14). Occasionally, lines painted on the face could create a geometric effect: hollowed cheeks could become regular triangles, exaggerated eyebrows (as in Jessner's *Der Marquis von Keith*) could add to the grotesque appearance. Primitive effects, like the blue skin of Holofernes in the 1922 production of Hebbel's *Judith*, were sometimes used, and colour symbolism sometimes extended to the make-up. Thus in Gustav Hartung's 1920 Frankfurt production of Unruh's *Platz* (*Place*) some characters had green or blue faces to symbolize the diseased decadence of contemporary society.

Any of these possibilities might be explored in the presentation of *Von morgens bis mitternachts*, but it seems in fact that this was one of the less adventurous aspects of early productions of the play.

Acting for the abstractionist theatre

Man and things shall be shown as naked as possible, and to better effect always through the magnifying glass.

Ivan Goll: 'The super-drama' (1920)

It was the sheer physicality of the human actor, despite efforts at disguise through costume, mask or make-up, that confronted the Expressionist theatre with its greatest problem. To portray Man on stage one still had to employ a man, an individual of flesh and blood, not a disembodied idea. All other art-forms could transcend the limitations of the human form to penetrate to the essential: the painter could transform men into geometric shapes, placing their features where this best served the artist's vision; the sculptor could distend and abstract, using the freedom of his medium to go beyond the individual case to project a universal image. But the unique quality of the theatre is the living presence of the individual performer; the word becomes flesh, and this human incarnation must remain in constant tension with the tendency to abstraction.

It was this very tension, this overcoming of the problem created by the physicality of the actor, that generated the greatest contribution of this period to the development of the theatre. However, of all the arts of the theatre acting is the one which has responded least well to the challenge of Expressionism. Particularly in America, but also in Britain, the art of acting is generally still undertaken with techniques devised for realistic writing, although this represents only a small proportion of world drama. Even where inappropriate, the psychological approach all too often dominates the Anglo-Saxon stage.

Within any performance an actor has to fulfil three often antagonistic demands: first, he has a duty to the written text, a responsibility to speak the lines with clarity and sensitivity; second, he must portray a character, communicate inner feelings; finally, he has a duty to realize the situation of the play, to subjugate his own personality to the central idea revealed by the action. The best actor will try to ride all three horses at once, creatively exploring all three elements, but this balancing feat is not easy. A Hamlet who approaches the 'To be or not to be' soliloquy may concentrate on the words, speaking the lines as though reciting a poem; or he may choose to reveal Hamlet's anguish, opting for an introverted style that chops the flow of the lines to produce a sense of tormented indecision; or again he may use the speech not so much as a piece of poetry nor as an indicator of his individual emotions but primarily to communicate the implications of the soliloquy, presenting rather than creating a character and inviting the audience to consider the passage as a debate on suicide.

It may be argued that the art of acting since the Renaissance has in fact evolved through these three stages. In the traditional declamatory style of previous centuries the emphasis was primarily on a powerful delivery of the text; gestures and poses were artificial and prescribed, the word was paramount. With the Naturalistic revolution in the theatre and the introduction of Stanislavsky's Method, the actor was encouraged to search within himself for the emotions that would inform the text. Truthful acting now became a question of psychological veracity; the prescribed gesture was replaced by what seemed most appropriate in terms of the actor's individual experience. The first two steps of Stanislavsky's Method, Emotional Memory and the As-If Metaphor, invited the actor to explore his personal past and an imagined future, and as such were products of bourgeois individualism.

When the Expressionist theatre made the bold attempt to go beyond individual psychology to discover essential Man, it laid the foundations for an acting style which, though known to the oriental theatre for centuries, was to be an innovative force in the theatre of Europe and to initiate the important explorations of Brecht.

In the early 1900s in Germany both the conventional prescriptive style of acting and the more recent psychological style of Naturalism were being practised. In a typical handbook like Adolf Winds's *Die Technik der Schauspielkunst* (*The Technique of Acting*, 1904) the author lays down the approved methods of indicating various types. In order to represent Dignity, for example, he advises as follows:[24]

> The posture is upright, the look mild, the lips gently compressed, the facial expression broad and relaxed rather than long and stern. ... Often this is accompanied by a slight nodding as if in greeting, while the corresponding movement of the hand, the gesture of authority, is firm.

As we have seen,[25] the Naturalistic style developed in Germany by Otto Brahm sought to replace this 'acting by numbers' by a much more truthful approach. It was an approach, however, that was avowedly anti-theatrical.

As in playwriting, the theorists of the Expressionist theatre declared war on psychological realism and its tendency to produce untheatrical performances. Felix Emmel recorded his dismay over a director who was so obsessed with psychological realism that he determined the volume at which an actor spoke according to whether the words might be overheard in a neighbouring room: 'He constantly destroyed the structure of the drama through a host of finely conceived psychological nuances, whereby all his productions were played at a terribly weary pace and the dramatic rhythm was perforce extenuated'.[26] Of this self-indulgent and petty realism of the Naturalist actor Jessner remarks: 'If there were no pockets in his trousers, he was unable to act'.[27]

Once again, Kaiser's writing demands an anti-realistic, abstractionist style appropriate to the two-dimensional figures he creates. The easiest way of achieving abstract effects in acting was by using a large body of actors. The physicality of the individual actor disappeared in an anonymous mass, and this mass could be shaped into geometric patterns. Already in his pre-war arena productions Reinhardt had explored the stylized quality of crowd scenes (*Oedipus*, 1910; *Jedermann*, *The Oresteia*, 1911).[28]

Now, in *Von morgens bis mitternachts* similar geometrical groupings could be used, especially in the Salvation Army scene. Here there is a significant change in the congregation from a collection of individuals to an anonymous mass. Initially, there are confrontations between single rowdy members of the congregation and Salvation Army officers, and single shouts are apportioned to individuals:[29]

OTHERS (*amused*): Speak louder. No, don't. Music. Bring on the band.
Bring on cherubs with trumpets.
VOICE Begin.
ANOTHER VOICE No, don't.
OFFICER Why are you sitting down there on those benches?
ANOTHER VOICE Why not?

Cynical laughter and jeers continue until the sudden embarrassed silence that follows the first direct appeal to testify. This moment of silence following so much noise of music, laughter and shouting is as effective as the sudden interruption of sound in the cycle race scene and is the first point at which the congregation acts uniformly. From now on there is only one more raucous comment (which causes the heckler an immediate sense of shame) and the minority that had been urging silence on their noisier fellows now gains the upper hand. As the testimonies proceed, first a 'man', then 'many' and finally 'all' demand to hear their sins confessed.

To stage this scene, each actor would be required to know at what point his 'conversion' takes place. Initially, if a sceptic he would adopt a relaxed body posture, an attitude of rejection. At the point of conversion he would align himself with the 'believers', his body would tense forward to strain to catch every word of those confessing. The demands by 'all' to hear their sins confessed are accompanied, according to the stage-direction, by wild gestures and shouts in unison.

This attainment of ecstatic uniformity sets the stage for the Cashier's confession, which is therefore given especial prominence not only by virtue of being spoken by the main character but also by the total concentration of attention given to it. When he flings his money into the hall, the straining attentive mass suddenly becomes self-seeking individuals once more, fighting with one another in their greed.

With this dynamic treatment of the congregation Kaiser exploits the monumental crowd effects so beloved of abstract Expressionism and visually familiar to modern audiences from the crowd sequences of Fritz Lang's film *Metropolis*. They are characterized by strong uniform gestures and body postures and by speaking in unison. In this way individual actors become a disembodied mass, a powerful component of abstract theatre but also an ominous antecedent of that other dehumanized spectacle, the Nuremberg Rally.

In the portrayal of the nameless types of abstractionist drama, the actor must similarly generalize his gestures and speech from the accidents of individual character to those characteristics which determine essence of the role he is playing. The Bank Manager, the Fat Man, the Gentlemen at the cycle race: none of these has a past or any existence outside the scene in which they appear. The only exceptions are the Lady and her Son who establish a relationship and generate an interest which are independent of the Cashier and out of all proportion with their function in the plot. Here Kaiser has in fact written a scene which it would be possible to play totally Naturalistically and which therefore threatens to disturb the stylistic consistency of the whole.

For the rest, it is simple enough to sketch in the figures with broad strokes, to create caricatures rather than characters. This will depend on certain principles of acting which recall the formal style of oriental theatre and Craig's proposals for the 'Übermarionette'. As Bernard Kellerman had already pointed out in 1912 in an article on Japanese acting: 'The first actors ... were marionettes. This consideration is a key to the whole of Japanese acting. For still today the strangely distended movements of the actor, his slightly distorted poses ... point towards this prototype'.[30] In his essay on 'Expressionism on the stage' of 1918 Karl Heinz Martin acknowledged the influence of this oriental style and urged the use of more formal gesture;[31] and in his play *Der junge Mensch* (*The Young Man*, published 1924) Hanns Johst prescribed in his stage-directions puppet-like movements for some of the minor characters.

The first principle of this acting style is economy. In contrast with the excess of detailed gesture and facial expression with which the Naturalist actor attempts to flesh out his role, the abstractionist actor selects only those signals which will emphasize his function in the scene, rejecting any which serve only to give psychological nuances to his role. This principle of economy extends to the stillness of the actor when silent; whereas again the Naturalist actor would be expected to register his individual reaction to events on stage, it became a convention established by Leopold Jessner that only an actor speaking his lines might move and gesture; the interlocutor normally had to remain still and hold his pose. As in dance or opera the focus was generously given to the leading performer.

It is this emphasis on focus which is the second major principle of this style of acting. While the Stanislavskian actor carefully concealed his 'super-objective' beneath life-like detail, the abstractionist actor is required to find a focus in the action and make this totally apparent. The single focus for the Cashier at the beginning of the play is the money he handles; he does not even glance at his customers, communicating only with raps on the counter. For the Son in the next scene his treasured painting is initially his sole focus, just as the royal box presents the initial point of concentration for the Gentlemen at the cycle race. This single-minded concentration makes for the intense stare and absorbed stillness which is characteristic of this type of Expressionist acting.

The third principle derives from the first two, that of exaggeration. By employing economy and clarifying the focus, each move and gesture becomes larger than life. An actor reaching towards a prized object, like the Son towards his painting, would reach not just with his hands but with his whole body, thus approaching the physical involvement of the dancer. The danger is that the bringing to the surface of inner emotion may render the expression superficial, thus creating melodramatic performances which fail to convince. But the important distinction between melodramatic and Expressionist acting is that the latter, while sharing the same boldness of gesture, proceeds from genuine inner conviction; it is a commitment to essential truth, not something produced from a bag of actor's tricks.

Ecstatic acting style

> One day there will be a higher kind of theatre, in which the *soul* will reign
> supreme – and the spirit.
>
> Friedrich Kayssler: 'It is the soul that acts' (1912)

While the abstractionist style is appropriate to the minor figures of an
abstractionist play, clearly something more complex than this marionette-like
quality is required for the central figure. His acting style must distinguish him
from the less enlightened beings around him. Thus the Cashier will begin with
the mechanical movements and intensity of focus that characterize his
repetitive and soulless occupation. But after his transformation he needs to
seek the ecstatic style of a more heightened mode of Expressionist acting.

Economy, concentration of focus and exaggeration are also elements in this
style, but whereas the two-dimensional quality of the minor figures is
expressed in disciplined angularity, the style appropriate to the central figure
results from a release of all controls on his passion. In place of the associative
symbol, communication now becomes intense and immediate. It is here that
even Kaiser moves away from abstractionism towards primitivism, where the
voice at times becomes the 'Schrei'.

Already, before the word Expressionism came into the language, there had
been actors, especially with Max Reinhardt, who performed in an expressive
and impassioned style. Tilla Durieux was praised in 1910, the year she played
Jocasta and the title-role in Hebbel's *Judith*, for her 'mixture of the bestial
and demonic'.[32] 'She does not act ecstasy, she experiences it, and so carries
her heroines into the realms of hysteria.'[33] Two years previously Paul
Wegener, whom Brecht declared in 1920 to be one of the two delights of
Berlin (the other was the underground railway), had performed the part of
Franz Moor in Schiller's *Die Räuber*, which both in visual appearance and
intensity of acting anticipated Expressionism (see Plate 3):[34]

> A raving fanatic with a shock of red hair, broad mouth and a complexion
> sallow enough to give you jaundice. Wegener is of the opinion that Franz
> Moor ... cannot be explained in human terms and so thrusts him into the
> realms of mental imbalance.

When, nine years later, Wegener turned to Othello, he discovered again the
primitive sub-structure of the character: 'Wegener is a negro who stands with
both feet in the animal world.'[35]

Although this violent and primitive acting was therefore not unknown on
the German stage, the new Expressionist playwrights were concerned that
most actors with their Naturalist mannerisms would make a nonsense of the
intensely lyrical writing of the new drama. As Hasenclever recognized, high
tragedy is often perilously close to the ludicrous. Citing the example of the
almost preposterous fight between Hamlet and Laertes in Ophelia's grave,

Hasenclever observed: 'When it is but a short step from the sublime to the ridiculous, then pain has become so sublime that it is almost ridiculous.'[36]

There could be no compromise in the performing of Expressionist texts: either the ecstatic lyricism could be rendered more acceptable by distancing it in an abstractionist manner by, as it were, placing the lines in quotation marks; or the production would have to risk mockery and scorn by unashamedly embracing emotionalism and allowing the text to explode with uninhibited force on the stage. The 'Schrei' performance, though vulnerable, maintained its integrity, whereas any compromise with realism or with conventional public taste pointed up the potential absurdities of the text, and the result was like the worst productions of Shakespeare on television, where the visual realism is constantly jarring with the imaginative power of the words.

Paul Kornfeld was aware of the dangers of an inappropriate acting style for his tragedy *Die Verführung (The Seduction*, written 1913). The action of the play appears excessively melodramatic. Melodrama rests on the enactment of a series of external incidents, and the cause of these incidents arises in hackneyed emotions or chance events; there is neither a psychological nor a metaphysical pattern to sustain their improbability and exaggeration. In a perilously similar way, the characters of Expressionist plays will often act out their innermost wishes with unreflective spontaneity: fantasy becomes a seemingly real event. As Sokel says: 'As in dreams, wish becomes act, emotion becomes event'.[37] So in *Die Verführung* the protagonist Bitterlich falls in love with Marie and promptly strangles her fiancé, while Marie cries in despair: 'If he kills him, I won't have a bridegroom any more'.[38]

Realistic acting would be clearly inadequate to cope with such unpremeditated violence and Marie's banal reaction. So the first recommendation of Kornfeld in his 'Afterword to the actor', appended to *Die Verführung* when it was published in 1916, was to reject all attempts to copy real behaviour. In place of the standard imitative skills the actor was to 'dare to spread his arms out wide and with a sense of soaring speak as he has never spoken before in his life. ... Let him not be ashamed that he is acting, let him not deny the theatre.' Indeed, it would be better for the actor to banish reminiscences of actual behaviour and to seek the One Experience: 'Let him abstract from the attributes of reality and be nothing but the representative of thought, feeling or Fate.' In place of Stanislavsky's Emotional Memory, therefore, Kornfeld sought means to create a universal image in performance: 'Think of opera in which the singer, dying, still sounds forth a top C and with the sweetness of his melody says more about death than if he were to writhe in agony; for it is more important that death is a tragedy [ein Jammer] than that it is horrible.'[39]

When, as one of the earliest attempts to stage an Expressionist play, *Die Verführung* was premiered in Frankfurt on 8 December 1917, directed by

Gustav Hartung, the acting fulfilled most of Kornfeld's demands. In a lengthy review Bernhard Diebold discussed the need to find a new style of performance:[40]

> The new actor has to remove himself as far from Naturalistic prose as from the pathos of blank verse; he must express himself immediately from his own soul without tricks of transformation, without imitating a character – for what meaning can psychology have compared with spiritual expression: its form is the melody of language alone, impelled by the rhythm of spiritual tension. The musical and sensitive amateur will here achieve more than the most talented court-actor or the cleverest realistic performer of Otto Brahm's. ... The major contribution of the evening was made by Herr Feldhammer, who as Bitterlich offered a perfect example of Expressionist technique. His arms by his sides, facing out towards the audience (at the same time lyrically turned in upon himself), he contained his gestures during the gradually mounting speech until the expressive scream of language and movement together.

Kasimir Edschmid considered that Feldhammer had gone even further than Kornfeld's advice: 'Feldhammer sang his whole part.'[41]

On a practical level there were three techniques introduced by this new style of acting. The first was a closer relationship with the audience. The actor no longer provided a pretty or a realistic spectacle, he bared his soul in an attempt at direct communication. The action was not confined merely to the relationships between the characters on stage; it now crossed the footlights, drawing the spectator into an active relationship with the play.

A paradigm of this breaking down of the fourth wall is provided by Hasenclever in Act 3, Scene 5 of *Der Sohn*. Here the Son addresses the assembled young revolutionaries to describe to them his years of suffering under his tyrannical father. At first his speech is subdued, almost inaudible, he does not move his hands. Then he throws his arms wide apart and leaves the dais to move amongst the audience. Finally, he tears his clothes from his body to reveal the weals of the whip-lashes administered by his father. The direct address to the audience, combined with a metaphorical, if seldom physical, disrobing, became a standard technique of Expressionist acting. Even Jessner, whose abstractionist performances tended to maintain a certain distance from the audience, would frequently change the lighting and have soliloquies delivered from the front of the stage direct to the audience, so reviving a technique familiar to most of the great ages of theatre, not least to the Elizabethans. In similar vein, the protagonist of Hanns Johst's *Der junge Mensch* (*The Young Man*, staged 1919) appeals in the eighth picture for the audience to applaud.

Such direct communication with the audience was problematic where the setting was inappropriate to this style. In Reinhardt's production of Goering's *Seeschlacht* (1918) Ernst Stern's realistic set created some sense of the claustrophobia of a naval gun turret. This was undermined by Paul Wegener's acting, now identifiably Expressionistic, which, though appropriate to the text, was out of key with the production:[42]

> The uncanny illusion ... was not helped by the figure of Herr Wegener with his brooding dreamer's look approaching too close to the audience. More important than this external detail was the fact that the performer did not release his hold of the audience. First came mysteriously evocative whispers, then the defiance burst through until a miracle occurred and flames shot up like roses around a heroic figure with great reserves of power.

Another danger inherent in uncontrolled and ecstatic communication is that it could lead to physical attacks on the audience. Although there are reports of this having taken place,[43] I have found no evidence for it, and it is unlikely that it took place at any major Expressionist performance.

In *Von morgens bis mitternachts* the Cashier is given a number of opportunities for direct address to the audience, stepping outside the limits of the play, becoming aware of his own performance, and so creating an example of metatheatre. In the hotel scene, when the Cashier is alone on stage with the Lady, he cries out: 'I've got my wits about me, ladies and gentlemen',[44] and in his monologue in the snowfield scene, when apostrophizing the Lady, he uses self-consciously metatheatrical language: 'That's your cue, silken lady. Give it to me, shimmering lady, why you're letting the show down. Stupid bitch. How did you get into the act? Fulfil your natural obligations, bear children — and don't bother the prompter!'[45] For the rest, while the speeches of the Cashier remain within the structure of the scene, their function as commentary implies a direct address to the audience, most obviously in his final confession to the Salvation Army congregation.

The second new technique of this heightened acting style derived from the discovery of the expressiveness of the body. While the old school of acting was concerned with the beautiful gesture, and while Naturalism, though aware of the expressiveness of the body as a means of complementing the inarticulacy of the realist character, remained locked in imitation, Expressionism returned to the origins of theatrical performance — to the dance. 'The actor has become an actor of movement',[46] asserted Herbert Ihering, and Josef Kainz described the actor's movements as 'the expression of a psyche, the illustration of an inner state'.[47]

While the movement qualities of abstractionism in its disciplined symbolism related most closely to the eurhythmics of Emile Jaques Dalcroze at Hellerau (1911–14), the unrestrained emotionalism of primitivistic acting seemed to develop from the expressive style of Isadora Duncan, who had founded a dance school in Berlin as early as 1904. A further influence was possibly provided by Rudolf Laban's system of eukinetics, and more especially by his pupil Mary Wigman. Wigman, who opened a dance school in Dresden in 1920 and later worked as a choreographer with Piscator, developed Laban's methods in a more expressive manner, going beyond formal and allegorical movement to develop a more intensely emotional style. In particular, she introduced to dance the technique, later popularized by Martha Graham, of moving suddenly from extreme tension to complete relaxation.

This spasmatic style, whether directly influenced by Wigman or not, certainly became characteristic of Expressionist acting. Friedrich Sebrecht argued in 1919 that the physical movements of the actor must project his inner feelings with total intensity:[48]

[He] could not feel ... a 'concealed longing pain' without spasmatically convulsing his shoulders while speaking; he could not experience vocally and viscerally a deep melancholia without first forcing his vacuous, 'chaotic and eternity-filled' eyes to bulge.

Two years earlier Walter von Hollander in his article on 'The Expressionism of the actor' emphasized above all the physicality of the actor:[49]

Impressionism [i.e. Naturalism] was bodily shame: the body clothed the soul, wrapping it round, hinting at what lay underneath, but never revealing it. Expressionism: the soul exposing itself in the body without shame. ... The soul communicating through the body means the grand gesture, stillness and strength and the evaluation of movement, it means too that a new body-language must be devised if it does not evolve by itself, must be learned if it has evolved. ... This new drama cannot be brought to life by the imitation of reality but through the expression of the body. Reality, however, does not find bodily expression in everyday gestures but only by the body's seizing hold of all means of which it is capable by shaping itself into a work of art.

What was therefore required of the actor was a total physical involvement in his performance: 'speaking with the body',[50] as Felix Emmel puts it, or, in Bernhard Diebold's words, 'Gestures alone create the geometry of performance.'[51] The questions an actor asks himself are no longer: 'Do I look pleasing to the audience?' nor 'Are my postures and gestures psychologically appropriate to the character I am portraying?' but simply: 'Is every part of my body reflecting and projecting my inner emotional state?' Thus a representation of anger would draw on all the most powerful signs of rage: the body in tension, bulging eyes, bared teeth; despair would be shown by the body collapsed and passive, the eyes sunk, the head bowed. Here we see the danger of the generalized style of Expressionist acting: this self-styled modern approach was coming perilously close to the overplaying and formality of the traditional declamatory style. The genuine emotional commitment of the actor alone preserved the Expressionist style from seeming merely a gross display in overacting.

Where this total commitment was achieved, the effect seems to have been overwhelming. Of Werner Krauss's performance in *Seeschlacht* Herbert Ihering wrote:[52]

The word was not accompanied by gesture, not amplified by movement: the word was gesture, the word became flesh. Krauss's acting was so intense that it was as though he had exchanged his senses: he saw the sound and heard the movement.

The third major technique developed by the 'ecstatic' actor was in the delivery of his lines, now no longer the prosaic dialogue of Naturalism but the clipped utterances of the 'Telegrammstil' ('telegraphese') and the lyrical outburst, often characterized in the text by attracting to it a row of exclamation marks. Ihering described this speech technique as follows:[53]

The manner of speech of the Expressionist actor was adapted to clipped responses, to striking sentences and the precise hammer-blows of single words. He did not speak in measured phrases or in a flowing style, but in an abbreviated and pointed manner. There seemed to be only nouns and exclamation marks. Initially this was a reaction against the Naturalistic slackening of rhythmic speech, against the division and chopping of verses by psychological and explanatory gestures. In contrast to this ramification, the actor spoke breathlessly, tensely, hastily, staccato. He spoke aggressively, fanatically, with emphasis, reproducing the punctuation rather than the melody.

What is then characteristic of primitivist Expressionist speech is the same quality seen in bodily movement: extreme energy, abrupt spasmatic delivery, and a total commitment of the actor so that the words seem to be exploding from within rather than being merely lines learned for a role.

In *Von morgens bis mitternachts* the intensity of the Cashier's communication is thrown into greater relief by contrast with the incomprehension and banality of the figures around him. His passionate declarations to the Lady are met with indignant rejection. The self-revelation about his transformation: 'I have bored my head through clods of earth ... one mighty leap – don't hesitate – and you are out of the pen – out of the treadmill. One mighty leap and here I am!'[54] is received by his family with the only acceptable explanation: 'He is ill'.[55] In the cycle race scene the essential contrast has to be established between the Gentlemen with their involvement in the event and the Cashier's excited observation of the crowd. This might be achieved by the Officials' mounting frenzy – a reflection of the general excitement in the stadium – contrasting with the stillness of the Cashier. On the other hand, since this might distract from the Cashier's speech, one might use the now familiar technique of the 'freeze'. As far as I can discover, it was Leopold Jessner in his production of *Der Marquis von Keith* who introduced this device: in the ball scene the dancers froze in their poses while the principals conversed. Here the Gentlemen could hold frenetic poses while the Cashier speaks, thus giving the proper focus to his words. It accords well with the imaginative quality of Expressionist theatre to represent violent and noisy movement with stillness and silence.

Contemporary reviews of early productions of *Von morgens bis mitternachts* suggest that the role of the Cashier was performed with appropriate intensity. The lead actor in the 1917 premiere, Erwin Kalser, had already distinguished himself a year previously by his ecstatic performance as the Student in Falckenberg's production of Strindberg's *Ghost Sonata*. Kalser had in fact become so totally involved in his role that at the dress rehearsal he physically attacked the actor playing the Old Man. As Kalser himself wrote in 1916:[56]

> What is the nature of the actor's training other than to force him against his will to abandon the obstinacy of his body, so that it may become totally and utterly the organ of his soul? The soul must reach deep into the hidden core of the body, so that all things become possible for the actor; he may completely surrender himself to his soul; it will do everything for him. ... The actor who is aware of his inner strength goes on stage like a being in search of sleep and treasured dreams.

In the Berlin premiere of 1919 Max Pallenberg, who had already played the lead in a raucous manner in Vienna in 1917, seemed under Hollaender's direction to have freed himself from the ranting of his earlier performance, combining now a grotesque comic quality with an intense delivery of the lines, a 'forcefulness, with which Pallenberg throws himself on each word and each thought'.[57] For Emil Faktor the grotesqueness worked only at the beginning, before the Cashier's regeneration; thereafter, 'If he turned to comedy, the tragic mania was lost; if he sought ways of affecting the audience emotionally, contradictions arose between his tendency to popularize and Kaiser's mystically accentuated spirituality'.[58] Alfred Polgar, however, found complete unity in the grotesque style of Pallenberg's Expressionistic acting:[59]

> a quite ghostly, unreal type and yet inwardly so full of living tension that sparks seemed constantly to leap from him and threaten to set the air alight. A melancholy clown, a depressive eccentric ... with a grimace of terrifying pain and rage against the divine and human order.

In this achievement Pallenberg, who was to become one of Piscator's leading actors, would seem to have discovered some sort of synthesis between the abstractionist and primitivist styles: using a two-dimensional grotesqueness he seems to have projected a sense of the ecstatic 'Schrei'.

The audience at the premiere reacted with considerably less enthusiasm than Alfred Polgar. They jeered and whistled, and hooted with laughter even when the down-trodden waiter in the night club scene was hit to the ground, and the lively Salvation Army scene, which even on stage almost drowned out Pallenberg's voice, became an opportunity for particularly loud and aggressive participation:[60]

The public responded to the crass effects with whistles and jeers, there were lively personal altercations leading to actual fights, and many of those present joined in the play. The director Hollaender appeared at the end and declared that he would report to the author on 'the lively reception' of his work.

The most successful realization of the role of the Cashier, at the Lessingtheater Berlin in 1921, owed much to the masterful direction of Victor Barnowsky, who had earned Jacobsohn's praise for his production of Kaiser's *Hölle Weg Erde* the previous year:[61]

The text, cleaned as white as a bone, poured out, unrolled, hummed forth as precisely as a machine from actors who for once did not need to be actors. Pace for its own sake was everything, not flesh and blood, and whoever showed too much of these had a disturbing rather than a beneficial effect. The director Barnowsky showed that he ... can force his actors to give up their own personality for the sake of an artistic experiment.

Barnowsky was well noted for the fast pacing of his productions (Ihering had commented: 'There is always movement in his performances, but this movement is movement at any price'[62]), and he also had a sound grasp of the new theatrical style required by Expressionistic writing. As he had written in 1920:[63]

To elevate solid bourgeois actors to an emotionally charged style is one of the hardest tasks of the director. All too easily a naturalistic gesture, hands-in-the-trouser-pockets-acting, creeps into the spiritual and heroic line.

Alexander Granach as the Cashier also possessed a great sense of pace, tremendous energy and the ability to produce the ecstatic emotional performance sought by Barnowsky. 'Pace is his thing,'[64] wrote Julius Bab, and Alfred Klaar described Granach's Cashier as 'an unleashed wild animal'.[65] The most complete description of his performance reads as follows: 'A drawn, haggard face with hollow eyes, emaciated hands with spidery fingers, and a shabby ill-fitting coat characterized the external appearance. But from within a hoarse and hungry despair cried out with hard jerky sounds.'[66] Emil Faktor was less convinced by this 'adventurous fanatic' and his throaty style of delivery and his acting 'more appropriate to a madhouse'. Faktor considered such unrelieved intensity a misunderstanding of true Expressionism: 'it only knows a state of frenzy and not caesuras, contemplativeness or points of relaxation'.[67]

Here Faktor points to one of the major directorial problems of Expressionist theatre: the undifferentiated ecstatic 'Schrei' becomes merely deadening, but if one lets the pitch drop to a more relaxed and Naturalistic level, the emotional peaks begin to appear false. The poetry must be sustained in theatrical terms, and the solution in a play like *Von morgens bis mitternachts* is to maintain the anti-realistic style (hard enough in scenes like the hotel scene) and to shift from the ecstatic to the grotesque, from emotional climax to cartoon-like comedy. In this way relief can be provided without ever slipping back into cosy realism.

Even if the critics were not in agreement over Barnowsky's achievement, the production became a great public success, perhaps not least because it coincided with Kaiser's trial in Munich for misappropriating his landlord's furniture. The play was now established as a major Expressionist work, and Granach was to be invited to play the role at a number of other theatres in Germany.

From now on the unrelieved, intense, haunted quality of Barnowsky's production began to give way to a lighter treatment, as Expressionism faded away before the advent of 'Neue Sachlichkeit'. In Berthold Viertel's production at the Schauspielhaus Dresden on 13 April 1922, the lead actor Erich Ponto, who was later to work with Brecht, took a quite different approach from Granach's:[68]

> Ponto did not place much emphasis on the man who is haunted by fear, who is already in despair ... he did not utter the piercing scream [Schrei] of the hunted beast, as we heard in Granach's performance. Ponto rather offered – in accordance with his nature – something of touching optimism at any price, something fearfully hopeful, something between disbelief and wanting to believe, something at once taut and free.

Here Ponto had introduced a complexity into the character of the Cashier, which may have made for a more interesting acting performance but was not in tune with true Expressionist style. The Cashier is a little down-trodden humdrum individual who bursts into ecstatic regeneration after the meeting with the Lady from Florence, the 'capitalist catalyst'. The change must be decisive and complete, and any half-tones or complexities blur the paradigmatic quality of the central figure.

Nevertheless, the era of theatrical Expressionism was past, and Fritz Mack, reviewing the Leipzig production of the play in 1924, said: 'it now seems almost historical'.[69]

The last inter-war production of the play in Berlin opened on 3 February 1925 under the auspices of the Volksbühne in the Schillertheater, directed by Albrecht Joseph, with Granach once more in the lead. 'Neue Sachlichkeit' seemed now finally to have quenched the Expressionist flames. Hugo Kubsch was disturbed by the intrusion of 'cold psychology' into the performance: 'The light of the seeker after knowledge flickers for a few moments, but it only flickers, it does not burst into flames.'[70] Gone then was the emotional ecstasy; the 'Schrei' had become a lecture:[71]

> You feel too removed from it all. It's as though you were attending a clever lecture in the Institute for Psychology ... and then again you feel as though you're in the cinema watching a well-made film.

Siegfried Jacobsohn summed up the problem in his review in Die Weltbühne:[72]

Why has no production caught on to the fact that the play rages like a tempest? Because in the phantasmagoria there are too many elements of realism, which no director and certainly no actor will be prevented from serving up in the old Naturalistic style, especially now that they have freed themselves from the bonds of Expressionism; and because the Cashier has monologues that need to be delivered. The new director Albrecht Joseph showed himself to be a pretty skilful eclectic.

The best documentation of the central performance is of Ernst Deutsch's portrayal of the Cashier in the film version of 1920, by which time Deutsch had already established himself as a leading Expressionist actor. His first major role had been the lead in the Dresden production of Hasenclever's *Der Sohn* in 1916: 'Ernst Deutsch moved trance-like through the play, the archetype of ecstatic man, hollow-eyed, incandescent, pulled by the strings of a higher power.'[73] He played the same part again at its Berlin premiere and also performed the lead in the 1917 premiere of Sorge's *Der Bettler*: 'His appearance and the fervour of his speech combined together in a compelling manner' (see Plates 4 and 5).[74] Calling him 'a modern ecstatic', Julius Bab said of Deutsch: 'The power of Deutsch is like electric energy, it is based on an inner transformation, it explodes suddenly like lightning. ... In him muscular energy is transformed into nervous energy.'[75]

In the *Von morgens bis mitternachts* film we may observe his use of the powerful gestures and violent facial expressions characteristic of Expressionism. Made up initially with heavily darkened eyes and lit so strongly on the crown of his head as to make his hair look pathetically wispy, he sits at the bank counter at the beginning, hunched one shoulder higher than the other, his hands poised like claws over the money he is about to steal (see Plate 14). After the transforming moment with the Lady his body straightens and his hands reach out to grasp symbolically his new regenerated life, until he finally decks himself out in evening dress and opera cape – a transformation into a dapper appearance, reflecting his growth into a new life. At the same time, the rather operatic quality of this new guise suggests an unconvincing superficiality; the Cashier's advance into a new life appears an illusion, and he only finally discovers reality in his suicide against the tottering cross in the Salvation Army Hall (see Plate 16).

At times Deutsch moves sharply and mechanically, like an automaton, as when his daughter helps him out of his coat, or when he turns full-face to the camera just before entering his home, only to break away suddenly to scuttle into the house. The ecstatic actor has here been refused the possibility of speech and so must communicate everything with his body and his facial expressions. The silent anguish of the Cashier revealed in his often twisted posture, bulging eyes and bared teeth, is a telling example of Expressionist acting.

Thus, despite the early date of its composition, Kaiser's *Von morgens bis mitternachts* contains all the ingredients that gave to Expressionist theatre one of its major styles: settings and characters abstracted from reality, the effective use of light and sound creating a total theatre calling for responses at many different levels, and, above all, an ecstatic central portrayal demanding an intensely expressive performance. Following the lead given by Kaiser and other playwrights of his generation, the theatre found its highest realization of abstractionist Expressionism in the work of a director whom we have already had cause to refer to frequently, Leopold Jessner.

The abstractionist theatre of Leopold Jessner

The whole of life is on the quest for a new form of expression, for an immediate and intensely effective form. The earlier form was awkward, its thinking contorted and so ramified, revealed as it was in everyday trivia, that it may have entertained and amused but it never convinced. So form turned into formality – uniform. Ideas demand the simplest, most immediately effective form of expression. In the theatre, where all artistic and technical possibilities meet in the common aim of creating the strongest effect, the striving towards a new form is at its most intense. ... Today the theatre is trying to free itself from the autocracy of detail, to present the writer's work and its effects in the purest, most convincing and deliberate form; it is not trying to act out something in front of the spectator but to force him to intense and delighted involvement, not trying to distract him but to force him to concentrate, not trying to bombard but to render precise – by seeking the strongest effect in simplicity of form.

Leopold Jessner, cit. in Adolf Winds: *Geschichte der Regie* (1925)

Leopold Jessner was a Jew, a Republican and a Social Democrat, three factors that made him the ideal representative of the new theatre of the Weimar Republic. Coming from relative obscurity in Hamburg and Königsberg in East Prussia, he was appointed to the most significant theatre post in the new Germany: the Directorship of the Staatliches Schauspielhaus or, more simply, Staatstheater in Berlin, which until the Revolution had been the Kaiser's own Hoftheater. Significantly, he opened the Staatstheater with that classical celebration of Republican freedom, Schiller's *Wilhelm Tell* (1804), the 'cultural visiting-card' of the Weimar Republic, as Ihering called the production.

Already in 1913 in his failed application for the Directorship of the Berlin

Volkstheater he had written: 'I also wish to present the freedom-cry *Wilhelm Tell*, that wonderful folk-song, but not as a realist peasant drama.'[76] He rejected the folksy realism of traditional presentations of the play: 'Away with the pictorial Naturalism of the Swiss landscapes that no civilized spectator can possibly believe to be real.'[77] With his designer Emil Pirchan, again a virtual unknown from Munich, Jessner sought to emphasize the essential theme of the play, the cry for freedom: 'not the story but the idea behind the story.'[78] By loosing Schiller's work from its specific historical situation and seeking to distil off its general political meaning, Jessner and Pirchan achieved the first major example of truly abstractionist setting in Expressionist theatre.

In place of the expected Alpine scenery of soaring mountains and green meadows atmospherically lit, the audience were confronted with a grey-green construction of ramps, stairs and bridges, forming a right angle behind an open playing area. This construction, and the dark side curtains and the geometric black mountain range on the white cyclorama, were always in view; and this permanent set was modified by simple additions to define locations. A grated door indicated Tell's home; a pillar-like tree suggested the proximity of Stauffacher's house; for the interior setting of Attinghausen's castle a rear wall with high Gothic windows was flown in; a single cross defined the Rütli meadow; a pole with a hat the meadow near Altdorf. It is now almost a commonplace of modern scenic design to use a permanent abstract set for a variety of scenes, whether outdoor or indoor; it makes for speedy scene changes and stimulates the imagination. In 1919 this way of staging a classic was nothing short of revolutionary.

To emphasize the architectural quality of the set Jessner made use of strong directional lighting. This was something which had been explored in depth by Appia in his creation of 'rhythmic space'. A three-dimensional set will lose much of its solidity if flattened by general lighting; so, for example, Felix Cziossek in his cubist design for Shakespeare's *Henry IV* in Stuttgart in the early 1920s reinforced the effect of the cubes and steps by lighting only one plane and leaving the rest in darkness. There is also the further consideration that, given a permanent set with minimal modifications to suggest a change of scene, a greater importance than ever before is attached to the lighting in assisting this change. A flight of steps can change its appearance radically if illuminated from different sides, and so can seem to become an entirely new setting. This architectonic quality of light meant for Jessner and Pirchan the abandonment of individual spotlights cutting through the darkness. This steady light source which created the setting rather than concentrating on the individual actor was particularly welcomed by Siegfried Jacobsohn in his review of *Wilhelm Tell*: 'at last constant light instead of those wandering spots'.[79] In addition to the architectonic use of light, Jessner employed it symbolically: the common people were lit by a steady grey light, while Tell was bathed in brilliant white.

Predictably, the audience were greatly discomfited by seeing one of their beloved texts treated in this way. Not only had Jessner deliberately cut from the play those over-familiar lines which made it seem like a repository of quotations, but he had also robbed the audience of any sensual enjoyment of the beautiful Swiss setting and the majesty and mystery of the natural elements. The annoyance and bewilderment of the public finally erupted in the famous 'Hollow Way' scene in which Tell shoots Gessler (Act 4, Scene 3). The Hollow Way was created by the simple device of drawing together two curtains at the back to allow just a narrow triangle of the cyclorama with its mountains to be seen. On the famous line, 'Auf dieser Bank von Stein will ich mich setzen' ('Upon this bench of stone I'll seat myself'), the actor playing Tell, Albert Bassermann, rested on one of the wooden steps in the foreground. It is perhaps significant that a detail of such triviality should have provoked the furore that halted the performance; for it was at this point that the traditional representational theatre and the modern imaginative theatre clashed most obviously. The 'bench of stone' would hardly in over a century of performances have been made of stone, but it would have looked like stone; Jessner and Pirchan had outraged the audience by blatantly admitting that their bench was of wood. An easy imaginative leap for children or for oriental audiences, this was jeered at angrily by the more vocal element of the public at the premiere of *Tell*. The curtain had to come down, and Bassermann emerged to bellow: 'Throw out these hired louts!' After the intervention of the police the performance was finally able to continue.

With his production of *Tell* Jessner had taken the abstract staging of the hitherto almost exclusively private Expressionist performances and thrust it boldly into the centre of Prussian theatre tradition, the Hoftheater. As Norbert Falk, mixing his metaphors with abandon, wrote in his review of *Tell*: 'He had the courage to slap a rotting tradition in the face and so with one heave has pushed the Schauspielhaus into the place where it belongs.'[80]

Having used a classic to let forth a cry of freedom in the name of the Weimar Republic, Jessner next turned to the depiction of modern society in a contemporary play, Wedekind's *Der Marquis von Keith*, originally premiered in Berlin in 1901. For this grotesque satire Jessner and Pirchan divided the stage into two levels, the upper half, the domain of the Marquis, white and brilliant, the lower half black, where the common people remained. The acting style also reflected these two worlds: while the aristocratic figures maintained a stylized manner of performance, the minor bourgeois figures acted in a totally Naturalistic fashion, so by an inverted process of alienation appearing particularly eccentric and trivial in their behaviour. Above the upper half of the stage there was no light, so the Marquis's abode seemed to be suspended in space. The spindly furniture and the symmetrical white screens, which the moody Marquis rearranged whimsically, reinforced this feeling of precariousness and insubstantiality. Similarly, the pictures were empty frames, the telephone a mere ear-piece, and doors snapped open before the actor reached them to swing shut immediately behind him. The reviewer Franz Servaes commented: 'The unreality of our modern life has now been pictorially demonstrated'.[81]

In order to transform his actors into the 'transcendental sculpture'[82] of abstractionist acting Jessner imposed on them a rigid discipline: 'Directing today means above all subjecting the individuality of the actor to strong guidance.'[83] In *Der Marquis von Keith* he went to the extent of turning them into marionette-like figures. Wearing extravagant costumes and make-up, the actors plunged on to stage as though thrown in from the wings. Instead of a bell, a drum-roll heralded their entrances, so that they appeared to be coming on as though, circus-like, to perform a turn. In a crucial scene from the last act, in which the Countess Anna leaves the Marquis for good, Wedekind gives the following line to the Marquis: 'If you leave me, I'll collapse like an ox in the slaughterhouse.' Characteristically for Jessner, he realized this threat in visual terms: on Anna's exit Kortner, playing the Marquis, sank to his knees in front of his table 'like an ox'. Lothar Müthel, in the part of Scholz, now entered, leapt on the table on his knees and seized the Marquis around the neck from behind. Scholz hung on as though his life depended on it, while the Marquis felt strangled by his grip. Most of the scene was performed in this awkward position, until the Marquis finally freed himself and the scene was played to its conclusion with a manic chase along the walls, intensified by giant shadows cast by spots at floor level.[84]

The high point of Jessner's and Pirchan's abstractionist style was reached with their next production, Shakespeare's *Richard III*, which opened at the Staatstheater on 5 November 1920. Once more it was not the psychological character of the hero or the specific historical situation that was the focus, but the image of a dangerous tyrant rising to power and being defeated – not Richard the individual, but his career. Jessner's production contained an anti-militaristic, anti-autocratic message for his fellow Republicans, and, as it transpired, a warning about another tyrant who was to reveal much in common with the ambitious Richard.

In order to clarify his vision of the play, Jessner made use of obvious and often symmetrically contraposed theatrical effects: for his opening monologue, Richard stood dressed in black in front of a black curtain; at the end Richmond, dressed entirely in white, moved forward on his final speech to allow a white curtain to drop down behind him. For his coronation Richard and his followers were clothed in red; the uniforms of Richmond's army were white. The entrance of the young princes was greeted with a blaze of white light; Richard at his death was bathed in a red spot.

In this production Jessner also carried Expressionist acting to a high point, both in Fritz Kortner's intensely emotional performance as Richard ('an incomparably earth-bound ballad-ogre. Gnashing teeth, poisonous looks, diabolical laughter, mysteriously energetic movements, an intelligence as supple as a snake, the body of a half-beast – all this not placed in the service of superficial theatricality but filled with the true blood of the performer'[85]) and in the abstractionist performance of minor figures like Buckingham, played by Rudolf Forster:[86]

> Buckingham's movements and attitudes were strangely conventionalized and were dominated by a restrained athletic grace and a statuesque im-mobility. Now his gestures became hieratic as when offering Richard the crown, now he made steps that seemed part of a solemn dance.

The basic design by Pirchan for *Richard III* consisted of a grey-green wall, about half the height of the stage, set across the back. This wall, which had a single arched opening through it at its base, was broad enough on top to allow actors to walk along it. This use of an upper level was particularly suited to Shakespeare, permitting the realization of Elizabethan stage-directions like 'Enter Gloucester, in a gallery above, between two Bishops' (Act 3, Scene 7).

Behind this wall was a second higher wall of equally muted colour surmounted by a long low rectangle of brilliant red sky. As in *Tell* this permanent set was adapted for various scenes; for example, hanging the back wall with tapestries to represent a room in the palace, or using the low arch in the back wall to represent Clarence's prison cell.

The bare staging was assisted by the use of striking lighting effects, as at the end of Act I, Scene 2 (see Plate 17). As Richard completed his monologue and turned to go, a light from the prompter's box threw a threatening shadow on to the rear of the stage, so warning of the diabolical power of the man and giving point to the lines:

> Shine out, fair sun, till I have bought a glass
> That I may see my shadow as I pass.

In this production Jessner also employed sound effects and music in an imaginatively Expressionist manner. He used music only expressively, never as decoration, and as a result would often prefer a truthful rendering which served the central idea to one that was aesthetically more pleasing. So, for instance, over-extended whining notes on oboes heralded the catastrophe of *Der Marquis von Keith*, and the song that follows the elevated Author's Prologue in Schiller's *Wallenstein* (staged 1924) was a raucous peasant affair, plunging the audience at once into the rough and tumble of the army camp. As Jessner wrote in 1925:[87]

> Stage music can no longer consist of a series of pieces which interrupt the action as independent works of musical impression. Music now has the function of integrating itself into the rhythms of the plot. It has become the source of those 'off-stage noises'. The roll of drums replaces machine-made thunder, which merely attempted to be a faithful imitation of nature. The flageolet tones of violins – in place of wind-machines – express the

blowing of storms. And where a huge thunder-sheet was used to reproduce the sounds of battle, we now use the dynamic effect of trumpets and percussion. ... However powerful the trumpets may be, however moving the sound of the violins, they are only elements of the total expression and must remain completely subservient to it. To conclude a melody for its own sake is no longer admissible. It must break off when the scene demands it.

The most striking scenic device, however, came in the second half of the play. As the curtain rose at the end of the interval after the third act, a monumental flight of blood-red steps was revealed, its base filling almost the whole breadth of the stage, rising in three narrowing sets to just below the height of the wall. It was these steps that were to become inextricably associated with the 'Jessner style' and to be imitated by abstractionist designers everywhere in Germany. When Jessner was asked what he had seen after returning from a visit to several provincial theatres in the mid-1920s, he wearily replied: 'Nothing but steps.'

Monumental steps were hardly new in theatre design. They were a virtually indispensable component of most Greek plays, they were a recurrent feature of Appia's designs, and the third act of Kaiser's *Die Bürger von Calais* (*The Burghers of Calais*), which was written in 1913 and premiered in Frankfurt in 1917, was played on broad steps leading up to the door of a church. What was new about Jessner's conception was the way in which the steps were employed.

They were first used as the setting for Richard's coronation preceding Act 4, Scene 2. Richard, in a long crimson robe, slowly mounted the red steps through two lines of bowing henchmen. As he reached the top to ascend his throne, the red of the steps was linked to the red of the sky by the crimson of Richard's gown, as though an electric charge of evil had leapt the gap between heaven and earth (see Plate 18). As Alfred Polgar wrote: 'It is as though the sky itself provides a bloody reflection of Richard's atrocities.'[88] Later, the same steps were used as the battlefield on which Richmond assembled his warriors (see Plate 19), on which Richard passed the nightmare-filled hours before battle, and on which the battle itself took place. The opposing armies, represented by just four extras each, faced each other on the steps and, to the rhythmic beating of a drum, mimed stylized movements of battle without ever making contact. Of a similar battle scene in Jessner's production of Grabbe's *Napoleon* in 1922 Ihering observed: 'Never have battle scenes been so far removed from the ridiculous and been subject to such a compelling rhythm.'[89]

As Richmond's forces gained the upper hand, off-stage was heard a repeated stammering shout like a child in despair: 'A horse, a horse, my kingdom for a horse.' Suddenly Richard appeared at the top of the steps, which were now aflow with the blood-red capes of his fallen soldiers. Naked to the waist, he held his crown under one arm like a severed head. Hopping down astride his sword, he plunged towards his death at the hands of Richmond's white-clad troops, who struck him down by stylized gestures with their swords without actually touching him. For Alfred Polgar the moment was as wild as 'an Indian war-dance'.[90]

This imaginative use of steps had many advantages. On a practical level it became easy to prevent actors masking one another, and the director could compose stage pictures which employed vertical as well as horizontal relationships. An actor's move from step to step was magnified by the addition of this new dimension, and so the performer was inhibited from making the trivial and unmotivated moves characteristic of the worst Naturalist acting. In their place much more powerful effects could be introduced. As Jessner himself stated: 'The erection of steps – as an autonomous architectural element – meant altering the base of the stage in accordance with its new function, which was now no longer to reproduce different rooms and landscapes but to be the abstract setting of mythical events.'[91]

So in his production of Grabbe's *Napoleon* the final scene shows the defeated Emperor, who had hitherto been on the highest step, now seated at the bottom, the sun sinking behind him and the common soldiers silhouetted against the sky above him. Another 'mythical' moment was made possible by the steps in the 1922 staging of Schiller's *Don Carlos*. The court entered over the top of the steps, slowly increasing in magnificent array as it poured over the highest step to descend slowly on the waiting Carlos, the figure of youthful freedom, who seemed swamped by this surge of splendour from above.

Besides offering such meaningful visual moments Jessner's steps also seemed to concretize the transcendent quality of Expressionism. The steps mounting into space seemed to be a correlative of the soaring lyricism and philosophical search for higher reality. As Alfred Polgar said of them:[92]

> They narrow towards the top and are free-standing in space. A sign that we
> are not to regard them as steps but as a vertical playing surface which we
> imagine stretching into infinity on all sides like a normal horizontal stage.
> This is surely the Platonic idea behind Jessner's steps: this elevation of the
> stage area from the horizontal to the vertical. The performance gains a new
> dimension; the characterless movement to right or left is replaced by ex-
> tremely meaningful moves up or down.

The three major productions of Jessner in his early years at the Staatstheater (he remained its Director until 1930, when Nazi pressure forced him to resign) were characterized by two principal features. First, even in dramas from another age, he sought some general contemporary relevance and so initiated the now common practice, exploited by Brecht, of the 'Aneignung' ('appropriation') of the classics: 'Basically, there are neither classics nor modern authors. Shakespeare, Schiller, Wedekind are to be regarded as much representatives of this generation as the latest writers.'[93] Second, in terms of staging, he developed what he called the 'Motivtheater' ('theatre of motifs'), a theatre that would dispense with all ornament, with all incidental detail of time and place, to project 'the idea' on stage. Subtle it was not, but of brilliant clarity.

Yet despite his clarity and pursuit of intellectual precision, Jessner was too much an Expressionist to deny an irrational and emotive strain in his work. So in his opening address to an actors' conference in 1926 Jessner stated: 'We all come from the same country, from the region of the irrational world, that is, the sphere of existence which is not subject merely to rational concepts. In this sphere of existence it is not reason which enlightens and directs, but only feeling.'[94]

While Expressionist abstractionism, then, appeared precise and cerebral, it was never entirely divorced from the powerful irrational primitivist strain; it was cool, but never cold. Even in its more extreme forms abstractionist set design sought to involve the spectator rather than distance him, sought to discover the abstract patterns of universal forms rather than to create the autonomous constructs of geometry.

4 · Primitivist theatre : the distortion of reality

The premiere of Toller's *Die Wandlung (Transfiguration)* in 1919

The play and its presentation

> We saw how vileness had an orgy,
> Europe, naked, dripping filth,
> Eddying lies gushed from trenches,
> Above our heads swirled mordant smoke,
> At our feet there rattled despair.
> A man screamed.
> from Ernst Toller: 'Eruption', poem prefacing *Transfiguration* (1919)

While Kaiser and Jessner struggled to give a voice to the 'Schrei', creating abstract symmetry in the presentation of ideas, other Expressionists in their intense response to the world about them sought to give more immediate expression to their anguish. One such was Ernst Toller.

Born in 1893 of Jewish parentage, Toller returned from his studies in France at the outbreak of the war and, without even visiting his home, volunteered at once for the German army. In his autobiography he records the horrors of war on the Western Front: how men killed beside him would be propped up against the side of the trench with little to distinguish them from the 'living corpses' of the survivors; how he and his companions stopped their ears to prevent their hearing the screams of a wounded soldier lying in the narrow strip of barbed-wire entanglements between the two trenches, screams that lasted three days;[1] how, when digging in a trench, his pick became entangled in the 'slimy knot' of a man's intestines. After thirteen months his nerves failed and, following treatment in a military hospital, he was discharged in 1916 as unfit for active service. Returning to his studies in

Heidelberg and Munich, he began to associate with socialist groups and to formulate his own revolutionary and pacifist idealism.

In 1917 he began writing his first play, *Die Wandlung*, and, when the metal-workers in Munich went on strike in January 1918, Toller distributed scenes from his play amongst the strikers. Arrested for his involvement in the strike, he finished *Die Wandlung* in military prison. He had become a member of the Independent Socialists (USPD), and when Kurt Eisner proclaimed the new Republic on the Munich Theresienwiese on 7 November 1918, Toller was at his side. In May 1919 he was arrested for his part in the attempt to set up a Soviet Republic in Munich and was condemned to five years' imprisonment. While serving his sentence, he wrote his three most important plays, *Masse Mensch (Masses and Man)*, *Die Maschinenstürmer (The Machine-Wreckers)* and *Hinkemann*, but was prevented from attending the premiere of any of them, just as he was unable to see *Die Wandlung* produced at its first performance at the Tribüne in Berlin.

Die Wandlung is clearly a semi-autobiographical piece. Its hero Friedrich is, like Toller, a young Jewish artist who seeks to submerge his racial isolation in blind devotion to his fatherland. He volunteers for the army, encounters the horrors of war, is wounded, is treated in a military hospital and is discharged. Returning to his studio, he begins to work on a statue celebrating the Fatherland. When two beggars appear, a syphilitic woman with a former comrade of Friedrich's, now crippled and insane, the 'transfiguration' takes place: he smashes the statue and leaves in search of greater fulfilment. By way of martyrdom in prison and a political meeting he finally publicly proclaims his message of freedom, love and renewal, and the people exit hand in hand, following his call for revolution.

In terms of content, *Die Wandlung* is a transitional work: its emotional intensity and the naive idealism of its vague proposals for a renewal of man are still characteristically Expressionist; on the other hand, the very real concern with contemporary problems and a search for some sort of political solution point forward to the political theatre of the 1920s. Despite the strikingly personal nature of its theme and hence its tendency towards lyrical outburst, it nevertheless possesses a sense of form far removed from the formlessness of the primitive 'Schrei', which is more evident, for example, in the short pieces of August Stramm. Just as Kaiser's abstractionist drama still has a place for the ecstatic utterances of the central figure, so Toller's more primitive work has a clearly defined structure. As in Kaiser, Friedrich's progress is traced through a series of loosely connected stations: the home, the Front, the military hospital, the studio, the People's Assembly, and the church steps where he makes his final public proclamation. Interspersed with these scenes are even less realistic 'pictures' or 'images' ('Bilder'), 'shadowily real, to be played with the internal distance of dreams',[2] in which occasionally a character with Friedrich's features appears, and which comment on the hero's progress: troop trains, barbed-wire entanglement, war-wounded, the Lodger, Death and Resurrection, the Wanderer and the Mountain-Climber. In addition there is a Prologue, 'which can also be played as an Epilogue',[3] revealing how even Death is ruled by war, no longer killing at random but with military precision.

Like Kaiser, too, Toller is primarily concerned with the central idea, 'the struggle of a man', as the play's sub-title has it. In 1930 he was to write: 'At that time my writing was concerned with only one thing: working for peace',[4] and so Friedrich's struggle is intended as representative, not individual:[5]

In Expressionist drama man was not a chance individual. He was a type. Standing for Many, devoid of superficial characteristics. Man was stripped of his skin, and under the skin we believed we would find his soul.

In this typical Expressionist declaration we encounter one of the inconsistencies responsible for a major weakness in Toller's play: while the central figure is stripped of individual psychology, he does not achieve any universality. On the one hand, it is impossible to become involved in his personal motivation: his decision to volunteer for the army and, more importantly, his later 'transformation' proceed from spontaneous emotional impulse; they are not clarified as consciously thought-out decisions, any more than is the transformation experienced by Kaiser's Cashier. It is above all not clear why, after all the horrors Friedrich has experienced, it is only with the appearance of the two beggars that his 'transfiguration' is effected. On the other hand, in his Jewishness and artistic sensitivity Friedrich is a very special type, with whom indeed a contemporary audience of alienated intellectuals may have been able to identify but whose particular concerns now seem very specific and dated. For the modern reader it is not Friedrich's transfiguration that is of interest; the wonder of it is that he was so blindly devoted to the fatherland in the first place.

The audience of the premiere in Berlin on 30 September 1919, however, understood only too well the impulses that drove Friedrich from station to station. *Die Wandlung* was moreover, incredibly, the only play on a contemporary theme being performed that autumn in Berlin, and the fact that Toller was imprisoned in Munich for his part in a revolution like that preached in his play added much to the interest and authenticity of the piece.

So it was with this premiere that the Tribüne achieved its first (and only) success in Berlin. The theatre had been launched only ten days previously by its director Karl Heinz Martin with two unsuccessful one-act plays by Hasenclever. The Tribüne had been founded, as its name suggests, as a platform for the new revolutionary drama of the Expressionists. While the monumental abstractionist dramas of Kaiser could be performed on the existing stages of the large municipal theatres, and indeed depended on their technical resources, the more intense primitivist works demanded intimate surroundings for their realization. Thus Stramm's works were staged on the small Sturmbühne in Berlin, and most of the Junges Deutschland season of new Expressionist plays were performed in the Kammerspiele of Max Reinhardt's Deutsches Theater.

The Tribüne was a converted hall in a student house in the Berlinerstrasse in Charlottenburg, an area some distance from the theatre and entertainment centre of Berlin at that time. It was tastefully decorated with pale yellow walls, green curtains and a small crystal chandelier. The auditorium was tiny by contemporary standards with a seating capacity of 296, thus allowing considerable intimacy to be established between audience and actor, who could remain audible with a whisper and shock even the back rows with a sudden burst of volume. To maintain this intimacy the stage was merely a raised platform, which was more broad than deep and was backed by green curtains concealing three entrances from the rear. There was no front curtain and the auditorium was connected to the stage by three shallow steps. There were no footlights, prompt box or orchestra pit, no sophisticated stage machinery nor any of the theatrical clutter which according to Martin merely erected barriers between the audience and the action on stage:[6]

The irresistible and necessary revolution in the theatre must begin with a remodelling of the playing space. The unnatural division between stage and auditorium must give way to the living unity of artistic space which will unite all the participants in the act of creation. We do not want a public, but a community within a single space ... not a stage, but a pulpit. ... Such a theatre without machinery and technical gadgets, without a cyclorama or sky-dome, without revolving or sliding stages can in its immediacy reveal the soul and its message without distraction or limitation.

Admittedly, Martin's idealized concept of establishing a 'shrine for a spiritual community'[7] was compromised by economic pressures. In order to make the undertaking financially viable, the small number of seats had to be sold at very high prices. Initially, season tickets were offered at 500, 400 or 300 Marks for ten premieres or at 120, 90 or 75 Marks for ten ordinary performances (at this time 1 dollar = approx 9 Marks). The cheapest individual seat cost 15 Marks. These prices, with up to 50 Marks being paid for a seat at the premiere, compared unfavourably with existing charges (even Reinhardt asked at most 20 Marks for his premieres in the Kammerspiele) and so excluded a large section of a potentially sympathetic public.

In other respects, however, the simple and intimate stage of the Tribüne was ideally suited to the premiere of *Die Wandlung*. Martin, who had already had considerable success with experimental productions in the provinces, in Frankfurt and Hamburg, and who had now taken the necessary step of coming to Berlin to establish a national reputation, approached the work with the intensity of focus on 'the idea' characteristic of Expressionism. His intention was 'to take a play as an *organic unity* independent of its author, to place it under the dominant aspect of its *central idea* and so to arrive at a conception for the production'.[8]

Already in the editing of the text Martin showed himself prepared to seek out the central idea independently of the author's intentions. For him the sub-title, 'The struggle of a man', revealed the major preoccupation of the play, so that Toller's ending of mass regeneration was replaced with the more personal conclusion of the birth of the New Man in a revised version of the 'Death and Resurrection' scene in the factory/prison. No prompt-book exists of the production, but from the many and detailed reviews it is possible to reconstruct the probable order of scenes as performed at the premiere:

Prologue: omitted.

Scenes 1–7: performed as in published text; i.e., up to and including the smashing of the statue.

Scene 8: second half, the introduction to the factory/prison, omitted.

Scenes 10 and 12: almost certainly omitted.

Scenes 11 and 13: revised by Rudolf Leonhard, Martin's Dramaturg, to form a composite scene of the People's Assembly.

Scene 9: factory/prison scene revised, so that the prisoner with Friedrich's features becomes Friedrich himself. He does not die however; his call for freedom is answered by the birth of a child.

Martin disregarded Toller's proposal that the non-narrative scenes should be played less realistically upstage. For one thing, the shallow stage of the Tribüne would not have allowed for a division between a downstage realistic playing-area and an upstage 'dream-world' area. For another, Martin decided to treat all the scenes in a stylized and unreal manner.

So, for example, Toller's essentially realistic if atmospheric stage-directions for the first scene were ignored: 'A room. Urban ugliness. Dusk blurs shapes and sounds. In the houses over the street the Christmas trees are being lit up. Friedrich leans against the window'.[9] Martin's designer Robert Neppach, whose sets for the premiere of Kaiser's *Gas I* in Frankfurt had already been acclaimed for 'achieving effects by primitive means',[10] provided a bare stage without any furniture, the set consisting solely of a large painted flat, about two metres by two metres, behind the actors. The top and sides of the flat had jagged edges, and it was painted with unfinished brush strokes in a bright (no longer ascertainable) colour. The window was a black trapezium painted on the left half of the flat.

All the remaining scenes or 'pictures' were defined by the use of similar flats, free-standing in front of the green backstage curtains: the troop-train was a flat with a grated window painted on it; the flat for the desert scene carried the image of a camp fire; for the barbed-wire entanglement an irregular triangular flat displayed in a crude receding perspective three shell craters surrounded by barbed wire – the impression is that of flames leaping from cauldrons. Here for the first time in the production stage furniture was introduced: two trestles, entwined with wire, on which the skeleton-figures hung at the beginning of the scene (see Plate 21). The next two scenes, 'The Military Hospital' and 'The War-Wounded', shared a plainly painted flat, in front of which stood three simple beds, each containing two patients. The studio scene was backed by a large rectangular flat, on which a big distorted window was painted (see Plate 22). There was no statue; it existed only in the imagination of the audience. The eighth scene, 'The Lodger', consisted of a flat and some form of bed, but no exact details of these are ascertainable. The backing for 'The People's Assembly' was probably a flat carrying posters, and a rostrum for the speaker was provided. The final scene of the production, 'The Factory/Prison', was represented by a tall narrow flat, on which jagged patterns and a particularly crude window were painted (see Plate 23).

In this type of design objects have lost their substance; they are no longer functioning elements in the environment as in Naturalism; no one can look out of Neppach's windows, characters cannot warm themselves at his fire. They do not even possess symbolic significance, as in the abstractionist sets of Pirchan; they exist only as images of the world as it is perceived by the central character – hence the jagged edges – for this scenery consists of fragments torn out of the plane of reality. Unlike the geometry of abstractionism it is not complete in itself; just as our perception of reality can never be total, so these Expressionist images of our environment are pieces wrenched from the whole. Hence too the oblique angles and unfinished brush strokes: the primitivist mind does not pursue a rational Kantian ordering of perceptions but lets the sense impressions bombard it with immediacy. Hence too the toppling buildings and walls, familiar from Expressionist cinema. The ecstatic hero feels crushed by his environment, for the world is out of joint and he, the victim and potential saviour, stands at the centre.

In the concentration on the central figure lighting had a major role to play. Already the use of the new hard-focused white spotlights had become common practice in Expressionist productions, as in Weichert's production of *Der Sohn* in 1918. As the contemporary reviewer Ernst Leopold Stahl commented: 'Herr Weichert ... places the Son – as the only truly physical presence – spatially in the centre of the action, a centre that becomes the objectified focus of the play because it is he that gathers the illumination of the spotlight about him'.[11] With this use of directional spotlighting the director could throw the central figure of a scene into unprecedented prominence, a device particularly appropriate to Expressionist plays treating of a protagonist moving through the darkness of a dream world about him. In addition, hard lighting from above cast unreal shadows on the face of the actor, so creating the chiaroscuro effect so beloved of Expressionism and frequently seen in the atmospheric lighting of the early cinema.

In order to light the forestage at the Tribüne, Martin had to place lights in the auditorium and shared the contemporary prudishness about exposing the source of illumination, perhaps in the belief that this would detract from the 'magic of the theatre'. Reinhardt in his Theater in der Josefstadt in Vienna tried to hide lights in a cut-away chandelier, and at the Grosses Schauspielhaus the arena lighting was concealed in 'an ugly red hood, which sticks out from the proscenium with no relationship to the rest of the house'.[12] Even as late as 1929 the American designer Walter Fuerst denounced the presence of lights in the auditorium as 'a makeshift which should be avoided if possible'.[13]

At the Tribüne there was a 'light-drum' suspended over the front rows of the audience. In *Die Wandlung* it was used to illuminate only the immediate playing area in front of the flats. In this way, the world of the central figure was again lifted like a fragment out of the surrounding darkness, a particularly effective device in the People's Assembly. Here the light spilled on to the front row of the common people listening at the edge of the acting area, so suggesting large numbers of the populace stretching into the darkness behind them. It was also, incidentally, Martin who, not having the use of a front curtain at the Tribüne, introduced, in Germany at least, the now well-established convention of denoting the end of a scene by using a blackout.

Scene changes were covered with eerie music composed by Werner R. Hagemann and played on a single violin, which achieved as great an effect 'as half an orchestra'.[14] The sound effects, like the rattle of the train in the second scene, were realistic and these, together with the Naturalistic groaning of the wounded in the hospital, were justifiably censured by one critic as not being properly in the style of the production.[15]

Both costuming and make-up were generally realistic as well, Friedrich's costume, for example, reflecting the stages of his development: the dark suit of the young civilian, the grey-green uniform of the soldier, the pyjamas of the invalid, the white coat of the sculptor and the drill-cloth jacket of the convict. The less realistic figures tended towards more symbolic costuming and make-up. The four male prisoners of the final scene wore sandals and crudely shaped tunics and trousers decorated with big rectangular patches. The skeletons of the barbed-wire entanglement scene were created with simple but effective means. The actors wore black leotards and tights on which were painted the bones of the skeleton. They wore white skull caps on their heads, their faces were whitened and their eye-sockets and noses blackened. Under the much subtler lighting than that required for the production photograph (Plate 21), only the luminescent bones and faces would have been clearly discerned, so adding considerably to the macabre effect.

The only other examples of exaggerated make-up were the characteristic hollow eyes and cheeks of the war-wounded and beggars. Again a critic complained of the excessive Naturalism of certain aspects of the make-up: 'Why did the actress representing a woman afflicted with syphilis have a whole atlas of skin diseases painted on her breast and cheeks?' (see Plate 22).[16]

As in abstractionist theatre, it was in the acting that the most decisive revolution took place.

Acting for the primitivist theatre

One day it may happen that the soul will explode into freedom from the constraints of the body, will pour forth into every vein and turn the body into its own instrument.

Walter von Hollander: 'The Expressionism of the Actor' (1917)

Because of the small acting area with its concentrated pool of light, the performance of the minor figures was generally static, which had the advantage of throwing into relief the ecstatic gesturing of the central figure. Group scenes were characterized by the control familiar from abstractionist productions, although Martin here used only a small number of actors to suggest a mass of people (only six in the prison/factory scene, probably not many more to represent the common people in the People's Assembly). Emil Faktor described the crowd in the People's Assembly:[17]

To one side, even before their cue comes, figures move into groups in corners, looking like natural statues. These act as representatives of the world outside, preparing the spectator for emotional climaxes and at the decisive moment proclaiming their life in flowing lines.

Herbert Ihering also praised the discipline and concentration of these crowd figures:

How individuals were subject to the dominance of the whole! Bodies became ecstatic, voices exploded. A student [played by Martin's wife, Roma Bahn] ... revealed such intensity of listening and participation in her forehead, chin, eyes and hands, that her words were of secondary importance.

This disciplined angularity was particularly evident in the more symbolic figures, like the skeletons or the prisoners of the last scene. The latter adopted strained poses, their wrists seemingly weighed down by chains, heads tilted, eyes cast upwards (see Plate 23). The woman who was to give birth to the child knelt at Friedrich's feet, her head bowed but turned towards the audience. Regrettably, no information exists to reveal how the birth of the child was effected. Since the mother wears a black cape, it may be speculated that she spread it open to reveal the 'child', or possibly the prisoners shielded her from view while the 'birth' took place.

The group of war-wounded was more individualized, according to their respective disabilities. They rose from their beds to stand in a row in a pathetic attempt at military discipline, one shaking with unrelieved nervous spasms. They then attempted to perform exercises as well as their deformities would allow. After returning to their beds, each in turn complained of his ailment until they finally let out a single united scream, at which the nurses fell moaning to their knees. The effect was so strong that Tucholsky recorded that some of the audience wept.[19]

The unified scream was characteristic of the uniform and disciplined treatment of groups under Martin's direction, which was therefore primitivistic in its effects rather than in its methods. As Faktor said of the choral speaking in the production: 'The many voices were compressed together so tightly that shouts seemed to leap from a single throat.'[20]

The most powerful group scene in terms of acting as well as in other respects was the barbed-wire entanglement scene. As the lights went up, the skeletons were discovered hanging on the barbed-wire trestles. With their first words they slowly turned towards one another. Their gestures then gained in size and definition, with jerky moves matching the rhythm of their falsetto speech, until they launched into a macabre dance accompanied by the banging of bones held in their hands.

Of the minor characters the most notable was John Gottowt in the role of Death, which appears in various guises throughout the play. Here again the angular gestures and body postures and the abrupt quality of his speech revealed the hallmarks of the abstractionist actor.

A strong primitivist element of the production and one of its most significant features was the ecstatic acting of the central figure, Fritz Kortner. Kortner, who on his own admission had had altercations with all the leading theatre directors of Berlin, was soon to become under Jessner the most famous Expressionist actor of all. It was his performance as Friedrich that turned him into a star.

The ideological division in acting styles between the abstractionist style of the minor characters and the primitivist self-release of the main performer (often embodying an extension of the author's own personality), together with the individualism at the root of Expressionism, furthered the star system in a manner embarrassing to the idealistically democratic claims of Expressionism. The leading Expressionist actors not only gained financial rewards out of all proportion to average salaries in the theatre: they also became the focus of most critical attention. The names of actors like Ernst Deutsch, Fritz Kortner, Heinrich George and Werner Krauss became better known even than those of the directors for whom they worked. At times this attention created almost intolerable pressures: Heinrich George, for example, once vomited with fright on seeing the critic Ihering enter the auditorium. More importantly, it impelled these stars to discover and maintain an individualistic style born of expressive energy.

Particularly in the delivery of his lines, Kortner revealed the explosive quality appropriate to what Toller called the 'pregnant, almost telegram-like'[21] style of his writing. As Ihering commented:[22]

Kortner turns sentences into arches, into buildings. Remove one syllable, and the whole structure would collapse. ... He uses pauses to maintain the tension between the lines. The exclamatory cry [Schrei] is not isolated, it is part of the rhythm: in the silence that precedes and follows it, the speech continues underground.

Kortner was well suited to the role of Friedrich for, as a young Jew himself, he could identify closely with Toller's hero: 'What I played at that time was myself: a young German Jew and rebel in conflict with the world about me.'[23] Initially, in his playing of Friedrich, Kortner's gestures and moves were precise and economical. As his intensity grew, his passion was revealed in the wild animation of his body and his sudden explosive bursts of speech: powerful gestures accompanied the rhythm of his lines, gestures which were in no sense graceful but sharp and sudden, recognized by critics as signals of the inner torment of the character. As Ihering noted:[24]

He is the most gifted actor in the ensemble and so sometimes – because of the power of his artistic temperament – he overstepped the mark. He reached out beyond the limits of the stage, exploding the space about him. He is an unusually talented, imaginative, fiery actor. ... Kortner does not give us transfiguration, but defiance. ... But he presents it to us with a power which is nourished from all the forces of the theatre, a power which rises up, spreads itself wide and shakes us hard.

As an example of primitivist theatre *Die Wandlung* is not completely typical. As we have seen, the costuming and sound effects were realistic and the acting style of the minor characters bore the hallmark of abstractionist discipline. The dramatically distorted sets of Neppach, and the ecstatic acting of Kortner, however, made Martin's production one of the most significant stages in the evolution of primitivist Expressionism. As Ihering commented:[25]

Expressionism could at first be recognized, like all new movements in art, by its excesses: in the theatre it had its break-through with the perform-ance of Toller's *Die Wandlung*. This play, already in the writing based on the 'Schrei', was given in the Tribüne the rhythm of ecstasy. And the abrupt intensity of this rhythm overpowered us all.

Abstractionist and primitivist theatre: an attempt at a synthesis

The Berlin premiere of Toller's *Masse Mensch* (*Masses and Man*) in 1921

In the soul of man there may be voices, raging, darkness, claustrophobia and starlight, but not walls, hat-stands and bedroom rugs.

Heinz Herald: 'Thoughts on *Naval Encounter* and *Saviours*' (1919)

Because the abstractionist architectural set demanded depth and space to achieve its effect, it was predictable that the Expressionist cinema should prefer the leaning angles and jagged outlines of the flat designs of primitivism. As a result, it is a commonly held misconception that the sets of a film like *The Cabinet of Dr Caligari* are typically Expressionist. In fact, as we have seen, the nightmarish distortions in *Caligari* represent but one of the styles, and by no means the most predominant, in Expressionist scenic design. As Helmut Grosse observes: 'The cliché conception of Expressionistic scenic design, the image of ragged leaning walls, of twisted and distorted doors, of reeling furniture and wild colours arose from the film, the cartoon and the reproduction of designs rather than from what actually took place on stage.'[26]

What was particularly striking about the Berlin premiere of Toller's second play was its blending of elements of both abstractionism and primitivism. *Masse Mensch* was given its first public performance by Jürgen Fehling at the Volksbühne in Berlin on 29 September 1921, with Hans Strohbach as designer. Again, Fehling and Strohbach did not make a rigid delineation between the realistic and the dream-like episodes. Instead, by raising all the action to the level of a dream they attempted to reproduce the feverish intensity of the play, which Toller had composed in two and a half days' frenetic creation, taking no food and having little sleep. The background alternated between producing a claustrophobic effect by means of an enormous dark curtain with heavy folds and creating a visionary quality with the use of an illuminated cyclorama, against which the characters acted out their parts like beings on the top of the world.

In the second scene, the stock-exchange, the curtains at the rear drew back to reveal a triangle of the cyclorama. Before this was seen a 'clerk on an impossibly high stool, writing on an impossibly high desk, almost in silhouette against the yellow-lighted dome'.[27] The grotesque inhumanity of the financiers speculating on the progress of the war was objectified by this distorted furniture, the clerk aloft scribbling his figures while humanity suffered far below in the mud of the battlefield. Here colour symbolism was used to particular effect. The cyclorama was initially blue, 'a beautiful yet sulphurous and sinister illumination'.[28] As the top-hatted speculators greedily bid for shares in the war-machine, the background turned a fiery red. Finally, as Sonja, the revolutionary figure, appeared to reproach them, the cyclorama turned to green, for Germans traditionally the colour of hope.

For the next scene, the revolutionary meeting, the back curtain fell into place, broad steps were placed in front of it and on these twenty-four agitators stood, closely bunched, facing straight out front, lit from the sides and above by hard-focused spotlights.

For the fourth scene, set in a prison yard, the cyclorama was revealed once more, shining with a greenish almost submarine light. Against this stood the dark and terrifying outlines of towering walls leaning inward on to a solitary figure playing a doleful tune on the concertina. The next scene, the rallying of the revolutionaries, again employed steps before the back curtain, the steps this time at an angle to the front, leading on a diagonal up to the dark emptiness of the black drapes. At the height of the meeting a rattle of machine-guns was heard, the revolutionaries fell sprawling on the steps, and the curtains centre right parted to reveal soldiers outlined against a yellow cyclorama, enveloped in a thin haze of smoke (see Plates 24–6). The separation of the sound of the guns from the appearance of the soldiers was an effective device: Fehling did not so much portray a massacre as communicate its idea.

The sixth scene, Sonja in prison, revealed the actress cooped up in a frail scarlet bird-cage just large enough for her to kneel in. Against the luminescent cyclorama shadowy figures moved threateningly.

In this production, regarded by many as the high point of Expressionistic theatre design and certainly one of the last examples of truly Expressionist staging, Strohbach achieved a remarkable synthesis of abstractionism and primitivism. While the distorted set of leaning walls in the fourth scene is clearly a product of the primitivist strain, the precise positioning and use of steps in the scenes of the revolutionaries is close to the work of Jessner and Pirchan.

By 1922 the styles begin to diverge, primitivism rapidly becoming a cliché of distortion and angularity, abstractionism being taken up in the striking but largely empty products of Constructivism, where set design became almost independent of the works for which it was created. Despite the exciting possibilities opened up by Expressionist scenic design, the theatre of the 1920s was to pass once more through trivial realism, before Brecht's genius would finally draw on its best qualities to create a viable style for the modern theatre.

Conclusion to Part One: The achievement of Expressionist theatre

> Instead of examining ... the complexity of what is all too transient, [we sought] to become aware of what is intransient in us.
>
> Paul Kornfeld

Short-lived as the Expressionist revolution in the theatre was, its achievements, as revealed in Kaiser's *Von morgens bis mitternachts* and in Toller's first two plays, were considerable.

Naturalist theatre was essentially a theatre of description. A milieu was presented, characters (products of the milieu) were introduced, and to create a plot, usually an outsider had to be brought in to set the action in motion. Aristotle had urged that a plot should have a beginning, a middle and an end. But real life contains only a middle; even death provides an end only for the individual. So the endings of Naturalist plays seemed frequently arbitrary: the suicides of Hedda Gabler or the Actor in Gorky's *The Lower Depths* were not catastrophes in the traditional sense. They changed nothing; in place of catharsis stood the trite recognition: 'life goes on'.

By turning from the description of the transient and by going beyond imitation, Expressionism restored to the theatre a storytelling function. Neither character nor setting were now as important as the episodes that created the action. As one of the earliest pieces of Expressionist playwriting, *Von morgens bis mitternachts* is very innovative in its precisely thought out structure. Here one will look in vain for complexity of character, for profundity of thought or for historical perspective. What one will find is clarity, model situations reflecting a central concern.

Particularly for those who regard the rich poetry and complex realism of Shakespeare as that towards which all theatre should strive, such clarity, which admittedly often borders on the obvious, seems hardly enough. Yet a theatre whose outstanding feature is its ability to present model situations shares this characteristic with some of the greatest periods of world drama, notably the theatre of the Ancient Greeks, of the Middle Ages and of the Spanish Golden Age.

Moreover, the major strength of Expressionist drama is its potential for creating powerful images to incorporate these model situations. While Naturalism was avowedly anti-theatrical, Expressionism exploded with vibrant theatricality. We recall the moment when Hedda Gabler burns Lövborg's manuscript, but do we actually see her 'burning his child' in the way that, from a mere reading of the plays, we see the Cashier flinging his money into the Salvation Army crowd or Friedrich smashing his statue? The bold violence of these images, together with the strong, clear lines of abstractionist settings or the distorted shapes of primitivism, with the restoration of music and dance-like movement to the stage, made the theatre once again a place of intense sensory experience. Realism, which was ultimately to find a more appropriate home in the cinema, seemed pale in comparison.

Von morgens bis mitternachts, *Die Wandlung* and *Masse Mensch* are virtually unknown works even in Germany, where there have been only two major post-war productions of Kaiser's play and a television version of *Die Wandlung*. Outside Germany, some amateur and fringe groups attempt Expressionist productions, often with considerable public acclaim,[29] but I am unaware of any professional production of these works. It is not so much a source of dismay that today's theatre seems to have neglected its significant antecedents – theatre should not function as a museum – but it is saddening that plays of such theatrical potential remain unperformed. They are not among the great works of world drama, but their revival might infect our contemporary theatre with a renewed spirit of theatrical adventurousness.

Part Two

The political revolution in the German theatre

We now ask you actors . . .
To change yourselves and show us the world of man
As it is: made by man and subject to change.
　　　　　　Bertolt Brecht: 'Address to Danish working-class actors'

5 · Piscator's theatre: the documentation of reality

Piscator's production of Toller's *Hoppla, wir leben!*
(*Hoppla, Such is Life!*) in 1927

The political function of theatre

> We came out of the filth of war, we saw a people that was half-starved and
> tormented to death. We saw how their leaders were ruthlessly murdered,
> we saw, wherever we looked, injustice, exploitation, torture, blood. Were
> we to go home and sit at our desks, drawing-boards or director's tables to
> dream about 'phantastic unrealities' or listen to the tinkle of sleigh-bells?
> Our art was created from a knowledge of reality and inspired by the will to
> replace this reality. We founded political theatre.
>
> Erwin Piscator: Letter to Die Weltbühne (1928)

When Erwin Piscator opened his first theatre in September 1927 with the
premiere of Toller's *Hoppla, wir leben!*, he had already spent several years
exploring and establishing the political function of theatre. His impulse to do
so came, as he readily admitted, from his personal experiences of the war and
its consequences.

Before and during the First World War the alienation experienced by the
German intellectual could hardly be alleviated by political activity: he rejected
the materialism and nationalism of his fellow bourgeois but felt unable
meaningfully to throw in his lot with the proletariat. It was understandable,
therefore, that he took flight into the realms of the spirit and softened his sense
of alienation by seeking privileged communion with his fellow Expressionist
artists.

By 1919, however, three things had happened to change this. First there
had been the war itself: much more so than was the case in Britain, middle-
class intellectuals found themselves in the ranks, fighting alongside workers

and peasants. It is an irony of history that a capitalist war probably did more to break down class barriers than half a century of socialist agitation. There is the famous anecdote about Piscator under shell-fire at Ypres, trying ineffectually to dig himself into the ground. An enraged NCO demanded to know what he did in civilian life. 'Actor', answered Piscator, and he suddenly felt his profession to be 'so stupid, so ridiculous, of such grinning mendacity, in short, so irrelevant to the situation ... and to the life of these times and of this world, that [he] was less afraid of the approaching grenades than ashamed of his profession.'[1] The traditional elitist Romantic view of the artist, already under challenge from writers like Thomas Mann, was now rendered absurd by the recognition that the artist's pursuit of the 'soul' was an irrelevance at a time when the body was being subjected to such violence.

Second, the Russian Revolution had taken place. Amongst many other things it proved to Piscator and others like him that the middle-class intellectual could play an effective political role: the alliance with the proletariat need not be merely a sentimental feeling of brotherhood.

Third, despite the failure in real terms of the Revolution in Germany, changes had been wrought in what seemed an unassailably conservative state: the monarch was banished, there was a new constitution and a nominally socialist government was in power. Movement had been slight, but it was movement none the less, and it provided the impulse to employ art to politicize the proletariat in the hope that the Revolution might be finally achieved.

Already, especially in the abstractionist tendency of Expressionism, the political function of the theatre had been recognized. Notably Jessner, who had staged *Wilhelm Tell* and *Richard III* as political parables, proclaimed the social relevance of theatre:[2]

> The most resounding melody was drowned in shouts from the street. The period wore a political face. So the theatre – unless it is to stand aside from the events of the period – will have to be political in that wider philosophical sense; roughly in the way that the theatre of the Greeks was religious in a philosophical sense.

Paradigmatic for Jessner's renewal of the function of the theatre was his staging of the play scene in *Hamlet* (1928). The setting evoked the Kaiser's pre-war court, weighed down by a court-ceremonial which hid the rottenness within. Claudius sat in military regalia in the box of an ornate court theatre, peering through his lorgnette, while the stage below revealed the truth behind the decorative façade. As Günther Rühle comments: 'Jessner used the stage to give concrete expression to the revolution in the court-theatre, for which he himself was a symbol: a troupe of players with political impact performed in opposition to the aristocratic theatre of entertainment.'[3]

Karl Heinz Martin's founding of the Tribüne was a further attempt to establish the theatre as a political force in the new Weimar Republic. Despite the critical and financial success of *Die Wandlung*, the Tribüne's role as a political forum was short-lived: in November 1919 there was an invitation by the newly-formed Bund für proletarische Kultur (Association for Proletarian Culture) to perform *Die Wandlung* before striking metal-workers. A number of actors at the Tribüne and the manager, Friedrich Mellinger, voted against such an obvious gesture of solidarity with the strikers, no doubt with one eye on the need to preserve middle-class support for their enterprise. Karl Heinz Martin and his co-founder Rudolf Leonhard withdrew from Die Tribüne, which thereafter became a purely commercial undertaking.

Martin's next step was to join the first Proletarisches Theater in Berlin, which had been founded earlier that year by a number of politically committed writers. Its only production was of Herbert Cranz's *Freiheit* (*Freedom*), performed in the Berlin Philharmonia on 14 December 1919. Despite its success in attracting a mass audience of workers, the performance was a failure. The play itself deals with eight so-called revolutionaries (in fact, idealistic pacifists) in a condemned cell. They gain the possibility of escape by seizing the key but then hand it back to their warders in order to achieve 'inner freedom'. Such Expressionistic idealism seemed a bourgeois luxury and an irrelevance to the proletariat. As Alfons Goldschmidt wrote: 'Like the play, the whole trend of the theatre was still only halfway proletarian. It was not a theatre for its time in the sense demanded by the proletariat.'[4] This 'Proletarian Theatre' deservedly failed after its one performance. Martin could blame the indifference of the proletariat, but the real reason lay in the inability of ecstatic Expressionism to relate to the needs of working people.

In fact, political theatre in the modern sense of the term had not yet been founded in Germany. Jessner was emphatic that his theatre, while political, was not 'party-political': when he unfurled a flag on stage at the end of his production of Bronnen's *Rheinische Rebellen* (*Rhineland Rebels*, 1925), it was the black–red–gold tricolour of the Weimar Republic. When Martin staged *Die Maschinenstürmer* (*The Machine-Wreckers*, 1922) in the Grosses Schauspielhaus, he may have arranged for political speeches to be delivered between scenes, but the play itself is an appeal for individual regeneration in place of political revolution.

When in 1920 Piscator began to direct for the Second Proletarian Theatre, there was therefore nothing particularly new about the notion of using the stage as a political platform. Where Piscator's work was decisive was in the gradual freeing of the theatre from its individualistic irrationalism. He dismissed Expressionist theatre as follows:[5]

Of course this drama was a 'revolution', but a revolution of individualism.
Man, the Individual, rebels against Fate. He appeals to the others, his
'brothers'. He seeks 'love' between all men, humility of one before the
other. This drama is lyrical, i.e. undramatic. In fact dramatized lyrical
poems. In the confusion of war, which in reality was a war of machines

against human flesh, passing through negation, the search was for the 'soul' of man. This drama was then essentially reactionary, a reaction to the war but against its collectivism, a return to the concept of self and to the cultural values of the pre-war years.

Table 4 *Expressionist theatre/political theatre of the 1920s*

Expressionist	Political
Idealism	Materialism
Liberal humanism	Marxism
Supra-rational	Scientific
Poetic	Prosaic
Subjective	Objective
Individualistic	Collectivistic
Regeneration within individual	Regeneration within society
Imagistic settings	Functional settings

Piscator's assessment is substantiated by Schreyer's definition of the revolution of Expressionism: 'Revolution means turning back, that is, a return to origins. In this sense our theatrical style was revolutionary.'[6]

For Piscator Expressionism was reactionary, bourgeois and individualistic; in his Proletarian Theatre he sought to create a theatre that was progressive, proletarian and collectivistic: 'We radically banned the word "art" from our programme, our "plays" were proclamations, with which we wanted to "make politics" and to influence day-to-day events',[7] for henceforth 'art and politics are inseparable'.[8]

The places of performance

Already the certainty is alive in the hearts of some of our best directors and actors that our theatre can only be freed from poverty and decline when wandering players once more travel through town and country, always and everywhere prepared to perform in squares, in tents, in halls, theatres or arenas.

Kurt Pinthus: 'The future of theatre?' (1923)

Having established his political programme for the theatre, Piscator still had to wait many years before he had the physical resources to cope with the complexities of a play like *Hoppla, wir leben!* Indeed, initially he rejected the concept of theatre as bourgeois artistic entertainment by turning his back on the opulent theatre buildings of the fashionable areas of Berlin and by taking his actors into the slums of Wedding and Neukölln: 'The decor was necessarily simple: Piscator travelled around with a handcart, a few pieces of scenery, black drapes and a spotlight.'⁹ Even the austere design of the Tribüne was luxurious compared with the halls in which Piscator and his band of mainly amateur actors had to work:¹⁰

Anyone who has had anything to do with these places, anyone who knows these halls with their smell of stale beer and gentlemen's toilets, with their flags and pennants from the last beer-festival, can imagine with what difficulties we introduced the concept of theatre here.

The critics from 'the bourgeois press' were banned from attending these performances, but a reviewer of the Berlin *Vossische Zeitung* who managed to gain entry reported on this early example of agitprop theatre: 'The men in the stalls kept their hats on, mothers brought their babies with them, and the whole audience commented vociferously on the events on stage.'¹¹

In the tone of both Piscator's and the critic's comments there is more than a little condescension: a wrinkling of the nose as the smell of the proletariat wafts towards them, a raising of the eyebrows that the men do not bare their heads before art and that these working-class women do not have nannies to leave their babies with. More seriously, the critic refers to 'the stalls' and Piscator speaks of introducing 'the concept of theatre', as though one were offering the gift of bourgeois culture and, however trying the circumstances, handing it over generously to those ignorant of the theatre. In fact, as we shall see, there already existed a vital tradition of popular theatre, which Piscator eventually recognized, aware that his mission of teaching the proletariat might be best fulfilled by learning from their vitality and unpretentiousness.

Economically, the Proletarian Theatre was not a stable enterprise: charging little for admission (and nothing at all to the unemployed), it was often unable to cover its costs, even when the hall was packed. In addition, the police granted the theatre a performing licence for only six months and, in April 1921, refused to renew it. However, even if it had been a financial success and had proceeded with the blessing of the authorities, it is likely that Piscator would have moved on. Apart from any personal ambition, and this would hardly be fulfilled in the relative obscurity of workers' theatre, he was eager to use the new technology of the theatre in the service of political agitation. Clearly this was possible only in the best equipped theatre buildings, and, after whetting his appetite with the facilities available at the Volksbühne and the Staatstheater in Berlin, he looked for his own purpose-built theatre in which to conduct his experiments.

The design which resulted was in its conception the most revolutionary contribution to theatre architecture of its time. Walter Gropius of the Bauhaus designed a 'Total Theatre' in response to Piscator's demand for a theatre related to the needs of a post-feudal society: 'The theatre structure which dominates our period is the obsolete structure of absolutism: the court theatre. With its division into stalls, balcony, boxes and gallery it reflects the social divisions of a feudalistic age.'[12]

As in Reinhardt's Grosses Schauspielhaus, therefore, the seating was on one continuous rake down to the acting area. Gropius's design, however, incorporated much greater structural flexibility than ever before. The circular stage could be positioned at the end of the auditorium in order to form a thrust before the proscenium opening, or it could be revolved to a central position, so creating an arena stage and with it the possibility of theatre-in-the-round. Indeed, since about a third of the seating was mounted on these 'revolving stalls', the shift from thrust to arena stage could have taken place during the performance. In addition, there was a circular acting area entirely surrounding the audience.

The technical equipment was equally extravagant. For example, in each of the twelve supporting pillars film projectors were to be concealed, so that the audience might be entirely surrounded by projected scenery or action.

Sadly, however, this exciting design was never realized, and Piscator had to aim his sights somewhat lower. With the generous patronage of a Berlin brewer, Piscator was able to take over and convert the Theater am Nollendorfplatz, and so in 1927 open the first Piscator-Bühne.

The financing of Piscator's theatre

> During the struggle for the lifting of the ban on Hauptmann's *The Weavers* the major argument insisted on by L'Arronge, the Director of the Deutsches Theater, was that the prices of his theatre seats were too high for the classes who might be incited by the play.
>
> Erwin Piscator: *The Political Theatre* (1929)

As we have seen, one of the major factors in the demise of Piscator's Proletarisches Theater was its economic instability. Even if the workers supported it in large numbers, they had not yet as a class achieved sufficient disposable income to make the project economically viable. Until such a time as the proletariat had sufficient wealth to afford their own theatres, some other financing would have to be sought.

Clearly the state was unwilling to subsidize subversive propaganda. Equally disinclined to offer much support, however, was the German Communist Party (KPD), of which Piscator was a member and whose political thinking he generally reflected in his productions. Understandably, there was some suspicion by the Moscow-controlled KPD of middle-class intellectuals playing at politics from the comparative safety of the stage. The KPD initially also propagated a quaintly bourgeois view of art, as though it were one of those middle-class luxuries like caviare or jewellery that the proletariat could appropriate only in a way consistent with middle-class values. The KPD organ, the *Rote Fahne* (*Red Banner*), reviewing a programme of the Proletarisches Theater, commented: 'The name of theatre creates an obligation to art, to artistic achievement! ... Art is too sacred a thing to let its name be used for churning out propaganda! ... What the worker needs today is a strong art ... such art may be of bourgeois origin, but it must be art.'[13] Eventually the KPD became better disposed towards Piscator's work and in 1925 even commissioned a mammoth political revue *Trotz alledem!* (*Despite Everything!*) to be staged in the Grosses Schauspielhaus for the party conference in Berlin. It played to packed houses for two nights and Piscator was eager to continue its run, but once more the KPD refused to give further support. As Piscator ruefully remarked:[14]

So the bitter experience was repeated for the umpteenth time that despite all the enthusiasm, all the success and the massive attendance which would have been the envy of every bourgeois theatre, this phase of the political theatre outwardly took us no further.

There was, of course, already in existence an organization for workers' theatre, the Volksbühne.[15] But for those committed to political theatre the Volksbühne appeared a reactionary force. Already Herbert Ihering had published a pamphlet entitled *Der Volksbühnenverrat* (*The Betrayal of the Volksbühne*), pointing out, for example, the inappropriateness of Reinhardt's earlier appointment as Director of the Volksbühne – the purveyor of 'sensuously beautiful theatre' in charge of an institution created to provide the workers with their own stage.

For Piscator the recognition that the Volksbühne could not be a suitable home for the political theatre came with the row that erupted after his tenth production for the Volksbühne in 1927. The play, appropriately named *Gewitter über Gottland* (*Storm over Gottland*), was set in the year 1400, but typically Piscator emphasized its relevance to contemporary Germany even to the extent of having the play's revolutionary figure Asmus appear made up as Lenin. The author Ehm Welk and the more reactionary elements of the Volksbühne saw to it that the play was taken off and Piscator dismissed: 'this type of production contradicts the basic political neutrality of the Volksbühne'.[16] The resulting *cause célèbre* became a focus for the debate on the role of theatre in the Weimar Republic, with figures as varied as the extreme left-wing Ernst Toller and the establishment director Leopold Jessner rallying to Piscator's support against the political censorship of the Volksbühne.

When Piscator eventually opened his own theatre in 1927, he came to a compromise arrangement with the Volksbühne. While the Volksbühne as a whole was not prepared to support his venture, it was agreed that politically committed members could join 'Sonderabteilungen' (special groups) who would provide a guaranteed audience in return for a season of plays at considerably reduced rates. Unfortunately, this arrangement proved a liability. In order to fulfil his side of the bargain, Piscator was obliged to present five major productions and a number of studio performances, as promised in his prospectus to the Sonderabteilungen and to private season-ticket-holders. First, this placed an intolerable pressure on him to stage a new piece approximately every six weeks — virtually unthinkable given the technical complexity of most of his work. Second, it meant that he had little flexibility in the length of run of any given production: just when it was playing nightly to full houses, it might have to be replaced by a less successful piece simply to fulfil the obligation to subscribers. Exactly this happened when *Schwejk* was enjoying immense popularity and Piscator took the fatal decision to lease a second theatre, the Lessingtheater, to house the next production, Lania's *Konjunktur (Oil Boom)*. Unable to finance two theatres, the first Piscator-Bühne collapsed, proving that it was impossible to combine the subscription system, deriving primarily from a philosophy of political education, with the marketing of tickets, based essentially on a capitalist view of theatre as show-business.

It was indeed capital that founded and sustained, as long as was possible, the Piscator-Bühnen. The considerable profits from the Schultheiss Brewery and other concerns allowed the financier Ludwig Katzenellenbogen to donate money to Piscator for the establishment of his theatre. Equally, it was the rich and the fashionable whose preparedness to pay anything up to 100 Marks each for tickets made it possible for the Sonderabteilungen to attend performances at only 1.50 Marks per head. So, the first-night audience of a play like *Hoppla, wir leben!* consisted of an extraordinary social spectrum: from the workers and students in the gallery to what Franz Pfemfert sneeringly called 'the jewellery-laden and frock-coated'[17] gentry in the stalls.

By 1929 Piscator was forced to utter two statements, whose juxtaposition is profoundly disillusioning. In a lecture to young members of the Volksbühne he repeated his belief in a truly proletarian theatre: 'A revolutionary theatre without its most vital element, a revolutionary public, is a nonsense.'[18] In the final chapter of *Das politische Theater* he was forced to admit, however: 'Like a thread running through this book and through the story of my ventures is the recognition that the proletariat, for whatever reason, is too weak to maintain its own theatre.'[19].

So Piscator, inspired by his mission to create a proletarian theatre, ended by founding a stage that was dependent on the goodwill of the middle classes. Capitalist society would tolerate this subversive child only so long as his tricks continued to amuse them. And while it amused them, one was treated to the curious spectacle of the bourgeoisie applauding their own subversion.

Forms of political theatre

Every evening in the ... theatre meant for us a waste of time. Every evening in the music hall ... rich rewards.
Lothar Schreyer: Expressionist Theatre (1948)

Part of the success of *Hoppla, wir leben!* was undoubtedly due to its montage
structure and its use of music and dance, all elements familiar to Piscator
from the popular forms of entertainment of the day.

At the turn of the century conventional dramatic form was a dull affair,
enjoyed only by a cultured elite. All the great ages of the theatre (with the
exception of French neo-classical tragedy) had been vital and popular,
incorporating music, dance and spectacle. But now, apart from opera, most
serious theatre was lacking in variety and excitement.

Expressionist theatre, with its montage structure, powerful visual images
and elements of music and movement, had done much to restore the
theatricality of theatre, but its high-flown style and idealistic sentiments had
prevented its becoming truly popular. But there were writers and performers,
both within the Expressionist movement and outside it, who trusted in
popular taste and sought to reflect it in their art.

One of the favourite places of working-class entertainment was, as in
Victorian and Edwardian England, the music hall or 'Variété', as it was called
in Germany. There was no doubt an element of sentimental condescension in
the delight of many Expressionists at the superficial and often tawdry offerings
of the Variété. But it possessed a number of features with which the theatre
practitioner of the early twenties could genuinely sympathize. It was lively,
and it was professional; that is to say, the performers were usually technically
accomplished; for here, unprotected by subsidies or the well-mannered
bourgeois audience, they required expertise to survive. There was also a
tremendous rapport with the audience and above all, as the name implied, an
abundance of variety, employing music, speech, colour and movement.

A more literary type of informal entertainment was provided by the
cabaret. Reinhardt had had his own cabaret, Schall und Rauch, and some of
the early Expressionist and proto-Expressionist works had received their first
readings in cabarets like Kurt Hiller's Neopathetisches Cabaret (1909) and
Das Gnu (1911).[20] Wedekind frequently appeared in such cabarets and was
famous for his 'Moritaten', ballads replete with horrific detail and moralizing
judgments, which formed a staple diet of street and fairground entertainment
and which Brecht was to exploit so effectively in his *Dreigroschenoper*
(*Threepenny Opera*, 1928). The Cabaret Voltaire in Zurich was the setting in
July 1916 of the first Dada evening, and it is known that Piscator had a brief
flirtation with the cabaret culture of Dada on his arrival in Berlin in 1919.[21]

The particular importance of the cabaret for the development of political theatre was that it opened up new possibilities of social and political comment through the use of songs and brief sketches. The first pieces of Piscator's Proletarian Theatre followed this formula, offering, as in Lajos Barta's *Russlands Tag* (*Russia's Day*), cartoon figures with slogan-like utterances to communicate a political viewpoint. As yet the form was not very adventurous: this first programme of the Proletarian Theatre was merely a triple bill of one-act sketches with the singing of the 'Internationale' thrown in for good measure. By 1924, however, as part of the Communist Party's campaign for the elections to the Reichstag, Piscator with Felix Gasbarra, who was later to become Piscator's chief Dramaturg, devised a much more successful programme. This was the *Revue Roter Rummel* or *Red Revue*, of which Piscator wrote:[22]

The revue form coincided with the decline of bourgeois dramatic form.
The revue has no unity of action, derives its effects from any that can be
associated with theatre, is loose in its structure and yet possesses something
tremendously naive in the directness of its presentation.

The programme consisted of some dozen sketches, linked by songs, and introduced by the stock figures of the 'compère' and 'commère', in this case representatives of the bourgeoisie and the proletariat, who emerged arguing from the audience.

Piscator's revue technique reached its high point with the programme *Trotz alledem!* Here the staging techniques were much more sophisticated, and the revue developed a much clearer line, treating as it did the development of Germany from 1914 to 1919. By restricting itself to the recreation of events of recent history it had some justification in claiming to be the first truly documentary drama.

Piscator's later work moved away from the loosely connected montage quality of the revue form, but he seldom abandoned the episodic structure or the use of song and movement which had attracted him to it in the first place. Above all, like Brecht, he had learned from music hall and cabaret the importance of projecting the action on stage into the midst of the audience:[23]

The author ... must cease to be the autocratic person of old, must learn to
put his own conceptions and originality in the background in favour of the
conceptions which live in the psyche of the masses, and in favour of trivial
forms which are clear and accessible to all.

Texts of political theatre

Playwriting limped behind the advance of the theatre, in ideology as in form. All the writers who shared our philosophy were still caught up in post-Expressionism, incapable of corresponding to our hopes for the theatre.

Piscator: *The Political Theatre* (1929)

With the development of the political theatre an interesting reversal occurred. In the earliest Expressionist experimentation, playwrights had explored new territory but had had to wait for the traditionally conservative theatre to catch up with these new ideas. Initially there was about a five-year time lag between writing and performance (e.g., Kaiser's *Von morgens bis mitternachts*, Hasenclever's *Der Sohn*, Sorge's *Der Bettler*), bearing out Otto Brahm's earlier contention: 'Modern literature is revolutionary; the theatre is conservative.'[24]

Now it became a recurrent complaint of Piscator that the political theatre had advanced far beyond playwriting. Usable texts simply did not seem to be available. The reason for this reversal was simple: the Expressionist revolution in the theatre had been almost entirely an aesthetic revolution, and it had taken time for the public to cultivate a taste for Expressionist styles. Piscator's political theatre, however, derived from a sociological revolution, from the need to create a theatre reflecting the concerns of the proletariat. But even left-wing writers — like Toller — could not free themselves from their bourgeois individualism, and the proletariat had not yet brought forth its own writers.

The result was that many of the texts Piscator staged were not only of little literary value but also never wholly satisfactory for his political ends: e.g., Alfons Paquet's *Fahnen* (*Flags*) and *Sturmflut* (*Tidal Wave*), Ehm Welk's *Gewitter über Gottland* (*Storm over Gottland*) and even, as we shall see, *Hoppla, wir leben!* Already he had taken considerable freedom in the use of these texts, but his first major adaptation occurred with his production of Schiller's *Die Räuber* (*The Robbers*), which caused a furore at Jessner's Staatstheater in 1926.[25]

Following in the footsteps of Jessner, Piscator felt that the classics must be made relevant to our own age. Replying to a newspaper survey of leading writers, directors and actors about the performance of the classics, Piscator answered in part:[26]

> The director cannot simply be 'loyal to the work', for the work is not something lifeless and final: once it is placed in the world, it changes with time, acquires patina and assimilates new awareness. So the director is given the task of finding that standpoint from which he can uncover the roots of the dramatic piece. This standpoint cannot be dreamt up and arbitrarily chosen: only inasmuch as the director feels himself the servant and interpreter of his time will he succeed in fixing the standpoint which he has in common with the decisive forces that shape the character of the age.

In the case of *Die Räuber* Piscator's standpoint was that the traditional hero-figure Karl Moor was 'a romantic fool'[27] who misused the revolutionary energy of the robbers for his personal ends, and that Schiller's villainous Spiegelberg was in fact the true revolutionary. So he cut and changed the text considerably and had the actor playing Spiegelberg made up to look like Trotsky.

Although Piscator never staged another classic in the pre-war years (the earliest work he directed otherwise was Tolstoy's *The Power of Darkness* of 1889), the freedom he took with the text of *Die Räuber* set a pattern for the free adaptation of established texts. In 1927 he set up a 'dramaturgical collective' under the leadership of Felix Gasbarra, the German-Italian communist who had worked with Piscator on the earlier political revues. In the hands of the collective, of which Brecht was an active member, texts like *Rasputin* and *Schwejk* underwent such a transformation that the authorship could only be accredited to a group and not to an individual.

Recognizing that 'no other art-form with the exception of architecture and orchestral music is so dependent on maintaining a like-minded community as the theatre',[28] Piscator laid down one of the foundation stones of political theatre, adopted by Brecht in the post-war creation of the Berliner Ensemble and central to the theory of all socialist theatre structure today: in place of the individual achievement of the bourgeois artist the work of the political theatre is produced by the collective. In this way the creative process itself became revolutionized in the theatre.

Technical innovations

Apart from the revolving stage and electric light the theatre at the beginning of the twentieth century was still in the same state as Shakespeare had left it: a rectangular opening, a peep-hole, through which the spectator might cast the well-known 'forbidden look' into a strange world. ... For three centuries the existence of theatre depended on the fiction that there was no audience present.

Piscator: *The Political Theatre* (1929)

One of the most notable features of Piscator's production of *Hoppla, wir leben!* was its use of stage machinery, film, and a complex construction on stage. Piscator named the lack of suitable texts for a political theatre as one of the chief reasons why he introduced so many technical devices into his productions,[29] and it is for this aspect of revolutionizing the theatre that he is now best remembered.

Although in tune with the technologically sophisticated character of the age, these innovations were not necessary components of a new political theatre, and in many cases now seem as dated as the spectacular horse-races or shipwrecks of Victorian theatre. Significantly, too, when the right material presented itself, as in Friedrich Wolf's *Tai Yang erwacht* (*Tai Yang Awakes*, 1931) Piscator seemed happy to return to a simple form of staging.

His first innovation was of a pedagogic rather than a technical nature. For the short political piece *Russlands Tag* the sole décor provided by Piscator's designer, John Heartfield, was a map of Europe. Not only did the map provide an easily portable backdrop; it also introduced a new concept into set design:[30]

It was no longer simple 'decoration' but at once a social, political, geographical or economic diagram. It was part of the action. It played a role in the scenic development, it became something like an element in the dramatic structure.

In Paquet's *Fahnen*, his first production at the Volksbühne in Berlin in 1924, Piscator extended this use of background visual information with projections of photographs and texts.

Already for *Fahnen* he had intended to employ film, but it was with the political revue *Trotz alledem!* that he first developed the documentary technique which became such a spectacular element in his theatre. The use of film in the theatre was not a new idea: as early as 1911 a revue called *Rund um den Alster* (*Around the Alster*) was introduced by a light-hearted film sequence, and film inserts are prescribed by the stage-directions of Ivan Goll's *Der Unsterbliche* (*The Immortal*) of 1920 and of Goll's *Methusalem* and Toller's *Der entfesselte Wotan* (*Woden Unbound*), both written in 1922.

Piscator's particular achievement was in using film not as a scenic interlude but to amplify and comment on the action on stage. The theatre, even with Reinhardt's huge casts, can only present a number of individuals; it cannot adequately portray mass movements nor show, for example, a nation at war. Film could reflect the new collectivist society by providing the historical background to the lives acted out before it. It was, above all, concrete evidence of the assertions of the performance: 'I need the means to show the interaction between the great human and supra-human factors and the individual or class. One of these means was film.'[31] The commenting function of film was compared by Bernhard Diebold to the chorus of Greek tragedy:[32]

When the ancient chorus appeared as ideal spectator, as soothsayer, as prophet, as judge, as the collective voice of the gods and the people, it created the general atmosphere for the individual drama of Orestes and Clytemnestra. ... Exactly the same psychic function is achieved with great effect by the Piscator film.

In *Trotz alledem!*, which depicted the years from 1914 to 1919, film was an indispensable component of the documentary revue. An audience not yet familiar with the newsreel was particularly receptive to the disturbing images of the First World War: 'These pictures perforce stirred up the proletarian masses more powerfully than a hundred speeches would have done.'[33]

In *Sturmflut* (1926) Piscator's somewhat random use of film was replaced by a more careful approach. For the first time film was specially made for the production and, using a number of projectors (six to ten were planned), the screen at the rear of the stage became 'a living wall, the fourth dimension of the theatre'.[34] In the scene depicting the sale of St Petersburg the handful of actors on stage stand before a film of a massive crowd, which extends the perspective of the stage. In a later scene a naval battle takes place in the background while individual sailors on stage prepare to fight (see Plate 30).

With *Rasputin* (1927) Piscator carried the use of film a stage farther. It did not now just extend the stage action in terms of general reference or physical space; it was used ironically, as a contrast to the action on stage, so creating one of the rare cases of genuine dialectic in Piscator's theatre. Thus, for example, the Tsar's authentic words from the front: 'The life I am leading at the head of my armies is healthy and bracing' coincided with a film showing the corpses of Russian soldiers.

The following year in *Die Abenteuer des braven Soldaten Schwejk* (*The Adventures of the Good Soldier Schweik*) Piscator used cartoon film created from the drawings of George Grosz. Already for Paul Zech's *Das trunkene Schiff* (*The Drunken Ship*) in 1926 George Grosz had drawn cartoons that were projected onto a triptych screen and provided a point of social reference to the events of Rimbaud's life. Now in *Schwejk* live actors conversed with cartoon figures like the ogrish military doctor in Scene 6.

Another innovative aspect of *Schwejk* was the use of conveyor belts. Again, their use in the theatre was by no means unknown, but Piscator transformed them from being a scenic gimmick into a necessary component of the action. The problem was to adapt a picaresque novel for the stage: the multiplicity of witty episodes would apparently make for a very disjointed stage presentation. As Felix Gasbarra reported:[35]

> It seemed impossible to manage the epic development of the plot by tradi-
> tional theatrical means. On a static stage one would constantly split up
> Hašek's episodes into individual scenes which would have completely gone
> against the character of the novel. Piscator overcame this impossibility by
> turning the static stage into a rolling stage. With a sure hand he discovered
> the stage technique appropriate to the epic development of the novel: the
> conveyor belt.

Thus the mobility on which Hašek's novel and his satirical view of war depend was created by moving actors or cardboard cut-outs, designed by Grosz, on the two conveyor belts that travelled the width of the stage. Plate 31 shows the rheumatic Schwejk being pushed by his landlady to the recruiting-office on the downstage belt and meeting an officer figure on the parallel band. Piscator claimed that his conveyor belts embodied 'the dramatic-epic principle' and asserted that in this way all novels might be turned into plays.[36]

It is certainly true that an 'epic' play which depends on mobility, like Brecht's *Mutter Courage*, benefits from a moving stage like the revolve at the Berliner Ensemble.

Compared with these technical innovations, Piscator's sets were generally unadventurous, being functional rather than decorative. For Gorky's *Lower Depths*, for example, a basically realistic set was surmounted by a city sky-line with the title of the play in lights hung before it. This was a mere design frill, and the impulse of Expressionism towards imaginative scenic design seems to have been resisted by Piscator, no doubt from suspicion of a too overtly 'artistic' element in his productions. While the sets may have been aesthetically uninspiring, from a functional aspect they were often impressive. Most striking was the segment-globe used for *Rasputin*: a silver image of the world, mounted on a revolve, and a surface on which films could be projected and in which sections opened to reveal different scenes. The effect was to offer glimpses into events all over the world, so using Piscator's favourite technique of simultaneity to make a general political comment.

Acting style

> The style which actors are to adopt must be of a completely concrete kind. … Whatever is said must not be sought for, be experimental, 'expressionistic' or intense, but be determined by simple, undisguised revolutionary will and purpose.
>
> Piscator: 'On the basis and aims of the Proletarian Theatre' (1920)

Just as the author and director had to abandon bourgeois individualism to discover styles appropriate to the new political theatre, so too the actor had to move from the self-release of ecstatic Expressionism towards a cooler, more objective mode of performance. No longer was he to bare his soul, because the individual soul had lost its importance; instead he was to explore his function as a member of a social and political structure.

This new 'hard, clear, unsentimental' style of acting was described by Piscator as 'neo-realistic'.[37] It contained a deliberate rejection of the Expressionist style, but this implied a turning away from primitivist acting only. The abstractionist style of Expressionist acting, while too stylized for Piscator's use, carried within it the de-individualized quality appropriate to collectivist political theatre.

Clearly, then, this 'neo-realistic' style was in no way a return to the undifferentiated psychological characterization of Naturalism, such as was to be revived for the performance of the 'Zeitstücke' or topical plays of the late 1920s. In place of Expressionist emotionalism and Naturalist psychologizing

Piscator sought a style of heightened realism: 'we demand a performance that is thought through so scientifically that it reproduces naturalness on a higher level.'[38] This natural style of acting depended therefore on the intellectual awareness of the actor: it had to correspond 'to the objective content of the role'[39] and the actor had to turn from being 'the embodiment of individual characteristics to become the carrier of universal historical ideas'.[40]

Given the need for a generalized style of acting, one might have expected Piscator to have released his hold on the 'natural' and to have typified roles into broadly-drawn cartoon figures. There were perhaps two reasons why he resisted this impulse. For one, the use of film in many productions gave an objective portrayal of background figures. However artificial the cinematic medium may have seemed at this early stage of its development, its 'naturalness' would have jarred with any strongly theatrical style in the acting. More importantly, any stylization would have been too reminiscent of Expressionist 'artiness'.

Characteristically, Piscator initially eschewed the prevailing style of acting by employing mainly proletarian amateur actors. It was only later, following the growing commercial success of his theatrical enterprises, that he began to employ stars. This in effect represented a further capitulation to the commercial pressures on him and remained something of an embarrassment.

In 1920 he had asserted that skill and talent would not be sufficient to fulfil the primary demand that the actor should 'allow each of his roles, each word and each gesture to become the expression of the proletarian Communist idea'.[41] By 1929 he was obliged to make room for the 'personality value' of the actor; i.e., an admission that the theatre thrives not on political ideas but on the living vibrancy of the actor. He still insisted, of course, that the actor's personality must not become an autonomous element of aesthetic charm (like a rococo desk in a functional living-room) but should serve an 'artistic and political function'.[42] Nevertheless, without the strong individual talents of stars like Kalser, Steckel, George, Granach and Pallenberg, the Piscator Theatres would not have enjoyed their artistic, albeit short-lived commercial success.

From this it becomes clear that Piscator had no very consistent conception of acting style, and despite his claim to be an 'actor's director',[43] he seemed repeatedly to be more concerned with staging techniques than with individual performances. Indeed some of his technical innovations made sensitive acting an impossibility. In both *Schwejk* and *Der Kaufmann von Berlin* (*The Merchant of Berlin*, 1929) the conveyor belts were so noisy that actors had to shout at the top of their voices to be heard. Despite his claim that 'all the new scenic discoveries that I used brought new dimensions for the actor with them',[44] the actors were frequently dwarfed by the stage-apparatus. Hans Reimann recalls a performance of *Rasputin* at which he wandered across the front of the stage without either the audience or the actors noticing.[45] It was therefore not entirely unjust of Meyerhold when he commented that Piscator 'has built a new theatre but makes old actors perform in it',[46] and one can give some credence to the anecdote about Brecht getting Piscator's actors to work for him. According to Fritz Sternberg the sociologist, Brecht proved that several leading actors would accept an engagement with him for less than they demanded from Piscator, in return for the promise of extra rehearsals.[47] Clearly, actors themselves were not very happy with Piscator's preoccupation with stage machinery.

Only relatively late in his pre-war career did Piscator — perhaps under Brecht's influence — seek for acting styles appropriate to the generalized concerns of the political theatre. Initially, the generalization was of a somewhat external nature, as in the Lenin make-up of Asmus in *Gewitter über Gottland* or Spiegelberg's identification with Trotsky in *Die Räuber*. Similarly, in *Schwejk* some of the figures were raised to the level of the 'clownlike symbolic'[48] by the use of exaggerated masks: a police-spy was characterized by a large protuberant eye and a colossal ear.

But it was in *Tai Yang erwacht* in 1931 that Piscator finally moved towards what was recognizably an 'epic' style of acting. He added to Friedrich Wolf's text a prologue in which the actors changed into their costumes and put on their make-up while relating the content of the play to the contemporary situation in Germany, a device to be taken up by Brecht in *Der kaukasische Kreidekreis* (*The Caucasian Chalk Circle*, 1948). Rhythmic movements, mime and symbolic dance all featured in *Tai Yang erwacht*, the last of Piscator's productions in pre-Hitler Germany; and with these means he seemed to have rediscovered the value of abstractionist tendencies in Expressionism:[49]

> The generalization of the dramatic action into intellectual slogans [ins Geistig-Plakatierte], into political awareness, makes specific demands on the actor. The actor must communicate the intellectual content which emerges in the action as points for discussion. These must operate like dramatic figures in dynamic opposition to one another within the framework of a new second level of action.

Ultimately, therefore, Piscator had aligned himself with this major development of German acting, from the abstractionist style of Jessner and Kaiser to Brecht's epic theories, the style that invites the actor to subjugate his personality to point to the situation beyond his own individual case.

Involvement, alienation and epic theatre

That is what is basically new about this theatre, that play and reality merge in a quite strange manner. You often don't know whether you are in a theatre or a political meeting, you think you have to intervene and help and heckle. The border between play and reality is blurred.

Critic of the *Red Banner*, 12 April 1921

For the immediate post-revolutionary activist, theatre predictably seemed to be more a matter of stoking the enthusiasm of the proletariat than of conducting a gradual programme of education. Equally predictably, therefore, Piscator initially seemed less concerned with objective reportage than with generating the involvement of his audience. Of the audience at the revue *Trotz alledem!* he wrote:[50]

The theatre had become reality for them and soon it was no longer the stage versus the auditorium but a single great meeting-hall, a single great battle-field, a single great demonstration.

Piscator clearly welcomed this emotional involvement that in a sense restored the illusionism of Naturalist theatre, but with the difference that the fourth wall was decisively removed to allow the audience to feel themselves a part of the action; they were no longer voyeurs but participants. At the same time he was aware of the need to maintain a critical viewpoint and so had to moderate the excitement of an emotionally charged audience:[51]

The theatre was no longer to have a purely emotional effect, no longer to depend on the responsiveness of feelings — it addressed itself quite deliberately to reason. It was to communicate not only elation, enthusiasm and ecstasy but enlightenment, knowledge and awareness.

In order to achieve critical distance, the stage illusion had to be destroyed, heralding the beginnings of 'alienation' and 'epic theatre', terms that were to become central to the theories of Brecht.[52] Piscator would jokingly relate that his designer John Heartfield was the actual inventor of epic theatre.[53] In the early days of the Proletarian Theatre, Heartfield arrived almost half an hour late for a performance, carrying with him a freshly-painted backdrop. He interrupted the piece, Karl Wittfogel's *Die Krüppel* (*The Cripples*), and demanded to be allowed to hang his backdrop on the stage. A discussion between Piscator, Heartfield and the spectators ensued, until it was finally agreed to put the backdrop in place, and the performance began afresh.

The technical apparatus of Piscator's later productions maintained the conflicting tendencies of involvement and alienation. On the one hand, technical devices like film allowed performances to be presented without breaks for scene changes: 'Until each climax the tension of the public must not be lost.'[54] On the other hand, the use of machinery and the different styles of presentation, from cinematic realism to song and dance, reminded the audience of the artificiality of the spectacle and so militated against uncritical involvement.

The truth is that, as with acting, Piscator did not think out his position in a coherent manner: for a man of the theatre, the enthusiastic involvement of the audience seemed to justify the validity of his work; as a political thinker, he knew that enthusiasm was hardly enough.

Hoppla, wir leben!: **Piscator's adaptation of the text**

All [the Piscator Theatre] had was a new dramaturgy; it had no new dramas.

Piscator: 'An account of our work' (1929)

The year 1927, when Piscator opened the Piscator-Bühne on the Nollendorfplatz in Berlin, was a year of new-found prosperity. The Dawes Plan on reparations had been in operation for three years, and Germany, far from being sucked dry, now became the recipient of considerable foreign investment (some 4 billion Marks). Unemployment dropped to 300,000, and bankruptcies occurred only a fifth as frequently as a year previously. Nevertheless, there were those who saw through the sham stability of the new Germany and tried to alert the nation to the dangers that lay ahead.

So it was appropriate − after the failure by Wilhelm Herzog, Piscator's disruptive Dramaturg, to furnish a usable script for the opening of the theatre − that Piscator should accept a proposal made by Ernst Toller: a play dealing with a revolutionary who emerges after eight years in a mental home and, like Toller on his release from prison, confronts the new Germany of 1927 and in particular the failure of a socialist government to achieve socialism.

Hoppla, wir leben! opens with a Prologue in a prison cell. It is 1919 and six revolutionaries, among them Karl Thomas, stand under sentence of death. When they are reprieved, the announcement proves too much for Thomas and he goes insane. One of their number, Kilman, is unconditionally pardoned. Act 1, Scene 1: It is now 1927, and Thomas is discharged from the mental asylum. 1,2: he goes to seek help from Kilman, only to discover that he has become a Social Democrat minister, courted by financiers and nationalist aristocracy. Thomas is bitterly disappointed at Kilman's compromise of his former revolutionary ideas. 2,1: Thomas now lives with Eva Berg, one of the original revolutionary prisoners, and is invited by her to join the Party in the fight for true socialism. 2,2: a presidential election brings the right-wing Minister of War to power. Thomas resolves to get rid of Kilman. 3,1: Kilman's life is also under threat from nationalist elements; Count Lande plots his assassination with a right-wing student. 3,2: Thomas, now a waiter in a hotel, resolves to shoot Kilman while he is dining there. While caught in indecision, however, the student assassinates Kilman. 4,1: Thomas pursues the student, firing two shots after him, and is arrested by the police. 4,2: the police-chief interrogates Thomas and concludes that he is mentally abnormal. 4,3 (cut in Piscator's version): Thomas is referred by the examining magistrate for a psychiatric report. 4,4: the psychiatrist examines Thomas and sends him back to prison. 5,1: Thomas finds himself in prison with three of the original revolutionary prisoners. 5,2 (cut in Piscator's version): Lande dedicates a memorial to Kilman. 5,3: the prisoners learn that Kilman's assassin has been arrested, but it is too late: unable to bear the thought of further imprisonment and destroyed by the failure of the revolution, Thomas has hanged himself.

The play's theme of exposing the Social Democratic Party's betrayal of its revolutionary origins was well suited to Piscator's purpose, but he was understandably suspicious of the Expressionistic elements in Toller's work. He had seen *Die Wandlung* at the Tribüne in Berlin and had planned his own production at Das Tribunal, the theatre he founded in Königsberg in 1919. His intention was to stage the piece as realistically as possible and to free the language 'from its lyrical Expressionisms'.[55] Now in 1927 Piscator was once more concerned with the way 'documentary was confused with poetic lyricism'[56] in Toller's new play.

It is impossible to know to what extent the text which was published in 1927 had already been affected by Piscator's proposals and recommendations that summer. Certainly, Toller in his autobiography considered the changes he had been persuaded to make both detrimental and significant:[57]

Today I regret having allowed myself to be seduced by fashion into destroying the architectonic quality of the original for the sake of the architectonic quality of the production. The intended form was more powerful than the one that was shown on stage.

It is not clear whether the word 'architectonic' refers to dramatic or linguistic structure, and anyway – even after the presumed changes made during the process of composition – Piscator continued to adapt both for the performance.

Most of these later linguistic changes resulted from Piscator's attempt to lessen the Expressionistic emotionalism of the piece in order to be able to analyse the material 'soberly, clearly and unambiguously'.[58] The more lyrical lines of Karl Thomas were cut; e.g., 'She is young. Hardly seventeen. For her, death is the cold black hole in which she must lie, for ever. And above her grave warm life, intoxicating, bright and sweet.'[59] Or, even more characteristically Expressionist, Thomas's reference to innocent men, 'in whose eyes, the heaven and the sun and the stars move, shining'.[60]

Other changes to the language for Piscator's production took place for overtly political reasons. In order to make the protagonist Karl Thomas more a man of the people all references to his bourgeois background, like the reference to his university career in Act 2, Scene 2, were excised; and some of his more cynical remarks about the proletariat and their revolutionary tendencies were suppressed, as for example in the following passage which almost exactly anticipates the Marquis de Sade's high-handed scepticism in Scene 25 of Peter Weiss's *Marat/Sade*:[61]

One runs away from his wife because she makes his life a misery. Another cannot come to terms with life and limps and limps until he finds a crutch that looks marvellous and gives him something of the appearance of a hero. A third thinks he can simply change his skin because he is fed up with it. A fourth just seeks adventure.

With regard to more basic structural changes Piscator had several reasons for tampering with the original. He was a little bolder than Toller in the cross-cutting of simultaneous scenes, so that, for example, at one point in Act 1, Scene 2 dialogue from three separate sources is intercut and overlaid. He also reasonably dropped the weakly satirical scene of the intellectual discussion group in the hotel (3,2). At other times Piscator sharpened the political bite of the original. Thus the original radio-telegrapher scene in the hotel begins with Karl Thomas hearing over the radio news of floods in America and jazz music from Cairo. In Piscator's version he immediately hears stock-exchange reports from Wall Street, the sound of American warships being launched (an insertion by Piscator), and the cries of starving masses in Romania (only briefly referred to in the original). What in Toller was a plethora of entertainment, advertising and news items, now becomes in Piscator a more critical view of the state of the world, the one major concession being the retention of the diagnosis of an airline-passenger's heart disease over the radio: clearly Piscator with his love of technological gadgetry could not let that one go, however little it might have to do with the world situation.

Another major textual change occurs with the arrest of Karl Thomas for the supposed assassination of his former friend Minister Kilman. In the original, two lengthy scenes deal with Thomas's arrest and interrogation. In Piscator the second scene is cut and the scene of the initial arrest is itself shortened and introduced by a telephone conversation with Count Lande, the person actually responsible for the assassination. Thus the traditional detective-story interest in Toller, which reassures us about the processes of justice, is here replaced by the suggestion of corruption and judicial arbitrariness. As Piscator noted in the prompt-book: 'The conversation gives the impression of mutual understanding. Talking 'between the lines'. It sharpens and prepares for Thomas's entrance.'[62]

The most significant restructuring was in the ending. According to Piscator, he, his dramaturgical collective and Toller considered three possible endings:

1 Arrest of Thomas. Police station. Mental asylum.
2 Thomas on the run. Voluntary return to prison. Film of Kilman's memorial, etc. and huge cannon directed at audience.
3 Arrest of Thomas. Police station. Mental asylum. Prison. Thomas hangs himself.

Toller claimed that he was opposed to the second version and preferred the first: an ending which would have identified the mental asylum as an instrument of state oppression and Thomas as a threat to the state. This conclusion was almost certainly the one used for the premiere of the play in Hamburg, which opened two days before the delayed first night at the Piscator-Bühne.

Piscator was unable to share Toller's positive view of Karl Thomas. Piscator saw him as 'an anarchic sentimental type who logically collapses',[63] and he finally managed to persuade Toller to allow the play to end with Thomas's suicide. This is the ending in the published version of the text, although Toller later expressed his dissatisfaction with it. Significantly, however, although Piscator felt that suicide was the logical outcome of the petit-bourgeois attitude of Thomas, he relieved the pessimism by adding a few lines to Toller's text: the final line of the original, 'He isn't answering', is deleted and is replaced by:

RAND (*shouting*): Hanged!!

MELLER: No!

KROLL: He shouldn't have done that; that's not the way for revolutionaries to die.

EVA: He was crushed by the world.

MELLER: Bloody world! We'll have to change it.

CURTAIN

Just as there is now no certainty about the extent of Piscator's influence on the published text of the play, it is also unclear how much of his theatrical practice determined Toller's conception of the staging. The hotel scene of the third act and the prison scene at the end are seen in terms of simultaneous staging in the published text, and Piscator applies this idea to the presentation of the whole piece. He had already tried out this technique in his production of *Die Räuber* the previous year,[64] but on this occasion the simultaneous and inter-cut dialogue had often left actors straining to hear their cues and had angered the critics because Schiller's text became frequently unintelligible. Perhaps for this reason the scenes of *Hoppla!*, while imagined to be simultaneous, are normally carefully separated, the shift of attention being achieved by blacking out one part of the set and illuminating another.

Hoppla, wir leben!: set design and visual presentation

> For years I have been working to get rid of scenery.
> Traugott Müller: Programme-note to *Hoppla, wir leben!* (1927)

For *Hoppla!* Piscator's designer, Traugott Müller, provided an entirely functional set. It consisted of a large scaffolding construction of 8-centimetre gas piping, 11 metres wide, 8 metres high and 3 metres deep, and weighing about 4,000 kilos. It was divided vertically into three areas, and the sides were further subdivided horizontally into three 'boxes'; the slightly narrower central area was three storeys high and was surmounted by a small room. There were therefore eight acting areas, with movement from one to the other made possible by narrow staircases both inside and outside the structure (see Plates 32–3). The whole construction was mounted on a revolving stage which allowed the side containing the action to be pulled slightly towards the audience in order to centre the action and to provide better sight-lines. It also rested on sliders so that the entire set could be winched back to create an open acting area in front of it. The construction was backed by white cloth on to which back-projections could be made to indicate the locality of each scene. In addition, the tall central area contained a movable screen which could be slid forward or back to make a smaller or larger central acting area inside the construction.

This scaffolding set was almost universally dubbed by the critics as an example of the Kreisler-Bühne (Kreisler Stage). This referred to a production in the Theater in der Königgrätzer Strasse, Berlin, in 1922 of *Die wunderlichen Geschichten des Kapellmeisters Kreisler* (*The Strange Adventures of Kapellmeister Kreisler*). For this episodic piece, the directors Carl Meinhard and Rudolf Bernauer with their designer Sven Gade managed its forty-two set changes by constructing a stage with six separate acting areas arranged asymmetrically above and beside one another. The intention of this set was purely to facilitate the flow of the piece, and no attempt was made to present simultaneous action (only one playing area at a time was illuminated). The relationship between Piscator's *Hoppla!* set and the Kreisler-Bühne was therefore a tenuous one.

A more probable influence was the production by Tairov of an adaptation of G. K. Chesterton's *The Man who was Thursday*, which was toured to Berlin in 1925. For this, Tairov used a metal scaffolding set with acting areas on different levels, but more in an attempt 'to express the mood and content (the atmosphere of the action) of this particular play'[65] than as a functional setting in the manner of Piscator's production.

There can be no question, either, of a direct influence from Meyerhold, similar to Piscator's though his approach was in many respects. Of the Russian directors, only Stanislavsky and Tairov were at all well known in the 1920s. Stanislavsky had brought his Moscow Art Theatre to Berlin in 1921; Tairov had made guest performances in 1923 and 1925 and his book *Das entfesselte Theater* (*Notes of a Director*) was published in German in 1923; it was not until 1930, however, that Meyerhold first performed in Berlin, at a time in fact when Piscator had largely abandoned the use of stage machinery, and it is known that Piscator never saw any Meyerhold performances during his visits to Russia. Significantly, an article written for the catalogue of the Theatre Exhibition in Vienna in 1924 explained to the German reader that Stanislavsky had been superseded on the Russian stage by a 'new generation' of directors, including Vachtangov, Tairov and Meyerhold.[66] Clearly, then, even by the mid-1920s there was still considerable ignorance in Germany about parallel developments on the Russian stage, and it would seem that the theatrical revolution that took place in both countries occurred independently rather than under mutual influence.

The furniture for the various 'rooms' of the *Hoppla!* set was kept to a minimum. Initially, Traugott Müller had intended to use collapsible furniture that would, by means of a 'scissor-mechanism', remain flat on the stage until required for a scene, when it would spring erect with cinematic suddenness. The idea proved impracticable, however, and furniture had to be set between scenes, usually while a film, song or dance sequence covered the pause. In practice, the play, which if paced reasonably fast would run for just over two hours, lasted a full four hours in Piscator's version.

The shift of attention from one acting area to another was effected by the lighting, either by front-of-house follow-spots or by overhead spots hung in the scaffolding, or by a combination of both. Throughout, the light was white and usually at full strength: it was dimmed only occasionally for atmospheric reasons and more often simply to allow the projections to be seen clearly. Like the set the lighting was functional rather than aesthetic. As Piscator wrote in 1927:[67]

> Lighting loses all its dependence on space, comes alive and wanders. With many gradations and rooted in natural contrasts, it achieves an important role in the composition of the scene by first creating a focus and then spreading boundlessly across the stage.

In theory, the simultaneous staging made possible by Müller's set should have been ideally suited to Piscator's political theatre, for here the stage could move away from the traditional portrayal of individual conflicts to present a broader, generalized view of society:[68]

> In his play Toller had already indicated the *social cross-section* in the choice and grouping of his scenes. We therefore had to create a stage form which would render this idea precise and concrete: a construction on several levels with many different acting areas above and beside each other, which would symbolize the social order.

In practice, however, by letting the light normally follow the progress of Thomas from acting area to acting area, Piscator did not present his audience with a social cross-section or simultaneity but with the traditional focus on an individual protagonist. As Reinhold Grimm acutely observes:[69]

> Toller's play ... does not create simultaneity; there is no juxtaposition of different strands of plot, but only the path of an isolated individual pressed into the confines of a single space. ... The cross-section of the hotel merely

provides a means to hound the hero Karl Thomas from place to place as quickly and as conveniently as possible and without any real motivation even though with apparent realism. In almost all the scenes he enters as a delayed wanderer in waiter's uniform; and the few in which he does not appear serve as mere colouring or prepare for his next entrance. What took place on Toller's and Piscator's extremely objective simultaneous stage was in fact an Expressionist 'Stationendrama'.

A major contribution to the political impact of the piece was made by the use of Piscator's favourite technique, film inserts. Some ten thousand feet of film were specially made for this production under the direction of Kurt Oertel and Walter Ruttmann (so named in the prompt-book, although Piscator refers to him as Simon Guttmann in *Das politische Theater*). These could be used as part of the narrative, as in the 'Film Prologue', which provides a kind of exposition to establish the background of the figures in prison. They were also used for specifically documentary purposes, showing, for example, the major events between 1919 and 1927, the period Thomas spends in the asylum: 'No medium other than film is able to show the passing of eight endless years in seven minutes.'[70] At this point Piscator had also wanted to indicate the passing of the eight years in a purely abstract manner: a film sequence in which a black surface would divide into lines and then into squares, representing days, hours and minutes. This idea, which was not realized, stood closer to the contemporary experiments in abstract film of Moholy-Nagy at the Bauhaus than to Piscator's previous documentary cinema. Significantly, Piscator did not use Toller's proposal of a film about female workers to preface the second act, since this would not have assisted the narrative and its documentary value would have been limited.

A more important use of film, as we shall see in the scene-by-scene analysis, was to comment on the action in progress on the stage, bringing the film into a dynamic and often purely atmospheric relationship with the theatrical presentation rather than using it merely as an interlude. In order to blend the action with the film, some of the front-projection was on to a gauze hung across the front of the stage. Although the picture was not as clear as it would have been on a flat reflective screen, it allowed the lights behind the gauze to be slowly brought up, so fading out the cinematic image as the actors began their scene. Although it had been known to the theatre for centuries that gauze seemed opaque when lit from in front, and transparent when illuminated from behind, it seems almost certain that Piscator was the first to use this idea for film projection.

Innovatory as the technical aspects of the production were, there is nothing in the prompt-book to suggest that Piscator was seeking anything but unspectacular realism in the acting. In the musical inserts the influence of the Variété made itself felt: in the song 'Hoppla, wir leben!' with lyrics by Walter Mehring, music by Edmund Meisel and sung by Käte Kühl, and in the dance sequences choreographed by no less a figure than Mary Wigman. But this vaudeville style did not carry over into the acting, and Piscator's directions, while by no means insensitive, contain no surprises.

Hoppla, wir leben!: presentation of individual scenes

> What [Piscator] achieved can be recognized in detail only from an exact reconstruction of his productions.
>
> Günther Rühle: *Theatre in Our Time* (1976)

The prompt-book, based on the Kiepenheuer Verlag edition of 1927, contains beside the text six columns indicating: Lighting, Music and Sounds, Film, Expression, Positions and Moves, Atmosphere. From this it is possible to attempt a detailed reconstruction of the production.

The performance began in conventional manner by dimming the houselights. As soon as the auditorium was dark, however, the lights came on again. This was repeated twice more, suggesting perhaps the traditional three blows of a stick in the French theatre and certainly having the effect of jolting the audience out of a complacent self-surrender to a theatrical experience. The curtains parted, not to reveal a stage set with actors but a large cinema screen, 10 metres wide by 8 metres high, which almost entirely concealed the scaffolding. There followed the 'Film Prologue', but not as described in Toller's text. Toller depicts the suppression of a popular revolt, without reference to place or time, as an explanation of the presence of the revolutionaries in prison. In its place, Piscator's film opened with a shot of the bemedalled chest of a general (cf.central projection in Plate 35). Although the head was not seen, the audience would have soon grasped that Hindenburg was being represented. There followed newsreel sequences from the Imperial archives: infantry and tank attacks, explosions, the wounded, huge military cemeteries, and the German army in defeat wearily returning home. Amongst these soldiers the figure of Karl Thomas could be recognized. Finally, the general's chest was seen once more, as his medals were torn off him, an act symbolic of the all too temporary end to nationalist militarism at the end of 1918.

Prologue As the film ended, a gauze was dropped in, and prison windows were projected on it. The film screen was raised to reveal the scaffolding structure with its slide-projections of prison walls and in the central area the six prisoners waiting in their cell, with Kilman drumming his fingers nervously on the wall downstage left (I have followed the practice in the prompt-book of denoting right and left from the audience's point of view). A film of a guard passing across the front of the prison was projected on to the

1 Reinhardt's production of Wedekind's *Frühlings Erwachen*, Berlin, 1906. Final scene with symbolic figure of the Man-in-the-Mask (played by Wedekind)

2 'Rhythmic space'. Adolphe Appia's design for Gluck's *Orpheus and Eurydice*, Hellerau, 1913

3 Paul Wegener as Franz Moor in Schiller's
   Die Räuber, directed by Reinhardt, Berlin,
   1908

4 Ernst Deutsch as Hasenclever's Son, 1916.
   Lithograph by Rochus Gliese

The first Expressionist productions

5   Ernst Stern's design for *Der Bettler*. Act 2: Son and Father

6   Hasenclever's *Der Sohn*: Ludwig Sievert's set for Weichert's production, Mannheim, 1918

7   Kokoschka: *Mörder Hoffnung der Frauen*. August Babberger's set for George's production, Frankfurt/Main, 1920

8 Primitivist: August Babberger's design for the premiere,
Frankfurt, 1918

9 Impressionist: Ernst Stern's design for Herald's production, Berlin,
1918

10 Abstractionist: Walter von Wecus's design for Lindemann's
production, Düsseldorf, 1920

'Von morgens bis mitternachts': the tree/skeleton

11 Fritz Schäfler's design, Munich, 1921

12 César Klein's design for Barnowsky's production, Berlin, 1921

13 Karl Gröning's design for Jessner's production, Altona, 1930

14 Ernst Deutsch as the Cashier. Bank scene

15 The repeated skull image. Bank scene

16 The Cashier 'crucified'. Salvation Army hall scene

17 Opening scene with shadow cast by spot from prompter's box.
Sketch by Robert Edmond Jones

18 Richard's coronation. The famous Jessner steps

19 Richmond and his troops in white

20 Jessner's production of Kaiser's *Gas I*, Berlin, 1928. Müthel as Engineer, Franck as Millionaire's Son, Granach as Clerk. An 'impossible' photograph

21 Scene 4: Barbed-wire entanglement

22 Scene 7: Friedrich and beggars

23 Scene 9: Factory/prison

24 Design by Hans Strohbach for Scene 5

25 Production photograph of same scene. Note deleterious effect of full lighting required for photograph

26 Robert Edmond Jones's impression of the same scene. Perhaps the most reliable visual evidence

27 Johannes Schröder's clinical design for Engel's production of *Gas I*, Hamburg, 1920, anticipates Constructivism

28 John Heartfield's functional setting for Toller's *Die Maschinenstürmer*, Grosses Schauspielhaus, Berlin, 1922

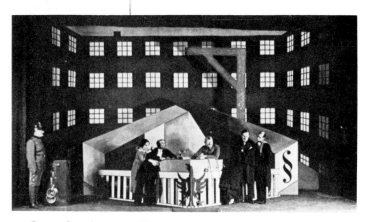

29 George Grosz's cartoon-like design for Viertel's production of Kaiser's *Nebeneinander*, Berlin, 1923

30 Back-projected film. Paquet's *Sturmflut*, Berlin, 1926

31 Use of conveyor belts. *Schwejk*, Piscatorbühne, Berlin, 1928

32 Collage showing Piscator (*top left*), the scaffolding set (prison scene) and moments from the play

33 Model of set with Piscator's silhouette

34 Design for Act 1, Scene 2: Ministry of the Interior

35 Act 2, Scene 2: the polling station

36 Act 4, Scene 4: mental hospital. Leonhard Steckel as psychiatrist,
Alexander Granach as Karl Thomas

37 1926 premiere in Darmstadt. Scene 8: Widow Begbick's canteen

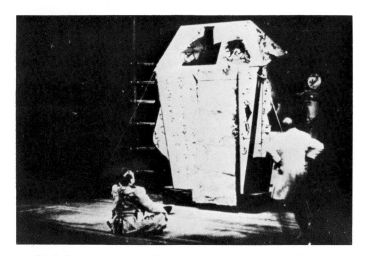

38 Brecht's 1931 production. Scene 2: the attack on the pagoda

39 Scene 7: Jeraiah Jip guards the pagoda. Note the half-curtain

40 Scene 8: Galy Gay proves himself fit to auction the elephant

41 Scene 8: Galy Gay refuses to recognize his wife

42 End of Scene 9: Peter Lorre as Galy Gay

gauze, and to the rear of the prisoners was seen a film of the warder Rand climbing the stairs. The massive head of Rand, seen in close-up, then passed over the actors' heads. Clearly, the film here did not possess any objective or documentary function, but was used simply to create atmosphere, to enclose the prisoners from in front and from behind with images of menace. In a note in the prompt-book Piscator emphasized the subjective nature of these film sequences in a curiously Expressionist manner: 'The actor reacts to the film images as though he were seeing them. They become *his* hallucinations, *his* terror; the events on film describe *his* imagination.'

Film was used also when Karl Thomas tried to loosen the bars of the prison window to allow the prisoners to escape (see group on the right of Plate 32). This was played to the front, imagining the window to be in 'the fourth wall'. As he reached up to the window, a front-projected film showed guns firing and a guard laughing, and at the rear Rand was also seen laughing. Film was used here to extend the action in physical terms.

Sounds were used effectively in this opening scene: there were continuous prison sounds (no doubt easily created on the iron scaffolding), which became louder when the cell door was opened. The loudest sound of the scene was the opening of the door on the entrance of Baron Friedrich, supposedly bringing the death warrant. The extra volume for his entrance was another unrealistic device, employed to suggest menace.

In the acting Piscator was concerned to express the fear of the prisoners, using directions like 'fearful tension' and 'climax of the nightmare', and by contrast emphasizing the pitiful enjoyment of the shared cigarette: 'This smoking to be made very personal. A single second of pleasure.' (See central group on Plate 32.) This cumulative tension prepared for Thomas's breakdown, while Kilman's over-confident behaviour made his attitude already suspect: he frequently stood separated from his fellows, and when he mocked the unnamed Sixth Prisoner for going to see the chaplain, Piscator required him to move quickly 'to make him appear "brave" '.

Act 1, Scene 1 Before the next scene the screen was lowered to show a film depicting the events from 1919 to 1927, including the election of Hindenburg as President in 1925 (a more immediately significant event than Toller's proposal for that year: 'Gandhi in India'). During the film Edmund Meisel, concealed with his orchestra in a box behind a red curtain, played appropriate music, and the stage was prepared for the next scene, the mental asylum in which Thomas had spent eight years. Once again the screen was lifted and replaced by the gauze, on which the image of the asylum was projected. In the central area the psychiatrist Lüdin sat at his desk, while in the bottom right area the warder handed Thomas the clothes for his departure (the date of discharge was changed each night to that of the performance, to make the events seem more immediate). Both rooms were defined by back-projections: shelves of files in the case of Lüdin's office and a wardrobe for the other room (cf. Plate 36).

An interesting aspect of the acting was the performance by Leonhard Steckel, later to become a leading Brechtian actor, as the psychiatrist Lüdin. Piscator exploited Toller's cliché suggestion that Lüdin was madder than any of his patients, an idea developed to its extreme in Act 4, Scene 4. Here already Piscator directed Steckel to develop the brief laugh indicated by Toller into almost continuous manic laughter.

Act 1, Scene 2 Before the next scene a film portraying the confusing world of the metropolis in 1927 was shown: Thomas was seen looking for lodgings and work, forced to sleep in a doss-house, trudging hopelessly from factory to factory. By contrast, the next scene was set in the opulent surroundings of the Ministry, and for the first time the full width of the set was used. Bottom right was Kilman's office with back-projected wallpaper and containing desk, sofa, chairs, a table with decanters, etc. The bottom left area was screened off to conceal the bedroom required for the next scene (the lack of a bridging film before Scene 3 made a fast set change essential). Above this, middle left, also with back-projected wallpaper, was an anteroom containing six chairs. From this room a staircase led steeply down into the central area, which represented a vestibule, with a huge back-projection of the Kaiser, a reminder that the political situation of 1927 had not radically altered from that of 1918 and a focus for the Minister of War's line: 'We need authority' (see Plate 34). A curious note in the prompt-book indicates how much Piscator was still operating within the limits of atmospheric realism: 'It is bright, but it is raining outside.'

The shift of attention was normally achieved by cross-fading the light from one acting area to another; only where exchanges of dialogue were very brief were the lights left on in more than one area at a time. Even when the lights were extinguished, the back-projections remained, so that figures could be seen in silhouette. There is no information available to indicate whether the actors when in silhouette held their pose or continued to act silently. Since the former would have lent a quality of unreal stylization to the performance, it is probable that actors continued to converse silently and without distracting. The prompt-book specifies a slow cross-fade of light from one area to another, so one may assume that the effect, far from reproducing cinematic juxtaposition, actually slowed the pace of the performance in a way that would be unacceptable to today's audiences. Only once did Piscator attempt to bridge the dead moment of the lighting change: as Count Lande and Baron Friedrich shared a joke in the anteroom, their laughter continued into the next scene between Kilman and his servant. When the lights faded on Kilman, the laughter began again, so leading the attention audibly as well as visually back to their scene.

Another lighting effect was achieved by using the two follow-spots to concentrate light on the intimate exchange between the two nationalists Lande and Friedrich: its concentration approximated to a close-up shot in the cinema and reinforced the privacy of their discussion. Similarly, after Thomas's entrance into Kilman's office, the stage was revolved two metres clockwise to bring this crucial scene more into the centre of the stage.

In terms of acting, the political undertones were repeatedly emphasized. Beside the Minister for War's line, 'Tricky situation', there is a prompt-book note: 'Economic situation'. This political interpretation of an ambiguous phrase could hardly affect the actor's performance: it would be impossible in two words to indicate that one was making a reference to the economic situation, but clearly Piscator considered this awareness of the general implication of the dialogue as something worthy of communication to the actor. The political impact is at its greatest in the confrontation between Kilman and Thomas, and here the prompt-book carefully plots the political undertones with notes like: 'Inability to bridge their lack of understanding', 'Thomas experiences colossal disappointment', 'The stages of the disappointment are the dramatic skeleton'. When Kilman refers to the new 'democracy', 'he emphasizes the word smoothly and complacently'. And when Thomas accuses him of being a traitor, Piscator gives Kilman the move to fetch a cigar, a supercilious gesture of detachment.

The other notable element of the acting in this scene was the performance by Paul Graetz as Pickel (the German word for 'acne'), an ineffectual provincial landowner. Here Piscator directed the part unashamedly for comedy, introducing business like the dropping of gloves, top-hat and umbrella as Pickel fumbled to pin a medal on his chest on the appearance of the Minister for War; or again, in Pickel's conversation with Lande and Friedrich, making use of the music-hall gag, in which a speaker gets so carried away with his rhetoric that he fails to notice that his interlocutors have walked away from him and so suffers comic deflation when he discovers he is alone.

Act 2, Scene 1 To prepare for the next scene, the room of Eva Berg, the central staircase was removed, the stage was revolved back to its original position, and the screen was removed from the bottom left area to reveal a room with bed, table, chairs, wardrobe and washstand. The back-projection on this was simply a white wall, while the areas above and beside it carried back-projections of a roof, a back street and factories. The scene began in darkness with the ringing of an alarm clock, whereupon overhead spots in Eva's room came on at full intensity.

A note on the tone of this scene is significant as an indication of the charged atmosphere of the rest of the performance: 'An unemotional mood. For once *here* it is not frenzied.' There are many careful directions to the actors, some stipulating the exact sequence of moves in the process of getting out of bed, washing and eating breakfast. Others concentrate on the psychological realism underlying the dialogue, while yet others emphasize the confrontation between Thomas's romantic idealism and Eva's practical revolutionary attitude. So Piscator notes beside the speech in which Thomas invites Eva to leave with him for a country of primitives where men know nothing of politics: 'Utterly Granach' – so inviting the former Expressionist actor Alexander Granach to abandon himself to ecstatic lyricism. Her response, which was to be delivered 'with wonderful simplicity', can be seen as a dismissal of Expressionist idealism: 'The paradise that you dream of does not exist.'

The climax of Thomas's anguish occurs when talking about the War and the Revolution to the two children who visit him. Rushing upstage to prevent them leaving, he cries out: 'What meaning have the suffering and understanding of millions, if the very next generation is deaf to them?' With a characteristically political reference, Piscator notes here: 'Climax. It is the bankruptcy of the passing years.' Thomas then collapses into a chair: 'The "Schrei" is over; yet another hope destroyed.' So Thomas's romantic revolutionary feeling is exposed, and Eva points the way towards serious revolutionary activity. Unfortunately, as we shall see, both the play and the production make Thomas's progress dramatically much more involving than the sober efforts of the party workers.

Act 2, Scene 2 The next scene, the polling station, was in terms of cast the biggest of the play, with some thirty actors and extras involved. It was introduced by a film, not as described in Toller's text, but depicting a presidential election. As the film ended, the screen was raised to reveal a working-men's bar on the day of the poll, with the ballot-box and electoral officers on a raised platform to the right. In the centre was the bar itself with the landlord facing away from the audience. To the left was a free-standing door in front of which stood three men canvassing for their parties (see Plate 35). In order to gain space for this setting the scaffolding was winched back about a metre, so extending the forestage. The only use the scaffolding was put to was to carry projections, party slogans to the left and right, and on the central screen a film of votes falling into the ballot-box, which continued throughout the scene. (The central projection shown in Plate 35 appears to be from the play's opening film sequence and was not in fact used in this scene.)

The opening of the scene was cinematic in conception. It began in darkness with a drum-roll. Light then fell on the three canvassers, calling their slogans in three different pitches of voice, tenor, baritone and bass. The central area was then illuminated, like a camera panning from left to right, to reveal a line of voters, queuing from the door to the voting table. Finally the table with the three officers, polling booth and ballot-box was lit. The voters continued to file forward to cast their votes (see group on left of Plate 32) then left by the door to make minor changes off-stage to their appearance, so that they might return as new voters. This activity continued throughout the scene, the focus on specific groups being achieved by concentrating the lighting.

There was only one film insert projected on the front gauze, that of a lorry arriving shortly before Kroll's entrance, presumably another attempt to contrast the patient unspectacular work of Kroll (played by Ernst Busch) and the party members in their electioneering with Thomas's dangerous idealism in his plan to assassinate Kilman.

The climax of the scene was therefore the discussion between Kroll and Thomas. To emphasize the significance of this, the stage was darkened to leave light only on the table at which they sat. The film of voting faded to a dim background, the 'election' music which had played intermittently during the scene ceased, and all movement of the voters was halted (the fact that a freeze was specifically prescribed here suggests that it was not the practice in other scenes). To make the confrontation clearer, Piscator concluded their discussion with the following additional lines:

THOMAS: Kilman must go.

KROLL: That sort of thing won't be any help to us.

The rest of the scene, dealing with the riot in which Frau Meller was injured, was sensitively paced, achieving a fine balance between fast tempo and telling silences. The scene ended with the announcement on the radio of the election of the Minister of War to the presidency. At this point the film, which had stopped with the ending of the voting, now began again, showing a pile of voting-papers out of which the expansive posterior of the Minister of War emerged. Slowly his whole body appeared and he turned to face the audience. At this point the stage lights went out, the front screen was lowered and a further film about the Minister of War was run. The interval followed.

Act 3, Scene 1 The second half began with the punchy 'Hoppla, wir leben!' song, with the singer Kate Kühl lit vaudeville-style by two follow-spots directed at her head alone. During the interval the stage had revolved through 90 degrees, so that the scaffolding was now sideways on to the audience. After the song a ten-second film showing the town by night was projected on to the open stage as the scaffolding was revolved through a further 90 degrees to stand at the back of the stage. In the area in front of it the student's room was simply created with table, chairs, cupboard and a free-standing door. The acting here was once more characterized by psychological realism with directions like: 'Anxious tension', 'forced and nervous', 'with resolve but shaken'.

Act 3, Scene 2 There followed the most complex scene of the production, the hotel scene, the only scene in Toller's text which specified the sort of simultaneous set that Piscator used throughout the production. While the scaffolding was revolved to the front, the sounds of the town by night were heard and the film used before Act 3 Scene 1 was projected again, once more across the open stage, followed by a film showing scenes of hotel life. During this all the performers ran up and down the stairs of the scaffolding to arrive at their places, so giving the impression of frenzied activity.

During the scene jazz music played continuously, becoming louder on the changes from one acting area to another. The areas used for the hotel were the middle-left area which was the private room in which the Banker entertained Kilman to dinner (furnishings of table and chairs; back-projection of wallpaper); below this, bottom left, was the servants' quarters (with tables, chairs and sideboard; back-projection of tiles); the top central area, used for the first time, was the Telegrapher's room containing suitable equipment; the central area, representing the foyer with a girl at a cash desk (here the screen was at the front of the area, so that the actors were seen in silhouette only); finally, the middle-right area, Room 96, for the scene between Lotte and Lande (furnished with a bed, table and chair; back-projection, suitably enough for their erotic relationship, a red wall). Neither the club-room nor the writing-room specified by Toller appeared in Piscator's set, because the intellectuals' debate and Baron Friedrich's address to the journalists were cut. A slightly different technique from the ministry scene was used here: the back-projections, except for the light in the central area, were switched off when there was no action in that room, so that one had even less sense of simultaneity than before.

Apart from the frenzied pace of the scenes in which Thomas appears (he gobbles his food and rushes everywhere), providing a meaningful contrast with the leisured indulgence of the guests, there is little significant direction until the scene with the Telegrapher. The placing of this scene is significant, because it is the political experience of the state of the world as revealed by the Telegrapher, and not so much personal anger over Kilman that triggers the attempted assassination. At the end of the Telegrapher scene Thomas hurtled down the three flights of stairs while the 'hotel' film was projected once more.

Act 4, Scene 1 The same desperate urgency occurred after the assassination. The Student switched out the lights, fired the shot, and there was a sudden flash like a short-circuit. Two follow-spots stabbed into the darkness to pick up the running figures of Thomas and the Student. The sound of a car engine was heard, the gauze was dropped in and the stage revolved 90 degrees anti-clockwise until the stairs at the left faced the audience. On to the gauze was projected the image of a park. While the assassin ran off, Piscator introduced a second student to delay Thomas, a device which gave the murderer time to escape in a waiting car.

Act 4, Scene 2 In the blackout after the previous scene, was heard the ringing of telephones and alarm bells. The scaffolding was revolved back to its frontal position and the top-left area was illuminated as the telephone box from which Count Lande phoned the police chief, who was situated in the lower-right area. His office was lit by overhead spots only, presumably to give a depressive atmosphere to the scene, and the screen at the rear was raised to allow entrances from the back. In terms of acting, Piscator clearly sought to contrast the comedy, provided by Pickel, with the seriousness of Thomas's situation.

Act 4, Scene 4 The scene in the mental asylum was played (as in Act 1, Scene 1) in the central area, with a back-projection of shelves of files. The psychiatrist Lüdin here revealed his own mental imbalance: as Piscator noted in the prompt-book, 'Lüdin appears almost mad, he seeks to convince with violence. He is carried away and loses control.'

The intercut scenes with the Banker, Hotel Servant and Telegrapher were all played in the same manner with only their heads lit by a sharply focused spotlight and grotesque images of their faces projected on to the front gauze. The nightmarish quality of this effect was intensified by returning to these images in rapid succession. When the raving Telegrapher declared himself normal, all chorused 'Normal, normal ...', while the light flashed onto the Banker, then the Servant, then the Banker again, and finally the Telegrapher, who short-circuited all the lights in the building. There was a flash and an explosion. The scene between Thomas and Lüdin continued at a faster pace, ending with Lüdin 'going quite mad', jumping from his chair at Thomas, holding on to him with his legs wound round him, the physically most exciting moment of the acting. As the warder entered, Lüdin tidied his clothing, straightened his tie and said in a matter-of-fact voice: 'Normal, normal' – a textual addition by Piscator.

Act 5, Scenes 1 and 3 Before the final act Mary Wigman's female dancers performed a Charleston. They were costumed as skeletons, and danced in ultra-violet light which gave a phosphorescent effect to their 'bones' and skull-like make-up. Besides filling an awkward gap in an entertaining manner, a Charleston performed by skeletons was a powerful comment by Piscator on the precarious nature of German prosperity in 1927: society was dancing in a charnel-house.

For the final setting each of the six side areas had been subdivided into three prison cells (see Plate 32). Frau Meller was at the extreme right of the middle-left area; immediately below her was Eva Berg; Thomas was on the right side corresponding to Frau Meller; and below him was Kroll. All the other cells were filled with extras. Each of these areas carried a back-projection of a prison cell. In the central area the screen was brought to the front. Throughout, it carried a back-projection of a prison wall (as in the

Prologue). Over this was projected from behind a film depicting the arrival of Eva Berg with the warder Rand.

This film sequence was followed by a simple but extremely effective device: the communication between the prisoners – until the final lines added by Piscator – continued purely by means of knocking on the scaffolding without the use of dialogue. To interpret the meaning of the knocks a film was projected from the front carrying the messages in caption form. The replacement of almost all the dialogue with rhythmic knocking created a powerful ending to the play and set off the spoken declaration of Frau Meller: 'Bloody world! We'll have to change it!' As one critic observed: 'Since Chaplin's dance with the rolls in *The Gold Rush* the suffering of humanity has not been expressed with such simplicity and impact.'[71]

Piscator's achievement

> For 3000 marks a month
> He is prepared
> To stage the poverty of the masses
> For 100 marks a day
> He shows
> The injustice of the world.
>
> Brecht: 'The theatre Communist' (*c.* 1925)

Piscator was a theatrical genius, and in common with many innovative geniuses who worked in the theatre – one thinks particularly of Craig and Artaud – he depended on and was held back by the inadequate technical capabilities of the theatre of his day.

Frequently he attempted too much and failed. Reports of chaotic conditions under which he tried to mount productions make amusing reading. So he describes the so-called dress rehearsal of *Trotz alledem!* as follows:[72]

Two hundred people were running around shouting. Meisel, who had just been converted by us to negro music, performed an unintelligible and diabolical cacophony with his twenty-man band. Gasbarra kept arriving every minute with new scenes until I made him sit down by the projector. Heartfield with jutting jaw was single-handedly painting all the flats brown from top to bottom. None of the film cues was right, some of the actors had no idea where they were meant to be, and, as for myself, the mass of material that still had to be sorted out began to seem entirely beyond my capabilities. People who had sat in the auditorium that evening left the theatre at three in the morning without the least idea of what had taken place on stage.

The same chaos characterized many other Piscator dress rehearsals, and few performances were free of technical hitches. The conveyor belts of *Schwejk* were so noisy that Piscator and his cast fell about in hysterical laughter when they were first tried out, and a liberal application of graphite provided only a modest improvement. The segments of the *Rasputin* globe sometimes failed to open, and the lifts of *Der Kaufmann von Berlin* were an actual danger to life and limb. Even the careful preparation for *Hoppla, wir leben!* did not prevent mishaps. Paul Fechter recorded:[73]

> At first the film-images shake terribly, desperately search for their screens,
> then don't fit on to them. This provides the major although admittedly
> totally unpolitical enjoyment of the evening. ... But this is not quite
> enough to compensate for four hours of bad theatre.

Even when all functioned perfectly, the technical complexities of some of Piscator's productions created almost impossible situations, as, for example, during the run of *Hoppla, wir leben!* and the rehearsals for *Rasputin*. Each night after the performance of *Hoppla!* sixteen men had to work for three hours dismantling the scaffolding. The next morning a similar shift erected the *Rasputin* set. At 4 pm the rehearsal ended, and twenty-four men had to prepare the stage for the evening performance of *Hoppla!* This represented a daily investment of some 150 man-hours, and it is small wonder that the first Piscator theatre went bankrupt.

The fact is that Piscator's inventiveness often outran what was financially or technically viable. He could direct simply, as in his production of Carl Credé's 'Zeitstück' on the abortion law §*218* (*Section 218*, 1929), but, as Brecht pointed out, Piscator was not happy with it: 'He was like a bacteriologist whose microscope had been taken away from him.'[74] Fortunately, as I have argued, the theatricalities of Piscator's theatre were not central to the development of political theatre and do not hold many lessons for subsequent theatre practice. The evidence of photographs and film was then an important aspect of documentary drama; now, in an age when we are surrounded by visual information from the media, especially television, such projections are usually redundant. Similarly, the stage machinery of Piscator's theatre seems to stand in the same relationship to modern hydraulic sectional stages as the wind-up gramophone does to quadrophonic tape-recorders.

If Piscator's major achievement was not in his technical innovations, wherein lay his contribution to the political revolution in the theatre? Above all, he asserted the political function of the theatre, relating theatrical experience to his own society in a way hitherto unknown. From this, all his other innovations followed: the use of photographic and cinematic material, the creation of documentary drama, the adaptation and 'appropriation' of established texts, and the establishment of collective methods of working. Brecht and the political theatre of today clearly owe a tremendous debt to Piscator, but this must not be allowed to obscure the contradictions in

Piscator's position. Although committed to the foundation of an objective political theatre, he began the first programme of the Proletarisches Theater with the words: 'Comrades! The soul of the Revolution, the soul of the classless society to come and of the culture of the community is our revolutionary feeling.'[75] The vagueness, the ambiguities and the emotive words are reminiscent of Expressionist idealism and do not suggest a very clear foundation for a new political theatre.

On his return to Germany in 1951 Piscator used a favourite term of the Expressionists to describe his work of the 1920s: 'Bekenntnis-Theater' (confessional theatre):[76]

> It was not I who invented my style of theatre; but the terrible experience of war, the despair of the period of inflation and of the post-war social struggles created it. Whether political or epic theatre — in my hands, almost against my will, all my plays and productions became confessions. If one had to find a word for this, the most appropriate would be: confessional theatre.

In place of the confessions of the individual writer, Piscator had substituted the communal confessions of a generation, but his collectivism ultimately offered hardly more satisfactory political analysis than the individualism of the Expressionists. We have already noted Piscator's dependence on bourgeois capitalism for the existence of his theatre; and Ernst Schumacher argues that this derived not only from financial necessity but from a confused ideology. Ascribing the failure of Piscator's theatre to win the support of workers' organizations to the fact that it was 'a radical left-wing petit-bourgeois theatre ... financially supported by capitalists', Schumacher condemns Piscator's style:[77]

> It was the involvement of the spectator in the action, the removal of the division between theatre and reality, such as Piscator strived for, which made the theatrical illusion total. The spectator was not allowed to think clearly, because too much reality, and a reality that had not passed through a real artistic medium, overwhelmed him.

So suspect indeed was the ideological position of Piscator that a proposal was made by Goebbels, through the mediation of Gordon Craig, that Piscator might return to Germany from his exile in Moscow to form a propaganda theatre for the Nazis.[78] Needless to say, Piscator turned down the invitation, but he remained full of self-reproach. In conversation with Professor Walther Huder he once admitted:[79]

> We used to arrive at the theatre with our dark suits and bowlers and rolled umbrellas, and outside on the streets the real politics were happening. We failed.

6 · Brecht's epic theatre: the challenge to reality

Brecht's production of *Mann ist Mann (Man equals Man)* in 1931

Brecht and Expressionism

> Expressionism was an artistic revolt against life, and the world existed in it only as a vision, strangely distorted, a monster created by perturbed souls. Expressionism, which considerably enriched theatrical means of expression and yielded hitherto unexploited artistic gains, showed itself quite incapable of explaining the world as an object of human activity.
>
> Brecht: 'On experimental theatre' (1939)

Brecht's *Mann ist Mann* spans more than a decade. He started planning it in 1918 under the title *Galgei*, began the first draft in 1920, finished it by Christmas 1925, saw it successfully premiered in Darmstadt on 25 September 1926 (the parallel premiere in Düsseldorf was a failure), had it performed at the Berlin Volksbühne in 1928 and produced it himself in a revised version in Berlin in 1931. So when Brecht started writing *Mann ist Mann*, he had completed only one play, *Baal*, a rhapsody of anarchic Epicureanism, and was revising a second, *Trommeln in der Nacht (Drums in the Night)*, a cynical view of the Spartacus uprisings. By the time he directed it himself, he had been converted to Marxism, was committed to epic theatre, and saw the piece as a weapon in the struggle against Fascism. Both in its writing and staging, therefore, *Mann ist Mann* is a transitional piece, reflecting well and not without contradictions Brecht's development from the cynicism and bawdy of his early plays towards the didactic content of 'Lehrstücke' of the late 1920s and early 1930s.

Much of the jeering amorality of his early writing was a response to the ecstatic elements in Expressionist theatre. Unlike Piscator, who condemned the Expressionists for their lack of political consciousness, Brecht rejected them for their lack of human relevance. After seeing Hanns Johst's *Der Einsame* at the Munich Kammerspiele in 1918, Brecht wrote his own *Baal*: contrasted with Johst's depiction of Grabbe as an idealized suffering artist-figure, Baal is a gross sensualist and a cruel seducer of women. Brecht's response to Toller's *Die Wandlung* was similar: 'Poetic newspaper at the very best. Flat visions, immediately forgettable. Flimsy cosmos. Man as an object, as a proclamation, but not as a man. Abstracted man, the singular of humanity.'[1] Brecht had already finished the first version of *Trommeln in der Nacht*, then entitled *Spartakus*, by the end of February 1919, so it cannot be claimed that *Die Wandlung* could have served as an impulse in the writing of his own play. Nevertheless, there are remarkable similarities and contrasts: like Toller's Friedrich, Brecht's Andreas Kragler is a 'Heimkehrer', a soldier returning from the war to face social unrest at home, and they both become involved in a revolutionary movement. But while Friedrich's revolution is idealized, pure and dependent on his personal leadership, the Spartacus revolt as portrayed in Brecht's play is real, confused and develops its own impetus. Toller's *Wandlung* proclaims the New Man in the birth of a child; Brecht's *Trommeln in der Nacht* ends with Kragler's fiancée confessing that despite an attempted abortion she is pregnant by another man. Friedrich leads his revolution; Kragler abandons his to go to bed with his woman, calling to the revolutionaries: 'You want my flesh to rot in the gutter so that your idea will get to heaven?'[2] At each turn Brecht reveals his vital if self-interested humanity compared with the abstracted proclamations of Toller.

In a note on Expressionism recorded in 1920 Brecht hit the Expressionists where it would hurt them most: 'Expressionism means: coarsening'.[3] If there was one thing the Expressionists were concerned with, it was refinement: to penetrate to the essence behind the world of coarse surface reality, to recognize 'what is divine in factories, what is human in whores',[4] as Edschmid had said. Brecht attacked them for doing exactly the reverse: 'Instead of revealing the soul (which they assumed to be misunderstood) in the body, they made the soul into bodies, coarsening them and turning even the spirit into matter.'[5] One need not take Brecht's concern with the soul and the spirit too seriously; he is merely scoring points off Expressionism by using their terminology. What is important is that Brecht here pointed to a very real fault in both abstractionist and primitivist Expressionism, namely that the refinement pursued by the Expressionists often resulted in crude simplification, that to abstract the individual took from him all the wonderful complexities that distinguished his humanity and in doing so rendered him an automaton.

On the other hand, Brecht owed a great deal to abstract Expressionism. He repeatedly excepted Kaiser from his denunciation of ecstatic Expressionism and grudgingly admitted his 'dramas to be of decisive importance ... the situation of the European theatre to have been transformed by him'.[6] In 1920, as local drama critic, he reviewed *Gas I* in Augsburg, was interested by the play, praised the performance, and regarded only 'the audience and a section of the press as a flop'.[7] A year later at the Neue Bühne in Munich he saw Fritz Schäfler's production of *Von morgens bis mitternachts*, and recorded in his notebook his interest in the piece and his dismay over Kaiser's glibness.[8]

What Brecht learnt from Kaiser by the time *Mann ist Mann* was written was above all the theatrical impact of creating a model situation and presenting it in a series of images: for instance, a Cashier who moves from one allegorical station to another, not in any attempt to explore his own personal psychology or to present an imitative picture of the world about him, but to reveal an underlying idea. So Brecht willingly embraced the non-psychological characters and non-realistic settings of abstract Expressionism, he adopted its montage structure and was strongly influenced by the incisiveness of 'telegraphese' dialogue. While happy to dismiss the Naturalist concern with individual psychology, however, he felt that Expressionists had put nothing in its place apart from vague mumblings about the soul and the spirit. What underlying idea could be revealed, if neither man nor his environment were being treated as real entities? The Expressionists, Brecht asserted, expressed 'the joy about a central idea, but no ideas'.[9]

Brecht therefore sought not to return to nineteenth-century realism but to investigate reality, not to return to depictions of the individual as a victim of his environment but to examine the individual's relationship to his environment with a view to changing both. He therefore continued the Expressionist protest about the inhumanity of the world, but recognized the real possibility of changing it instead of running from it to seek refuge in the human soul or in poetic images of an idealized and universal revolution. In this incitement to change, the Naturalistic preoccupations of bourgeois individualism could no longer serve Brecht's purpose; his characters, like those of the Expressionists, had to be (occasionally unnamed) representative types, representative no longer of universal Man but of men in a specific social situation. From man the psychological animal and man the spiritual animal Brecht turned to man the social and political animal.

From Expressionist theatre practice Brecht learned two further important lessons. The first of these was the willingness to be boldly theatrical. In a note on make-up written in the late 1930s he stated: 'You get annoyed in the theatre if you are not aware of what is intended. (Being discreet is a question of honour, in other words a bourgeois snobbery which has nothing to do with the theatre.)'[10] In his pursuit of clarity Brecht abandoned 'bourgeois discretion' and subtle nuances in favour of the theatrical exaggeration of Expressionism, admittedly eschewing the emotional exaggeration of their ecstatic lyricism.

Second, from abstract Expressionism Brecht learned the clarity and effectiveness of abstractionist set design. It is known that after he settled in Berlin in 1924 Brecht attended Jessner's rehearsals. Not only did he take from him the notion of 'appropriating' classics, but he also adopted many of the principles of the set designs for Jessner's productions. Indeed, a permanent abstract set with small modifications to indicate a change of scene would now be described by many theatre critics as 'Brechtian',[11] so strongly has Brecht become identified with this type of abstractionist staging.

Brecht and Piscator

There is a tendency to regard Piscator's attempt to renew the theatre as revolutionary. But it is revolutionary neither in terms of writing nor of politics, but only in terms of the theatre.

Brecht: 'Piscator's Theatre'

The development in Brecht's writing towards a greater political awareness, which is reflected in the sharper political accent of the 1931 revised version of *Mann ist Mann*, owed much to the influence of Piscator. As a member of Piscator's collective from 1926 he collaborated on the writing of *Rasputin*, *Schwejk* (which he later claimed was almost entirely his own adaptation) and *Konjunktur* (*Oil Boom*). It was also while preparing a play about wheat for the Piscator-Bühne that in 1926 he first began to study Marx. He had attempted to research the mechanics of international wheat trading but soon discovered that no one could actually explain how the market functioned. Amazed at the self-perpetuating irrationality of capitalist economics, he began to investigate its mysteries with the aid of Marxist analysis. However, it was probably only in 1929 after the experience of seeing May Day demonstrators being shot by the police that he became an active socialist, although unlike Piscator he never joined the Communist Party.

In addition to the political influence exercised by Piscator, Brecht shared with him an enthusiasm for the entertainments of the common people and wanted to enliven the theatre with their colour and vitality. Brecht himself loved watching sport, especially boxing, was a great fan of Charlie Chaplin, and worked with the famous Munich comedian Karl Valentin. In another attack on the Expressionists he blamed them 'for converting the theatre from a biology or psychology lecture-hall into a temple'.[12] 'A theatre without contact with its public is a nonsense',[13] he wrote in 1926 in a newspaper article entitled 'Mehr guten Sport' ('Emphasis on sport'), and he compared the fun of sports arenas with the unexciting atmosphere of the theatre-temple. Like Piscator he exploited the fun and variety of the revue format, of stage music and of lively comedy, all of which are important elements in *Mann ist Mann.*

It was through Piscator's work, too, that Brecht became acquainted with the term 'epic theatre' and with some of the techniques he was later to adopt. Alfons Paquet's *Fahnen*, Piscator's first production at the Volksbühne in 1924, bore the sub-title 'An epic drama', but this implied here only that the play presented a fairly objective and documentary account of a historical event, in this case a strike in Chicago in the 1880s. As with other obvious contenders, like the dramatization of *Schwejk*, Piscator's epic drama did not contain the major elements upon which Brecht was to insist.

The term 'epic' has particular problems for the English reader, because it carries associations of the panoramic view of history or of grand spectacle, as in the cinema jargon 'a Hollywood epic'. But for the German, 'epic' merely means any form of narrative fiction (as opposed to the other two literary genres, 'dramatic' and 'lyric'). Brecht distinguished between 'dramatic' or 'Aristotelian' theatre, which depicts events as though they were taking place in the present, and 'epic' or 'non-Aristotelian' theatre, which shows actions as having taken place in the past. An essential component of Brecht's epic theatre was the audience's awareness that what was thus narrated on stage happened as a result of alterable causes; the 'dramatic' theatre, he argued – often with happy disregard for the facts – all too easily showed that the processes leading to the conclusion of the play remained unquestioned and seemed inevitable. It is the incitement of the spectator to view the action on stage critically that distinguishes Brecht's particular conception of epic theatre from Piscator's use of the term.[14]

The particular staging techniques of Piscator adopted by Brecht were concerned above all with the demystification of the theatre, with encouraging instead of suspending disbelief. One such technique first used by Piscator in his staging of Paul Zech's *Das trunkene Schiff* (*The Drunken Ship*) in 1926, was to change the sets in full view of the audience (this had occurred at the Tribüne for the production of *Die Wandlung*, but only because of the absence of a front curtain, not as a deliberate alienating device). Already in 1920 Brecht had imagined introducing into theatrical performances a pair of clowns who would comment on the action and rearrange the set between scenes:[15]

> In a tragedy the scenery will be changed on the open stage. Clowns will
> walk about on the stage giving instructions: 'Yes, he's heading for a fall.
> Make the light darker! Those stairs create a tragic impression.' ... In this
> way many things on stage shall become real again. For God's sake, *things*
> themselves should be criticized, the action, the words, the gestures, not just
> the way they are presented.

With the clowns' ironical comment on the need to darken the lighting for the tragic fall, Brecht anticipated a further technique which he adopted from

Table 5 *Piscator's theatre/Brecht's theatre*

Piscator	*Brecht*
Documentary theatre	Epic theatre
Involvement	Alienation
Neo-realistic acting	Epic style of acting
Theatrical surprise	Intellectual surprise
Elaborate stage effects	Simple stage effects
Director who influenced playwrights	Playwright who influenced directors

Piscator: the use of hard white light throughout. A poem written in 1950 begins:[16]

Give us some light on the stage, you electricians!
    How can we
Playwrights and actors in semi-darkness
Present our copies of the world? Dusky twilight
Sends you to sleep. But we want our audience
Awake and alert.

While Brecht therefore took up some of the alienating devices of Piscator, including the use of projections and film, he was less convinced by Piscator's love of stage machinery, even suspecting the use of film if it did not encourage a critical viewpoint. Far too often, Brecht felt, Piscator's stage effects provoked a delighted and uncritical response, producing reassuring involvement in place of the challenge of alienation. In 1928 he directed a particularly outspoken, though at the time unpublished, attack on Piscator's type of theatre:[17]

Requisitioning the theatre for purposes of class struggle represents a danger for the true revolutionizing of the theatre. It is not by chance that this requisitioning was the work of directors and not of playwrights. The artistic methods of these self-styled revolutionaries had to resort to new devices (like jazz and film) from the start and could not achieve a revolutionizing of the theatre itself. The presentation of a revolutionary spirit by means of stage effects may be politically meritorious. But if these effects merely produce an exciting atmosphere, they cannot revolutionize the theatre and must be regarded as something provisional which cannot be pursued but can only be replaced by a truly revolutionary theatre. Such a theatre of effects is basically anti-revolutionary, because it is passive and imitative. It depends on the mere imitation of existing types, i.e. the ruling or bourgeois classes, and has to await the political revolution to find new models to imitate. It is the last form of bourgeois Naturalistic theatre.

For Brecht the spectacular stage effects of Piscator, like the realistic acting of his performers, were ultimately anti-revolutionary because they reinforced accepted attitudes instead of challenging them: they presented propaganda not argument. This insight of Brecht explains the remarkable and – for the Soviet apologist – embarrassing fact that Nazi Germany and Stalinist Russia imposed the same style of socialist realism on their artists. In 1920 Lenin had proclaimed: 'The All-Russian Proletkult Congress rejects ... all attempts to invent one's own particular brand of culture,' and he saw the future of revolutionary art in 'assimilating and refashioning achievements of the bourgeois epoch'.[18] To this day in Eastern Europe the simplest all-purpose condemnation of an artist is that he is 'formalistic', i.e. not aligned to the realist tradition.

Although in the 1930s Brecht just once lent support to the condemnation of formalism,[19] his real feelings were better summarized in the following, at the time unpublished, pronouncement: 'If certain people see new forms, they bellow in accusation: "Formalism!", but they are themselves the worst formalists, worshippers of the old forms at any price.'[20] Brecht was disturbed to discover that no real revolution had taken place in theatre itself; it was still as bourgeois as before the Revolution:[21]

The passion which [actors] showed when their stage-wives were unfaithful is now shown by them when the stage-capitalist reduces wages. The public is no longer in suspense whether Romeo gets Juliet but whether the proletariat gets the power.

The post-revolutionary emphasis on maintaining the bourgeois tradition of nineteenth-century realism, something which experimenters like Meyerhold resisted at their peril, is simply explained. As Wilhelm Worringer had pointed out as far back as 1906,[22] the culture that feels at home in this world will celebrate it in Naturalistic imitation. Fundamentally, reality will be accepted and approved. Clearly the leaders of post-revolutionary Russia wished their reality to be approved and so encouraged the assimilation of bourgeois realism. As long as the revolution persists (and it is clear that Brecht did not regard it as having been finally achieved by any nation), reality needs to be challenged. For this it is necessary to evolve an anti-Naturalistic form, one that does not accept reality as given but presents its possibilities in a dialectic manner: 'Reality, whatever its complexities, must first be changed by its artistic presentation, so that it may be recognized and treated as changeable.'[23]

Despite these insights, Brecht's critique of Piscator's theatre of involvement did not immediately result in the questioning view of reality he intended. It was a source of some dismay, if also of income and prestige, that *Die Dreigroschenoper (The Threepenny Opera*, 1928) became a resounding success in cities round the world with the very bourgeoisie the piece was supposedly attacking 'chewing their chocolates in time with Brecht's music',[24] as Edward Bond put it. Similarly, in *Mann ist Mann* there are still elements which too easily reward the spectator with comfortable entertainment without the more satisfying pleasure of seeing the world with new eyes.

Man ist Mann **as an epic play**

> If you hit a car with a coachman's whip, it won't get it going. Our plays are totally unsuitable for rescuing the old theatre. They themselves imperiously demand a new theatre, and they also make it possible.
>
> Brecht: 'The crisis of the theatre' (1928)

Mann ist Mann, set in colonial India, tells in simple episodes of the 'transfiguration' of an Irish porter called Galy Gay, 'a man who can't say no'.[25] Since the name in German is pronounced 'Gully Guy', Brecht, who had a fair working knowledge of English, may have intended a reference to a 'guy who is gulled'. Leaving his wife one morning to buy a fish, he is bribed by three soldiers, who have lost their companion, Jeraiah Jip, while plundering a pagoda, to stand in for the missing man at roll-call and so avoid incurring the wrath of their bullying Sergeant, Fairchild. When the soldiers find it still impossible to retrieve Jip, they plot together to turn Galy Gay permanently into Jip's replacement. They involve him in the auction of a fake elephant with the connivance of the canteen owner Widow Begbick, arrest him for attempting to sell army property, try him and sentence him to death. After a mock execution Galy Gay is ceremoniously 'buried' and, relieved at finding himself still alive, is only too glad to assume Jip's identity. As Jeraiah Jip he now becomes an efficient fighting machine, leading his companions into victory against a fortress on the northern frontier.

The meaning of this parable is straightforward: a simple and kindly fellow is misled by his easy-going nature and acquisitiveness into losing his identity and becoming merely a part of a war-machine. The problem in ideological terms is that Galy Gay would avoid his fate if he retained a more secure hold of his individual personality; and yet Brecht's socialism made him suspicious of such individualism: the individual should be prepared to surrender himself to the collective. However much irony was present in Brecht's 1927 preface to *Mann ist Mann*, he would in other contexts certainly have subscribed to his assessment of Galy Gay: 'He becomes the strongest character only after he has ceased to be a private person, only in the mass does he become strong.'[26]

Clearly Brecht did not approve of Galy Gay's transformation from a peaceable, homely character into a bloodthirsty killer, but the only alternative offered in the play is the perfectly acceptable maintenance of Galy Gay's individuality. There is no alternative collective for him to turn to, no suggestion, for example, of a porters' union, dedicated to changing an economic situation which allows false trading with an elephant to be such an attractive proposition. Nor is the 'collective' of soldiers presented in such a negative light that one is impelled to reject it totally. Like the crooks of *Die Dreigroschenoper* they are jolly, courageous, randy, and themselves underdogs.

It is also difficult to be utterly dismayed over Galy Gay's transformation into a good fighter: there is something undeniably fearless and heroic about his single-handed destruction of the mountain-fortress, and the 'distant voice' announcing that the fortress had given shelter to 7,000 refugees, 'most of them friendly, hard-working people',[27] is hardly sufficient to balance the shouts of joy that greet Galy Gay's victory. In a version of the ending which remained undiscovered until four years after his death, Brecht attempted to give more emphasis to the suffering by cutting Galy Gay's final speech and by defining the cry from the fortress as 'a cry of horror'.[28] In *Mann ist Mann* Brecht seems to retain something of the attraction he felt towards the vital and irresponsible grossness of characters like Baal and Kragler while now being more aware how socially destructive such irresponsibility could be. It was only later, in the more considered statements of his mature work, that contradiction became dialectic: Mother Courage shares with Galy Gay the same acquisitive instinct, but with her there is no doubt what this costs in personal terms.

Because he was aware of the ambivalence in the content of *Mann ist Mann* Brecht undertook certain revisions for his production in 1931. Significantly, he cut the last two scenes, so that the play concluded with a roll-call added to the end of Scene 9, Galy Gay appearing for this literally armed to the teeth (see Plate 42).[29] Clearly, this cut removed the danger of seeing Galy Gay in a heroic light in the final episode; the sight of him laden with weapons was contrasted with the mild-mannered man of the beginning. Furthermore, Brecht cut some of the more farcical elements and the rowdy Kiplingesque songs but added most of the verse passages and Begbick's 'Song of the Flow of Things' and gave more prominence to her Interlude speech by using it as a prologue:[30]

Tonight you are going to see a man reassembled like a car ...
Indeed if we people were to let him out of our sight
They could easily make a butcher of him overnight.

Here it is clear that Brecht was issuing a warning to his fellow Germans not to surrender their individuality to the Fascists; the emphasis he intended was the avoidance of the false collective not the retention of a bourgeois concept of individualism.

The structure of *Mann ist Mann*, like its ideology, is not wholly consistent. Ostensibly it employs the montage technique characteristic of epic theatre: the

story is told in a series of episodes ('each scene stands on its own' as opposed
to: 'each scene depends on another'[31]). At two points the epic structure is
particularly striking: during the elephant auction and its consequences, and
then again on Sergeant Fairchild's visit to the canteen owner Leokadia
Begbick. In the first, the leading soldier Uriah takes on the function of a
master of ceremonies calling out the stages of the scene: 'Number One: The
Elephant Deal ... Number Two: the Elephant Auction',[32] and so on. This is
an obvious reference to the turns of the circus or variety show or to the rounds
of a boxing match, a device Brecht had already used in *Im Dickicht der
Städte* (*In the Jungle of Cities*). By introducing the incidents of the scene in
this way, the action is repeatedly interrupted and the audience is invited to
view the events with critical involvement. At the circus or boxing match the
excitement may be intense but it does not prevent the spectator from judging
what he sees; indeed, his assessment of what is taking place is central to his
enjoyment and he may well be at his most voluble when evaluating the
judgment of the boxing referee.

The appearance of Fairchild, drunk and in civilian clothing, is such an
autonomous scene that it could be omitted or placed at another point in the
play. In practice it comes after the fourth 'number', the mock-execution of
Galy Gay. Apart from Galy Gay's 'corpse' everyone leaves the stage, only to
return immediately to begin the Fairchild scene which is in fact consecutive
on the previous one. The effect of this is to reverse a theatre convention.
Traditionally, when the same actors leave the stage and reappear in the next
scene, it alerts the audience to the fact that either time has passed or the locale
has changed. Here neither is the case, and the departure and return of the
actors defines the Fairchild scene as a scene arbitrarily inserted into the flow
of the action.

Despite the notably epic quality of these devices Brecht, on the other hand,
introduces an obvious example of conventional dramatic suspense: on the
outbreak of war the order is given that all troops must be entrained before
moon-rise. Throughout Scene 9 the urgency to convert Galy Gay into Jeraiah
Jip becomes a race against the clock; e.g., 'Galy Gay, the porter from Kilkoa
has ... to be transformed in double quick time into the soldier Jeraiah Jip';[33]
'Once they start loading the elephants if you lot aren't ready you can be
written off';[34] 'Is that the moon? Yes. – It's getting late';[35] 'The whole
operation must not last more than nine minutes, as it's already a minute past
two';[36] 'The trains are whistling ... the convoy leaves in six minutes'.[37] In
fact, during the last nine minutes stage time corresponds to real time so
closely as to be the envy of the Naturalist writer. The disadvantage of this
kind of suspense for the epic theatre is that the spectator becomes too involved
in the outcome: 'will they manage in time?' rather than in the process: 'how
will they manage to do it?' As with Mother Courage's haggling over the
financial cost of saving the life of her son, the pressure of time can sharpen the

issues involved; on the other hand, the excitement of experiencing the suspense of action in the present undermines the critical distance of seeing action presented as though in the past.

Another device of epic theatre is the use of songs. Whereas the music in a play like *Von morgens bis mitternachts* arises from the action of the scene, in *Mann ist Mann*, as in the 'Hoppla, wir leben!' song of Piscator's production, the songs stand on their own. While it would be acceptable in Kaiser's play for the family to applaud the piano-playing of the Cashier's daughter or for the Salvation Army congregation to cheer the music of the band, it would be as inappropriate for the characters to applaud the singing of a Brecht song as it would be for the cast of an opera to clap an aria. If applause comes, it will be from the real audience, whereas such applause would break the illusion of more traditional drama. As Brecht wrote in 1950:[38]

> Separate the songs from the rest!
> ... The actors
> Turn into singers. Adopting a different posture
> They turn to the public, still
> Characters in a play, but now also
> Openly sharing the views of the writer.

The music in Brecht is not a musical offering within the play but serves a commentary function. The soldiers' song introduces Begbick's canteen, while Begbick's songs tell of her past: the loss of her good name and her transformation from married woman to a self-sufficient hard-headed businesswoman, a transformation paralleling that of Galy Gay.

Alienation and early Brecht productions

> The audience was no longer to be abducted from their own world into the world of art, no longer to be kidnapped; on the contrary they were to be led back into the real world with their senses alert.
>
> Brecht: 'On experimental theatre' (1939)

The stage technique appropriate to epic theatre is the employment of 'Verfremdung'. This term, which began to appear in Brecht's writings about 1939 although he had begun to explore the concept a decade and a half before, is the opposite of 'Einfühlung' (empathy); it is best translated as 'estrangement', because the more common version 'alienation' too often suggests a deliberate intention to thwart the enjoyment of the audience. 'Alienation' is, however, the term best understood with reference to Brecht, and so I rather reluctantly continue to use it here. Perhaps the not infrequently expressed view that Brecht is boringly didactic derives in part from a misunderstanding of 'Verfremdung'. Brecht's definition is quite clear:[39]

alienatie

> To alienate an incident or character means simply to remove from the incident or character all that is taken for granted, all that is well known and generally accepted and to generate surprise and curiosity about them.

In terms of stage design alienation meant 'that the stage and auditorium are cleansed of all "magic" and that no "hypnotic fields" arise'. There must be no attempt 'to create the atmosphere of a certain space on the stage (Room by Twilight, Street in Autumn)', no attempt 'to put the public into a trance and to give it the illusion that it is viewing a natural and unprepared event'.[40]

The three major pre-war productions of the play all attempted to employ some degree of alienation. The premiere at the Landestheater in Darmstadt on 25 September 1926 was directed by Brecht's friend, Jacob Geis. Geis had been sacked from his post as Dramaturg at the Munich Kammerspiele over the row resulting from the premiere of *Im Dickicht der Städte* in May 1923, when nationalist thugs had thrown tear-gas in the auditorium and caused fights in the foyer. In his comments on the production Geis said he intended[41]

> to show the play's underlying sense by making the surface meaning as clear as possible. In other words, no implications, hidden meanings, ambiguities, half-light; but facts, brilliant illumination, light into every corner, absence of feeling, no humour with tears to fall back on. The theatre as craft rather than art, no private issues – these should emerge only secondarily, as self-evident.

The Berlin premiere of the play took place under Erich Engel's direction at the Volksbühne on 4 January 1928, with music by Edmund Meisel, the composer of Piscator's production of *Hoppla, wir leben!*, and with Heinrich George in the lead-role (Figure 3). Engel's directing style, a combination of precision and vitality, was ideal for Brecht's plays. Ihering described Engel as 'teaching like a schoolmaster while dancing on a grave, a pedant and a sage, a cautious chess-player and a light and elegant entertainer, a mathematician and man of the theatre, a man who orders the mind while shaping his art'.[42]

Brecht's production at the Staatstheater in Berlin on 6 February 1931 marked the first time he had directed a piece of his own for a Berlin theatre. His first attempt at directing a play had ended disastrously. He had been invited by the Deutsches Theater in Berlin to stage Arnolt Bronnen's *Vatermord (Parricide)* in 1922. He at once launched into an attack on the Expressionist style of the actors: 'In came this thin, rather under-sized Augsburger and told them in dry, clearly articulated syllables that all their work was so much crap.'[43] He finally reduced Agnes Straub to floods of tears and caused Heinrich George to refuse to continue working with him. Berthold Viertel had to be called in to take over the production, and George's role of the Father was given to Alexander Granach. Bronnen sided with Brecht,

Figure 3   Sketch by K. Isenstein of George as Galy Gay, 1928

however, and sought his assistance the following year on the adaptation and production of Hans Henny Jahnn's *Pastor Ephraim Magnus*, which opened at Das Theater, Berlin, on 24 August 1923. Although Bronnen was named as the director, it seems that Brecht's influence at rehearsals was quite strong.

In 1924 with the premiere of his adaptation of Marlowe's *Edward II*, *Leben Eduards des Zweiten von England*, at the Kammerspiele Munich on 18 March, Brecht formally directed for the first time and began his life-long collaboration with former school friend and designer Caspar Neher.

Two years later he made his directing debut in Berlin, but only in collaboration with his leading actor, Oskar Homolka. This was the Berlin premiere on 14 February 1926 of Brecht's first play, *Baal*, staged for the Junge Bühne at the Deutsches Theater.

In the following year he was involved with productions of his more obviously didactic pieces: the premieres of *Das kleine Mahagonny* (*The Little Mahagonny*) in Baden-Baden in 1927; of *Das Badener Lehrstück vom Einverständnis* (*The Baden-Baden Cantata of Acquiescence*) in Baden-Baden in 1929; of *Happy End* in collaboration with Erich Engel at the Theater am Schiffbauerdamm, Berlin, in 1929; of *Der Jasager* (*He Who Said Yes*) together with his composer Kurt Weill in Berlin in 1930. In addition, he worked with Jacob Geis on the first staging of Marieluise Fleisser's *Pioniere in Ingolstadt* (*Pioneers in Ingolstadt*) at the Theater am Schiffbauerdamm in 1929, the nearest Brecht came before the war to directing a play not of his own composition.

The 1931 production of *Mann ist Mann* was therefore a significant step in Brecht's career in the theatre. His opportunity was given to him by Ernst Legal, the Intendant or Chief Director of the Staatstheater who had replaced Leopold Jessner after the latter's resignation in 1930 under nationalist pressure. Legal had long been a supporter of Brecht and had played the role of Galy Gay at the Darmstadt premiere. Besides, the Staatstheater was under a contractual obligation to Brecht, having taken an option on *Im Dickicht der Städte* a few years previously with the guarantee to perform it or another Brecht piece by January 1931.[44] In the event Legal agreed on *Mann ist Mann*. On the production Brecht collaborated with Emil Burri (a one-time boxing second with whom he was to direct the premiere of *Die Mutter* (*The Mother*) in the following year), Slatan Dudow (a film and theatre director), Elisabeth Hauptmann (Brecht's life-long collaborator, perhaps best known for translating Gay's *Beggar's Opera* and so supplying Brecht with the material for *Die Dreigroschenoper*), and Bernhard Reich (a former Dramaturg with Brecht at the Deutsches Theater); he worked once more with his designer Caspar Neher and with the composer Kurt Weill, whose music for *Die Dreigroschenoper* had contributed so much to its success. Unfortunately, Weill's music for *Mann ist Mann* disappeared after Hitler's takeover.

In the 1931 production of *Mann ist Mann* Brecht and his team attempted for the first time to explore fully the alienating devices of epic or non-Aristotelian theatre, and so it is of major importance for the development of Brecht's theatre practice, especially in terms of design and acting.

Mann ist Mann: set design and visual presentation

> It's more important nowadays that the set tells the audience that they are in a theatre than that they are in Aulis.
>
> > Brecht: 'The set'

The set design for the Darmstadt premiere had already introduced a feature which Brecht used in his own production and which became as closely associated with him as steps were with Leopold Jessner; for this was the first time that Caspar Neher employed the half-curtain. The half-curtain is a plain white curtain suspended on a wire stretched across the stage about two metres above the floor and usually some way behind the proscenium arch, so creating a small forestage (see Plate 39). When the half-curtain is closed, the lower half of the stage opening is hidden from view, while part of the background scenery may still be seen above the curtain. This part-screening of the stage had been used for centuries in Kathakali Indian folk-theatre, where a hand-held curtain conceals a new character before his entrance and so increases the sense of anticipation in the audience. In Europe it appears as the crude provisional curtain erected in front of fairground side-shows. These popular associations were, of course, particularly welcome to Brecht, and it may well be that Neher and he borrowed the idea from the 'Jahrmarkt', the annual fair and market which takes place in every German town and village, although there had been one precedent on the legitimate stage: in 1916 Knut Ströhm had used the half-curtain in his production of *Hamlet* at the Düsseldorf Schauspielhaus.

The advantage of the half-curtain is that it allows sets to be changed and actors to get into position while both concealing this from view and at the same time reminding the audience that it is going on. Theoretically, it would be possible to change sets behind the half-curtain while a scene is played in front of it. In practice, in the three major pre-war productions of *Mann ist Mann* there was a pause while the sets were changed, a pause that was filled at the premiere by singing a verse from the *Mann ist Mann* song, later dropped from the text.

In the traditional proscenium arch theatre the front curtain cuts the stage off from the auditorium: it encloses the theatrical action in a magical sphere, entire unto itself. As Peter Szondi says, such a stage 'becomes visible, that is, only begins to exist when the play starts, and so seems to be created by the play itself. At the end of the act, when the curtain falls, it disappears from the spectator's view, is removed by the play and so is shown to belong entirely to it'.[45] With the half-curtain, the audience is no longer encouraged to view the stage as a separate world into which the spectator must be transported; on the other hand, it allows a modicum of surprise at each new setting or tableau and prevents the unnecessary distraction of seeing the set changed in full view. As Brecht was to write some twenty-five years later:[46]

> Make my
> Curtain of medium height, don't shut off the stage!
> Leaning back, the spectator will observe
> The bustle of preparation which is being
> Cunningly made for him, he sees
> A tin moon float down, a shingle roof
> Is carried in. Don't show him too much

But show him something! And let him be aware
That you are not magicians, but
Workers, my friends.

In the text of *Mann ist Mann* there are no descriptions of the set, merely
the name of each locality at the beginning of a scene. The last of these is a
characteristically epic phrase, more reminiscent of a novel than a drama:
'Deep in Remote Tibet Lies the Mountain Fortress of Sir El-Djowr'.[47] This
stage-direction is also characteristic of the geographical and historical
confusions of the play. When the fortress is destroyed, the army prepares to
march into Tibet, so the fortress must stand on the Tibetan border and not
'deep in Tibet'. This phrase, however, possesses the quality of a Karl May
adventure story and presumably for this reason was retained, inconsistent
though it may be. Similarly, the action takes place in India, but Jeraiah Jip is
lost while raiding a Tibetan pagoda attended by Chinese worshippers. The
date is 1925, but there is a queen on the British throne. The group of soldiers
forms a machine-gun squad and yet Galy Gay destroys the fortress with single
rounds from their weapon. Such fairy-tale indifference to historical detail
imposes a non-realistic style on the design. The emphasis must be on the
action not on local colour; the sets must be areas where events happen, not
picture postcards of the scenery.

Another alienating device was the use of projections. A standard feature of
Piscator's productions, projections were first used by Brecht when he
directed *Leben Eduards des Zweiten* in 1924. They gave dates and
background information to introduce each scene, and were condemned by at
least one critic for turning the play into a history lesson. Projections were used
at the premiere of *Mann ist Mann*, and Erich Engel in his production
projected slides of the actors on to large flats, a reminder to the audience
that the characters are representative images and not real people. The so-
called 'Regie-und-Soufflierbuch' (director's prompt-book) of the 1931
production[48] contains a list of the projections used in Brecht's own staging.

The first scene is entitled simply 'Kilkoa', the home-town of Galy Gay,
and Brecht's projection was: 'The porter goes to buy a fish'. This scene
would have taken place in front of the closed half-curtain, the only set
consisting of a stool each for Galy Gay and his wife, which they can remove
on their exit. It is not important to know exactly where they are – inside their
house or in front of it – and their economic situation is clarified in the
dialogue, so need not be determined by the setting. As Brecht wrote:[49]

In areas where work is going on, one often reads, 'Access forbidden to
those not employed here'. Stage designers should hang this sign over their
sets. What is on stage must play a part, and what does not play a part must
not be put on stage.

The second scene, 'Street outside the Pagoda of the Yellow God', was introduced with the projection: '$4 - 1 = 3$', a reference to the loss of Jeraiah Jip in the raid by the four soldiers, a neat formulation but hardly intelligible to the audience at this stage. In Brecht's production the pagoda consisted of a structure like an upright coffin, probably made with a wooden frame covered in card or canvas, stabilized by guy-ropes attached to the top corners (see Plate 38). Access to the skylight/upper window appears to have been provided by a simple metal ladder, free-standing beside the pagoda. An interesting feature of the set was the presence of a petrol-pump marked 'Shell'. In order to emphasize the relationship between capitalism and colonial conquest, Brecht drew attention in this way to the oil interests backing the army. Thus the last projection, which replaced the final scenes cut by Brecht, read:[50]

Deep in remote Tibet lies the mountain fortress of Sir El-Djowr. On behalf of Royal Shell it is taken by the scum, including the soldier Jeraiah Jip. They realize they can use him for any purpose they want. Nowadays he is used for fighting wars.

It is important to recognize that the petrol-pump is not a symbol. Brecht was alert to the dangers of symbolism as practised in abstract theatre:[51]

If you symbolize capitalism with a lump of gold, it is an empty trick, because gold itself is not capital and the lust for gold is not the lust for exploiting labour. Such symbolizing lends support to the superstition, put about by those who profit from it, that mankind is ruled by certain ideas or subject to primitive drives of an everlasting kind.

Therefore, 'the art of abstraction must be used by *realists*', for 'There is a big difference to be made between symbolic decorations and the design of non-Aristotelian drama, which makes use of realistic elements'.[52] The petrol-pump exists in its own right; it is not an improbable street accessory in the town of Kilkoa; it has a meaning but its presence on stage is not dependent on it.

In Scene 3 'Country Road between Kilkoa and the Camp', the stage-directions stipulate a shed for characters to hide behind while they observe others. In practice, the half-curtain would fulfil this function adequately.

Scene 4, 'Canteen of the Widow Leokadia Begbick', was prefaced by Brecht with the projection: '$3 + 1 = 4$' − Galy Gay makes up the number of the squad. This was the most important setting of the play, being needed for some three-fifths of the full version and for almost four-fifths of Brecht's truncated 1931 version. It also required several tables, chairs and a bar. In the 1926 premiere the background was created by a staggered arrangement of flats of different heights, deliberately proclaiming itself as a stage set (see Plate 37). The furniture was substantial, and even, like the Viennese rocking-chair, verging on the elegant. Neher's design for Brecht's own 1931 production suggested a much cruder and more temporary canteen: simple chairs and trestle tables, at the back a wooden framework standing in front of black curtains or a darkened cyclorama; and suspended over the stage on a metal grid billowing sheets suggesting a provisional roof (see Plate 41). None of the pre-war productions made any attempt to indicate the railway carriage in which Begbick travels from place to place with the army, although this was an imposing feature of the Berliner Ensemble production after Brecht's death, the carriage, executed in considerable detail, occupying almost half the stage.

To judge by the programme of Brecht's production,[53] which lists neither sacristan nor worshippers, and by the production photograph, which shows Wang's drawing of the four matchstick men in the canteen (see Plate 40), it seems most probable that Brecht omitted Scene 5, so that Scenes 4 and 6 became one consecutive scene in the canteen.

For Scene 7, 'Interior of the Pagoda of the Yellow God', a flat was placed behind the half-curtain, bearing the inscription 'Guard of the Pagoda of the Yellow God' (see Plate 39). The text of this scene in the 1931 production was reduced to a single verse-speech by Jeraiah Jip, as he sat munching his steak and drinking his beer.[54]

Scene 8, introduced by the projection '1 = 1', i.e. man equals man, takes us back to the canteen once more, where we remain for this and the next long scene. In Brecht's production the 'numbers' of this last canteen scene (Scene 9) were separated by the use of projections, beginning with the announcement of the outbreak of war and followed by 'No. 1', 'No. 2', 'No. 3', 'End of No. 3', and so on. An even more alienating device was employed to introduce the Fairchild scene immediately after Galy Gay's mock-execution. In Brecht's own words:[55]

Sergeant Fairchild's transformation into a civilian (No. 4a) was clearly marked off as an insertion by the half-curtain closing before and after it. The stage manager stepped forward with the script and read interpolated titles all through this process. At the start: 'Presenting an insertion: Pride and demolition of a great personality' ...

After this interruption Galy Gay recovered, and two drawings of him were projected on to flats either side of the stage, one showing him as the harmless porter and the other depicting him as the bloodthirsty soldier he was to become. As the scene continued, projections marked the passing of time usually at 2-minute intervals, and by repeatedly interrupting the flow of the action prevented the spectator from becoming too involved in the suspense of the situation.

Another interesting scenic device employed here by Brecht is the dismantling of the set as part of the action. Already in Scene 4 the soldiers shift the tables to provide Galy Gay with a screen to change his clothes behind, a much more theatrical moment than an off-stage transformation. Now in Scene 9 Begbick's canteen has to be packed together for the departure. This is not only visually interesting but also supported by typically

Brechtian motivation: for the elephant auction to succeed, Begbick's co-operation is required; she will co-operate only if the soldiers help her to pack up her canteen. Her participation in the action is therefore dependent on the removal of the set, a remarkable integration of the actor with the stage design. It is an imaginative use of the theatre to end the play, as was the case in the 1931 production, with a bare stage. It was as though Brecht, by removing the very last illusion of the stage, was also finally destroying any illusion about the unassailable integrity of the individual. As he was later to write in exile: 'The construction of the stage in movable sections corresponds to a new way of viewing our environment: it is seen as changing and capable of further change, as being full of contradictions in its wavering uniformity'.[56]

One of the more striking aspects of the dismantling of the canteen was the lowering, washing and folding of the sheets suspended as a roof above the stage. Begbick unhooked them with a long pole while delivering her first lines in Scene 9, the story of her life, directly to the audience. She washed them while singing the song about the loss of her good name by lowering them into a trap in the stage. She moved them as though they were in water and then pulled up clean sheets substituted for the dirty ones beneath the stage. On the reprise of her song she folded the clean sheets with the soldier Uriah. This activity, which is not dramatically necessary (the soldiers could pack up the sheets with the rest of the canteen), seems to serve two functions. First, by accompanying the verse and song commentary with work, the actress can avoid letting her lines appear either didactic or sentimental. Second, it seems that Brecht experienced a simple visual pleasure in such activity, quite apart from any functional quality.

The two final scenes, not performed in Brecht's 1931 production, are 'In the Moving Train' and the Mountain Fortress. The first of these (Scene 10) could be played in front of a suitable flat with the half-curtain drawn back sufficiently to define the limits of the carriage. The final scene presents greater technical problems if one is to follow the stage-directions, which indicate that the fortress begins smoking and then burning. The simplest way of presenting the scene is to allow the hill from which the soldiers launch their attack to obscure the fortress, so that all that is required is a smoke machine by the cyclorama with a flickering red light to suggest flames. The problem here is that the destruction of the fortress is too comfortable a stage device and so none of the horror of killing is communicated. This was a reservation Ihering had about the scene in Engel's 1928 production:[57]

The end of the play, as in Brecht's text ... is merely an image or epilogue. It indicates that the transformed Galy Gay is now *functioning* as Geraia Jip [sic], but this is lost in the musical and ballad-like adornment of the stage (relapse into atmospherics).

If one rejects Brecht's decision to omit this scene, there might well be a case here for using film material of war scenes as a backing to the scene to remind the audience of the reality underlying the ballad-like heroism of Galy Gay.

The additional piece, *Das Elefantenkalb* (*The Elephant Calf*), which formed part of the original conception of the play, but which Brecht later designated as 'An interlude for the foyer', was never performed as such in Brecht's lifetime and so need not be considered here.

Like the stage furniture, the stage properties had to be real, not 'realistic'. A stage set can never be real, unless the setting of the play happens to be a theatre, but the properties can be authentic, and Brecht, as in the tactile delight he showed in the washing and folding of the sheets, would certainly in his later work with the Berliner Ensemble, insist on well-worn objects and their proper use. Thus, in *Mann ist Mann*, the soldiers must know how to assemble their gun with the efficiency acquired from long experience; for the actors to bungle this would create the wrong kind of alienation.

The costumes, too, for *Mann ist Mann* should be functional and look as though they have been worn regularly by the characters, while not necessarily making any attempt at historical realism. Engel's production, in particular, distinguished itself by its subdued range of colours: against Neher's black and white set, 'which made wonderful use of the empty space, at once real and unreal',[58] were set the khaki uniforms of the soldiers and drab colours of Galy Gay and his wife; even Helene Weigel as Leokadia Begbick wore riding-breeches and boots.

In Brecht's production the costumes were a significant element in his conception. In order to make the soldiers less jovial and more disturbingly grotesque, he placed Uriah (Theo Lingen) and Polly (Wolfgang Heinz) on stilts, increasing their height by at least fifty centimetres, padded out Jesse (Alexander Granach) and gave some of the soldiers, including Fairchild, false noses and hands (see Plate 41). An unpublished note of Brecht reads:[59]

> masks stilts gigantic hands etc served both the parable-like clarity of the transformation and the depersonalization of the actors, who were thereby forced to bring to the surface through external gestures through most obvious behaviour emotions that otherwise remain hidden. in this way the 'natural face' of the lead actor could be used effectively at a certain point in the action.

Certainly, the transformation of the natural-looking Galy Gay into a grotesque figure like the soldiers, achieved by dressing him in uniform, whitening his face and covering him with weapons, including a knife between his teeth, provided a powerful visual image.[60] Unfortunately, the exaggerated costumes of the soldiers not only depersonalized them, but also differentiated them from one another. If Galy Gay sacrifices his individuality to become uniform with the soldiers, then they must already possess uniformity themselves. As Bernhard Diebold justifiably complained: 'Brecht seems to accept individuality on stilts', and pointed out: 'The Tiller Girls – now that would be the true equality of *Mann ist Mann*'.[61] While Brecht's use of grotesque costumes was, therefore, theatrically striking, it militated against the meaning of the play.

White make-up for soldiers was first used by Brecht in his production of *Eduard II*. He had been unhappy at rehearsals about the way the soldiers went off to war. He asked Karl Valentin what soldiers do before a battle, and the Munich comedian answered: 'They're scared, they look pale' ('Furcht hams, blass sans'). This matter-of-fact answer gave Brecht the clue he was seeking: he made the soldiers up white, a characteristically theatrical metaphor for a psychological condition. So Peter Lorre as Galy Gay whitened his face after recovering from his mock-execution in preparation for his transformation into a soldier. Brecht and he discussed the possibility of whitening the face earlier to indicate his fear of death, but 'between fear of death and fear of life he chose to treat the latter as more profound'.[62]

Brecht's adoption of Piscator's use of full white light is particularly striking in this play, because most of the action takes place at night, and characters comment on the late hour, the rising moon and the darkness: 'It's so hard to see in this light'.[63] Diebold praised the strong lighting of the 1926 premiere: 'The stage was bright: praise be to God, there's light and shade in the modern theatre again. You could see every wrinkle of the actors'.[64]

Of particular importance to Brecht was that the source of lights should be visible to the audience.[65] To a modern audience well used to sitting beneath an array of spotlights, his insistence on this only makes sense if one recalls the extravagant efforts made by theatre architects and lighting designers until the 1930s to conceal lamps from view in order to preserve the 'magic' of the theatre.[66]

Mann ist Mann: **music**

You need only cast a single glance at the audience in a concert to see how impossible it is to use music that produces such effects for political and philosophical ends. We see entire rows of people who are in a state of strange intoxication, totally passive, lost to the world, apparently suffering from serious poisoning. ... The worst gangster film treats its audience more like thinking beings.

Brecht: 'On the use of music in an epic theatre'

The music for *Mann ist Mann* underwent several changes. For the premiere Brecht himself seems to have been responsible for the music, and it was played by three half-caste daughters of Begbick, 'who form a jazz-band'. By the 1928 production only one daughter, Hiobja,[67] remained, and it seems that for this and Brecht's production all the music was played off-stage.

It is impossible to assess the particular quality of Kurt Weill's contribution to the 1931 production, since it is no longer extant, but one may safely assume that he would have used the parodistic jazz-rhythms familiar from his other scores of this period. There is an interesting note by Brecht, however, on the function of the music. At the end of Scene 4, Begbick sang her song off-stage through a megaphone, and then apparently Weill's 'Night music' was played to bridge the missing Scene 5, while Galy Gay dozed on his stool:[68]

> three elements combined without merging entirely: stage set, story and music. the set offered a pure visual effect rather than an illusion, the story receded as an experience and permitted meditation, the music did not arise 'out of the mood' but from the wings and preserved its concert character. writing, music and design appeared as independent arts in a clear event.

Mann ist Mann: acting for the epic theatre

> Whoever does not instruct entertainingly and entertain instructively should stay out of the theatre.
>
> Brecht: 'Instructions for actors'

The new style of acting which Brecht was creating for his epic theatre must be accounted one of his major contributions to the revolution of the German theatre. Already in 1923, if Rudolf Fernau's memory is accurate, Brecht spoke of 'alienated' acting. Certainly, as Fernau shows, the concept if not the term was already familiar to Brecht: in response to Fernau's ecstatic performance as Goethe's Tasso, Brecht commented:[69]

> That wasn't Tasso ... that was an overheated locomotive. You must open all your valves and let the steam out. ... Don't read things into the role, read out of the role, until in your mind you are standing beside the character. Don't go begging for sympathy, point at Tasso (look, that's the way he is!), so that people think about it. ... Ecstatic Expressionism has got a lot to answer for. You have to alienate the character, so that he becomes credible.

When, a year later, Fernau was coached by Brecht in the role of Kent in *Eduard II*, the lesson was similar. Brecht gave Fernau a bread-roll to chew on while he spoke his lines:[70]

> 'Say the text again and eat at the same time. It'll loosen you up. This betrayal must be communicated as drily as a military despatch.' 'But it's supposed to be tragic,' I dared to interpose. 'To Hell with tragedy,' replied Brecht. 'Only the event itself is tragic and that's what the people should be concerned with.'

Already at this stage, then, Brecht had established the basic principles of his new acting style. Basically, there are three interrelated elements in this style:demonstration, emotional restraint, and a critical view of the character.

Just as Brecht invited Fernau to demonstrate Tasso rather than to create the character, so he repeatedly encouraged his actors primarily to show the event rather than to be concerned with their individual emotional reaction to it. However different the resultant modes of expression, this movement from personal psychological response to a generalized demonstration had already been effected by Expressionist acting. As Paul Kornfeld had observed, the opera singer in the throes of death can still sound a top C; 'for it is more important that death is a tragedy (ein Jammer) than that it is horrible'.[71]

As a model situation for epic theatre Brecht proposed the Street Scene, in which an eye-witness describes a traffic accident to a crowd of bystanders.[72]

It is of the utmost importance that a major characteristic of conventional theatre has no place in our Street Scene: the creation of an illusion. The performance of the person demonstrating the accident possesses the quality of repetition. The incident has happened, now it is being repeated. If the scene in the theatre follows the Street Scene in this respect, then the theatre no longer hides the fact that it is theatre, just as the demonstration on the street corner does not hide the fact that it is a demonstration (and does not pretend to be the incident itself).

Therefore the Brechtian actor should not try to get 'inside the skin' of his role, any more than the man describing the accident should attempt to convince his audience that he is himself the driver:[73]

In short, the actor must remain a demonstrator; he must present the character he demonstrates as a stranger, he must not exclude the '*he* did that, he *says* that' element from his performance. He must not allow himself to be completely transformed into the person he demonstrates.

While in exile Brecht began to set down certain methods by which an actor can learn how to 'demonstrate' in the epic manner, and it may be that they were based on techniques he used while directing in the 1920s and early 1930s, especially during the rehearsals for *Mann ist Mann*.[74] These techniques include: (1) transposing the dialogue into the past tense, (2) transposing the dialogue into the third person singular, (3) saying the stage-directions out loud, (4) demonstrating a role to another actor, and (5) performing a scene as though to a group with special interests. It is clear that the first two of these must create a distance between the actor and his role. The performer of Hamlet might be asked to say at rehearsal: 'he had of late – but wherefore he knew not – lost all his mirth, forgone all custom of exercises; and, indeed, it went so heavily with his disposition that (what he had hitherto regarded as) this goodly frame, the earth, seemed to him (now) a sterile promontory'. Because the actor is forced to describe the past action of another person, it would be absurd for him to re-experience Hamlet's emotions. And yet the actor is not a mere narrator; for he is representing on stage the figure he is describing, and in performance will be speaking in the present tense and first person singular. It is Brecht's conviction, however, that once such alienation has been experienced, the actor will never again be tempted to identify totally with his role.

A similar learning process can be achieved by devising and speaking stage-directions. This was a method Brecht recommended in his 'Anweisungen an die Schauspieler' ('Instructions to actors') of the late 1930s:[75]

> The actor shall think up directions and commentaries to what he says and does, and speak them out loud at rehearsal. For example, he shall preface his line with: 'So I said angrily, since I had not eaten', or: 'At that time I knew nothing of what was going on and so I said'.

Indeed, for his post-war production of *Antigone* Brecht wrote 'Brückentexte' ('bridging texts') for his actors to use to introduce many of their speeches at rehearsals. As with the transposition into the past tense and third person, this device made characters seem to belong to the novel rather than drama; they became in fact 'epic' figures.

The fourth method of developing the 'demonstrational' style is for the actor to coach someone else in his own part. By showing another actor the way a character walks or how he speaks and by getting that actor to imitate and be corrected, the performer is forced to analyse the elements that have gone into the creation of that character and avoid close identification by externalizing them.[76]

The fifth method involves playing a scene in such a way as to serve as a demonstration to people of particular interests:[77]

> The first scene of *King Lear* with its division of the kingdom could be conceived as a demonstration before a commission of lawyers, doctors, experts in court ceremony, members of the family, historians, politicians, and so on. The details would have to satisfy the requirements of such different groups of interest.

Such an exercise would impel the actors towards a much clearer form of presentation, replacing 'I am feeling this now' with 'I am showing why this happened as it did.'

There are many opportunities in *Mann ist Mann* for demonstrational acting. The play opens, in Brecht's own translation, as follows:[78]

> GALY GAY (*sits one morning upon his chair and tells his wife*): Dear wife, I have decided in accordance with our income to buy a fish today. That would be within the means of a porter who drinks not at all, smokes very little and has almost no vices.

The stage-direction sets the tone of the scene: although phrased in the present tense, the words 'one morning' establish the narrative quality of the situation. That the chair is 'his chair' suggests a repeated situation. (The conventional form of stage-direction, which would read 'sitting on a chair' cannot be as specific as in Brecht, because in conventional theatre the chair only exists within the unique and observable situation and cannot initially be recognized as being the chair on which he regularly sits.) Finally, 'tells his wife', in terms of conventional theatre, is redundant; its purpose here is solely to remind the reader and actor that this is a piece of epic theatre.

Galy Gay's opening speech shares the same demonstrational character. The language, as stilted in the original as it is in this translation, is a deliberately impossible way for a docker to talk to his wife. The diction is that of a legal document, not that of an uneducated worker. In addition, the reference to himself in the third person ('a porter who drinks ...') creates the same distancing effect as in Brecht's acting exercise described above. Finally, he describes his own characteristics objectively. In a conventional drama, a character who declares that he has 'almost no vices' would normally only do so as a form of denial; indeed, it would be the kind of statement that immediately throws doubt on its own content. Only in a few cases, like Myedvyedenko's self-introduction at the opening of Chekhov's *The Seagull*, will the audience accept such statements at their face value, but here the facts are anyway relatively unimportant; it is the character's indulgent self-interest that engages the attention. But with Galy Gay we are neither invited to question his statement nor to regard such self-revelation as an idiosyncrasy of his character. Brecht's intention is much more simple and much more closely related to reality: the actor tells the audience about the character he is to portray.

Such self-introduction is characteristic of Brecht's style in *Mann ist Mann*: 'Here we are, along with a hundred thousand other soldiers, all of us thirsting to restore order on the northern frontier;'[79] 'It is many moons since I, Bloody Five, known also as Tiger of Kilkoa, the Human Typhoon, a sergeant in the British Army, experienced anything as marvellous as this';[80] 'I am the Widow Begbick and this is my beer waggon'.[81]

Another important opportunity for realizing to the full the demonstrational style of acting is in the direct address to the audience. This occurs most obviously in the songs and verse-passages when a character is alone on stage; e.g., Galy Gay's speech beginning:[82]

Now I could go away, but
Should a man go away when he is sent away?

Of such passages Brecht wrote: 'If there is an address to the audience then it must be a direct address and not the "asides" or soliloquizing technique of the old theatre'.[83] What is required therefore is that the actor humbly and simply shares his thoughts with the audience, employing neither the 'aside', which usually contains within it an element of condescension ('I, the actor, will share this with you for a brief moment before returning to my role'), nor the soliloquy where the actor conventionally talks to himself rather than to the audience.

Apart from the sung or spoken monologues, there are other lines which are best addressed to the audience. When one of the soldiers collapses from lack of beer, Polly comments: 'Just as the powerful tanks of our Queen must be filled with petrol if we are to see them rolling over the damned roads of this oversized Eldorado so can the soldier only function if he drinks beer'.[84] Polly's words are hardly addressed to his companions, since they already know what he says and it is anyway not the idiom normally used by the soldiers. The information is for the audience's benefit and should be projected out to them, somewhat in the manner of a Corporal giving a brief demonstration to his men.

The second major characteristic of Brechtian acting, emotional restraint, follows necessarily from the demonstrational quality of epic acting. The explosive and passionate style of Expressionist acting, which had been such a welcome change from the tedious Naturalism or hollow histrionics of existing styles, in turn soon became a fashionable self-indulgence, lacking the original commitment that inspired it. Wrily recalling his experience as failed director of Bronnen's *Vatermord*, Brecht denounced bad Expressionist acting:[85]

In place of real ability they make a display of intensity while being merely tense. ... From the start the actor is ... in such an unnatural flow that it seems the most normal thing in the world to attack his father. At the same time you see that the acting places a terrible strain on him. And a man who is under strain on the stage will, if he is only moderately good, put all the audience under strain too.

Even where the excesses of Expressionist acting were eschewed in favour of a more conventional approach, the emphasis was still on emotional self-expression:[86]

If you visit our drama schools you see how little is required to turn someone into an actor. ... Old plays are rehearsed, and from the very start value is placed on the student introducing as much passion as possible into his acting and 'coming out of his role' as little as possible. It is assumed that the talents, which are needed for everything that plays demand and contain, are inborn: the passion (and manner) with which Romeo loves, and the passion (and manner) with which Lear wishes to be loved, Hedda Gabler's pride and Lady Macbeth's ambition. It is expected of the actor that he will so to speak infect the audience with his passion and it is expected that the audience will be satisfied with this.

That Brecht's description is no exaggeration is suggested by the latest word on acting in the catalogue of the Vienna Theatre Exhibition in 1924: 'Acting without side-glances at conscious relationships – completely surrendered to the moment – that is to act like a great artist and like a – child!'[87]

It was precisely this intensity, this passion, this self-surrender to the moment that Brecht was so suspicious of in the theatre. Quite apart from any personal embarrassment about displays of emotion – and his life provides many examples of apparently callous treatment of his women friends – he had a philosophical view of emotion which seemed a direct inheritance of the thinking of the German Enlightenment: 'Emotions are in no way common to all mankind and timeless';[88] 'Feeling is a private affair and limited. By contrast, the intellect is consistent and relatively comprehensive'.[89] For Brecht, the emotions were individual, limited, and dependent on a specific historical and class situation. Reason, if not actually universal, was certainly a more dependable means of communicating truth and the only viable means for our scientific age.

Two more immediate causes made Brecht declare that 'it is perhaps the essential quality of epic theatre that it appeals not so much to the feelings as to the reason of the spectator'.[90] The first was precisely his recognition of the dangerous power of emotion and its abuse by the Fascists:[91]

> Fascism with its grotesque emphasis on the emotions and perhaps no less a
> certain decline in the rational quality of Marxist doctrine caused me to
> place a stronger emphasis on the rational.

Moreover, Brecht also drew cunning parallels between the emotional self-indulgence of the bourgeois theatregoer and his economic acquisitiveness. Dismayed by the emotionally charged performances in the 1935 New York production of *Die Mutter* (*The Mother*, 1932), he wrote:[92]

> Just as the businessman
> Invests money in a concern, so you think the audience invests
> Feeling in the hero: they want to get it back again
> If possible doubled.

For all these reasons, whether personal, or philosophical, or in response to the historical and economic situation of his society, Brecht undertook 'perhaps the greatest of all conceivable experiments',[93] the abandonment of empathy in the theatre. On other occasions he was obliged to admit that empathy was – within limits – appropriate to certain characters; for example, to the central figure of *Die heilige Johanna der Schlachthöfe* (*Saint Joan of the Stockyards*, 1932).[94] In fact, despite some of his more extreme pronouncements, it is clear that Brecht was never opposed to emotion but only to emotionalism:

> The epic theatre does not attack emotions, it examines them and does not
> hesitate to produce them.[95]

> Only opponents of modern drama, champions of the 'eternal laws of
> drama' will maintain that the modern theatre dispenses with emotion when
> it dispenses with empathy. In fact the modern theatre liquidated only a
> worn-out, outmoded subjectivist sphere of feeling and makes way for the
> new, complex, socially productive emotions of a new age.[96]

This new style of acting is best illustrated in Brecht's description of Helene

Weigel's performance as the Maid in Leopold Jessner's production of Sophocles' *Oedipus* in 1929:[97]

> Recounting the death of her mistress, she shouted her 'dead, dead' with a penetrating voice quite devoid of feeling, her 'Jocasta is dead' without any lament, but with such unrelenting determination that the naked fact of her death had at that moment a deeper effect than any personal grief would have achieved.

What Brecht describes here is not absence of emotion, nor even absence of empathy. It is simply more truthful and thoughtful emotion than the cliché emotions of inferior actors. Weigel gave here, as Brecht phrases it elsewhere, not only an experience but an insight.[98]

In *Mann ist Mann*, given its demonstrational, almost cartoon-like style, there would be little risk of emotional indulgence by the actors. Nevertheless, there are moments in the play which are illustrative of Brecht's technique of alienation, where insight is more important than experience. One example is the attack on the pagoda. Just as the soldiers are about to rush at it, Uriah calls 'Wait!' In performance there should be a pause here as the soldiers stop in their tracks and the audience wonders why the command has been given: has Uriah had second thoughts? Is some sign of danger approaching? In fact, Uriah continues: 'Hand over your paybooks first. A soldier's paybook must never be damaged. You can replace a man any time, but a paybook is sacred if anything is'.[99] A moment of excitement is interrupted to fulfil the bureaucratic precautions of the army, an insight appropriate to the theme of the play and one that replaces a feeling of tension with a moment of intellectual recognition.

Again, Galy Gay's mock-execution could be played so as to engender sympathy from the audience, but there are various ways in which Brecht reduces this possibility to a minimum. The first is the invitation to treat the episode as a parody of high tragedy (and here Brecht may have been thinking of the totally serious mock-execution of Kleist's *Prinz von Homburg*): '*Galy Gay ... strides like the protagonist in a tragedy*'.[100] Such parody (that is, the use of a conventional form with a new content) undermines the potential involvement with Galy Gay's plight: the gap between him and a traditional tragic hero is so great that his attempt to assume the characteristics of the latter is incongruous and therefore laughable.

Second, while Galy Gay believes in the threat of execution, the audience is reminded that it is merely staged: Polly in his enthusiasm loads a live round by mistake and has to be reprimanded by Uriah. In this way, the audience recognizes that Galy Gay's fears are only imagined and so cannot develop empathy with his state of mind.

Third, Brecht introduces broad slapstick: '*Polly runs up behind Galy Gay and raises a big club over his head*'.[101] Such a clown-like visual gag clearly undermines at once any potential empathy with the central figure. Thus, although the speech in which Galy Gay pleads to be spared from death could be acted with intensity of emotion, the context in which Brecht has placed it would inhibit such a style.

Such demonstrational, non-empathetic acting creates the conditions for the third major characteristic of the Brechtian acting style: the encouragement of a critical view of the role. For Brecht, conventional tragedy ('Aristotelian drama') depended on a view of humanity and its institutions as unchanging and unchangeable:[102]

> It is not possible to experience empathy with men that can change, actions that can be avoided, pain that is unnecessary, and so on. As long as the stars of Lear's fate live in his breast, as long as he is regarded as unalterable, as long as his actions appear determined by his nature, totally unable to be prevented, in fact fated, so we can have empathy with him. Any discussion of his behaviour is as impossible as it would have been for men of the tenth century to discuss the splitting of the atom.

For the modern scientific age Brecht insisted that the writer must abandon his mythical view of man in favour of a historical perspective. Instead of accepting the rightness of Lear's anger, the actor must question it himself and invite the audience to question it; in this way the spectator will begin to perceive that the events he is being shown do not proceed from inner necessity but are dependent on certain historical circumstances − in the case of Lear, an outmoded feudal view of kingship.

This stimulation of the spectator to become a critical participant in a theatrical performance was justifiably regarded by Brecht as his major contribution to revolutionizing the theatre. The neo-classical tragedies of the court theatre and the works of Naturalism had presented intra-personal conflicts, created and resolved by the characters on stage; the audience looked on as voyeurs, passively responding to the emotional stimuli emanating from behind the proscenium arch. Brecht also creates conflicts on stage but indicates that their resolution can only be sought outside the theatre. Here the audience enters into a new relationship with the action on stage: instead of abdicating their responsibility for the conflicts they witness, they are called upon to prevent such things happening in their own lives. Hence the 'Aristotelian' drama 'provides sensations' and 'exhausts the capacity for action' by teaching resignation; the epic theatre 'forces decisions' and 'arouses the capacity for action' by stimulating a critical attitude.[103] In the conventional theatre the spectator is an observer of transactions being conducted on stage; in the Brechtian theatre he himself becomes involved in those transactions:[104]

> Empathy must be avoided as a way of communicating with the audience.
> An exchange takes place between actor and audience to the point where the actor finally addresses the audience in a distanced and estranged manner.
> In order to establish this exchange, based on a new respect for the public,

the actor has to abandon his traditional role of 'hypnotist'. In an article on epic acting, written in 1940, Brecht quotes the words of an American actor, Rapaport, who urges the actor to transform objects in his imagination: 'Take an object, a cap for example; lay it on the table or on the floor and try to regard it as though it were a rat; make believe that it is a rat, and not a cap ... and, at the same time, learn to compel the audience to believe ...' On this Brecht commented drily:[105]

> You might imagine that this was a course in conjuring, but it is in fact a course of acting, allegedly according to the Stanislavskian Method. One wonders if a technique which equips you to make the audience see rats where there aren't any can really be so suitable for propagating truth? Without any acting, but with sufficient alcohol, you could make anyone see rats – or at least pink elephants.

Instead of using conjuring tricks the actor must invite the audience to question what it sees taking place on stage:[106]

> Human behaviour is shown as alterable and man as dependent on certain economic and political conditions and, at the same time, as capable of changing them. To give an example: a scene in which three men are hired by a fourth to a specific illegal purpose (*Mann ist Mann*) must be portrayed by the epic theatre in such a way that one can imagine quite different behaviour by the four men than that shown here; i.e., that one can imagine either political and economic conditions under which the men would speak differently or an attitude of these men towards the existing conditions which would make them speak differently. In short, the spectator has the opportunity to criticize human behaviour from a social point of view, and the scene is played as a piece of history. ... This means, from the aesthetic standpoint, that the social gest of the actor becomes especially important. ... The imitative principle is, so to speak, replaced by the gestic principle.

The reference to *Mann ist Mann* is curiously phrased: Brecht must surely have intended to write 'a scene in which a man is hired by three others ...' But this does not affect the point he is making: the actor, in order to awaken the critical faculties of the spectator, must indicate the social context of his action: he must no longer be imitative but 'gestic'. Brecht's notion of 'Gestus', for which I have adopted Willett's sensible translation 'gest',[107] was defined by Brecht as follows:[108]

> By *gest* I understand a complex of gestures, facial expressions and usually statements, which is directed by a single person or a group at a single person or group.

Clearly there is nothing new about the concept of the gest (the word itself had been used by Lessing in the eighteenth century[109]), for it forms the basis of all acting. It is, however, a term frequently used by Brecht when he wished to emphasize the communicative role of the actor in preference to his expressive role. While the Stanislavskian actor tried to immerse himself more and more deeply in his part in the faith that such total commitment to imitation would result in clear and truthful communication, Brecht, by emphasizing the gest, called on his actor to seek consciously for the clear demonstration of certain behaviour. In this respect, despite the difference of approach, the product of Stanislavskian and Brechtian methods may be remarkably similar: in order to demonstrate what it is like to be a Russian mother in the early years of this century (*Die Mutter*), the Brechtian actress must discover some empathy with the role; in empathizing truthfully with the role, the Stanislavskian actress will demonstrate what it is like to be such a mother.

The difference is that while the Stanislavskian portrayal will remain imitative, individualistic and idiosyncratic, the Brechtian portrayal will use empathy only as a means to generalize about the situation of the Mother. The actress must discover a series of social gests to communicate this situation to the audience.

In order to cultivate this ability to criticize a role from a social standpoint, Brecht proposes three further techniques for his actors. The first is the memorizing of first impressions. He suggested that an actor should retain the surprise and tendency to contradict that he felt on first reading through his part. Far from abandoning these critical responses to his role, he should carry them forward into performance, inviting the audience to share in the same surprise and desire to contradict which he initially experienced. Indeed, in order to overcome the spontaneous and unreflective style of acting, he originally urged his actors to spend a long time 'rehearsing at the table'.[110] Later, at the Berliner Ensemble, he preferred to avoid lengthy discussions and to devote almost all the rehearsal time to active exploration: it is recorded that during some two hundred hours of rehearsal on *Der Hofmeister* the cast spent less than a quarter of an hour talking about the play.

A second technique, similar to the coaching of another actor referred to above, is to objectify a performance by seeing it mirrored. This can be done literally by performing in front of a mirror, preferably masked, and so having the opportunity to criticize and select his own gestures and intonation. Alternatively, one can exchange roles with another actor and so see one's own character and the way he is portrayed from another viewpoint.

Third, Brecht recommends the application of the 'not – but' technique:[111]

The actor shall at all essential points not only show what he is doing but also work out, designate and communicate what he is not doing. He does not say, for example: 'I forgive you', but: 'You'll pay for that!' He does not fall in a faint, but he comes to life. He does not love his children, but he hates them. He does not move upstage right, but downstage left. The actor performs what follows after the *But*; he shall perform it in such a way that we also become aware of what follows the *Not*.

This style of acting destroys the inevitability of the behaviour of a character in an 'Aristotelian' drama and makes us repeatedly aware of alternative courses of action. How, one may ask, can this be achieved in practice? If the character debates the alternatives with the audience, whether it is Hamlet soliloquizing on suicide or Galy Gay musing on the possibility of going or staying, the task is easy. But if an actor moves downstage left, how can he show that he might have chosen to move upstage right? It seems that just as Stanislavsky assumed that if an actor invested time and thought in clarifying a picture of his physical surroundings, something would show through in performance, so too Brecht seems to believe that if an actor has investigated the alternatives, something of that critical awareness would be communicated to the audience.

Both men may well be right. Recent behavioural studies[112] suggest that human communication is strongly influenced by signals that pass unnoticed by the conscious mind: body posture may reveal more than the words spoken, the amount of eye-contact may say more about a relationship than statements by the people involved. Therefore Stanislavskian sub-text or the Brechtian 'Not-but' may be communicated without conscious effort by the actor. If the actor himself is sufficiently aware of possible alternatives, he will send out almost imperceptible signals, a hesitation here, an exaggeratedly decisive move there, and the audience will perceive the possibility of variant action and so maintain its critical awareness.

In practice, the acting style which Brecht explored for his 1931 production of *Mann ist Mann* met with a great deal of incomprehension:[113]

a quite extraordinary piece of directing. ... The actors talk like automata or schoolchildren reciting a poem.

Alfred Kerr commented that Lorre was saving up his talent for humour for another occasion[114] and a certain B.W. described the lead actor as 'a neurasthenic Kaspar Hauser'.[115] Even Brecht's great ally amongst the critics, Herbert Ihering, while praising Helene Weigel's performance as Begbick, complained that Lorre lacked 'clarity and the ability to speak in a plain and expositive manner'.[116]

In a letter to the *Berliner Börsen-Courier* of 8 March 1931 Brecht attempted to answer the two major criticisms of Lorre's performance, 'his habit of not speaking his meaning clearly, and the suggestion that he acted nothing but episodes'.[117] Clearly Brecht regarded Lorre's performance as an important step towards finding an appropriate acting style for the epic theatre, and he indicated that it was not incompetence on Lorre's part but a lack of understanding that attracted so much criticism to the performance. As he wrote in an as yet unpublished note:[118]

the attempt was made to use for certain effects a style of speaking which was however divided up (as though into stanzas). the actr lorre [sic] must be congratulated for his courage in giving up a general effect which he could have easily achieved in favour of one which was appreciated only by the few.

His defence of Lorre's manner of speaking is based on three points: first, the need to bring out the gest (the meaning of individual phrases and sentences had to be sacrificed for the sake of the general meaning). Second, the actor had to resolve the inner contradictions in Galy Gay's dialogue. This he did by rejecting the temptation to lead the spectator carefully through Galy Gay's thought-processes; instead he delivered his lines flatly, loudly declaiming one or two significant sentences:[119]

This was the case with the sentences 'I insist you put a stop to it!' and 'It *was* raining yesterday evening!' By these means the sentences (sayings) were not brought home to the spectator but withdrawn from him; he was not led but left to make his own discoveries.

Brecht's argumentation is difficult at this point: it is hard to see how the loud declamation of these sentences created a distance from the spectator. But the general tendency is clear: the spectator is not to be spoon-fed by the actor's interpretation but to seek out his own meanings from the clues given by the actor. Nevertheless, it seems that in Brecht's experimentation he failed to make these clues sufficiently clear, but succeeded only in alienating most of his audience in the negative sense of the word: instead of arousing their critical response, the monotonous style of Lorre's speaking seemed to deaden any response at all. Helene Weigel knew better how to maintain the interest of the audience without resorting to an acting display, and her cool, intelligent and sensitive style was to help Brecht in his post-war work to go beyond the partly failed experiment of *Mann ist Mann*.

More convincing is Brecht's defence of Lorre's handling of the protest against the announcement of the verdict:[120]

The impression intended was of a man simply reading a case for the defence prepared at some quite different period, without understanding what it meant as he did so. And this was indeed the impression left on any of the audience who knew how to make such observations.

Here Brecht applied the non-empathetic style of reporting in the past tense. As he said in his 'Instructions to Actors': 'Instead of trying to create the impression that he is improvising, the actor shall reveal the truth: that he is quoting'.[121]

To the accusation that Lorre was an episodic actor Brecht countered that this was exactly how the epic actor should present himself:[122]

As against the dramatic actor, who has his character established from the first and simply exposes it to the inclemencies of the world and the tragedy, the epic actor lets his character grow before the spectator's eyes out of the way in which he behaves.

Clearly such an episodic presentation, which Brecht here considers to characterize Chaplin's style, was appropriate to Brecht's view of man as alterable, and particularly suited to the theme of the play, the ease with which one man can be replaced by another.

The importance of *Mann ist Mann* is that it was the first time Brecht was able to explore fully the relationship between actor and audience in the epic theatre (the 'Lehrstücke' were staged primarily for the benefit of the participants rather than of the onlookers). As Ihering observed, not all aspects of the exploration were productive, and in particular it seems that in the pursuit of a new non-empathetic style in Lorre's performance, clarity was lost rather than gained.

Emil Burri in a programme-note for the 1939 production[123] gave a balanced view of the acting style that Brecht was trying to achieve. He first commented on the actor's difficulties with the new style of direction:

ACTOR: 'What kind of a character am I?'

DIRECTOR: 'You don't have to worry about who you are. If you're interested, you can perhaps find out afterwards from the public who you
were.'

The bewildered actor, however, persists in his questions:

ACTOR: 'What line shall I follow? I'm not meant to be a character and I'm
not meant to create a mood or atmosphere, and hardly any sentence
I'm to say in the way I am used to? How am I to speak my lines?'

To this the Director answers that in the epic theatre the lines have three functions:

1 Explanatory lines, which should be spoken direct to the audience.
2 Lines that carry forward the action. These are spoken amongst the actors and need hardly to be understood, so long as the story emerges clearly. Certainly, they require no special effect.
3 Passages that call for the actor's art, 'that is, that consist of gestic sentences'.

Burri concludes by pointing out:

It is quite obvious that an actor who gets under the skin of a character in the Naturalist manner is unable to speak the first two types of sentence with the right attitude and in the right style. But it is precisely this style which is essential to epic acting, whose style is in itself the combination of these different styles.

Therefore, in addition to the new epic mode of addressing the audience and in making intelligibility gestic rather than purely verbal, there was still room for the traditional skill of the actor in sharing with the audience the feelings and attitudes of the character portrayed. The full range of epic acting is therefore by no means limiting or stultifyingly intellectual. Indeed, it is the very richness of epic styles that allowed Brecht later to create such complex figures as Mother Courage and Galileo without abandoning the critical standpoint central to his theatre.

Conclusion

The world of today, as it appears to us, can hardly be contained in the form of Schiller's historical drama, if only because we cannot discover any tragic heroes but only tragedies which are staged by arch-butchers and carried out by mincing-machines. You cannot make a Wallenstein out of Hitler or Stalin. ... Art penetrates only to the victims, if it penetrates to people at all; it can no longer reach the powerful. Creon's secretaries dispose of the case of Antigone.

Friedrich Dürrenmatt: Problems of the Theatre (1955)

The technological advances of the past century and a half have forced modern man to reassess radically his view of himself. Industrialization, improved communications and increased mobility have brought about a political and social complexity that throws into question the whole concept of the individual. Philosophical scepticism, behavioural psychology and genetic research further beleaguer this threatened concept. No longer is man – as was Schiller's tragic hero Wallenstein – free to make moral choices and incur moral guilt in anything but the trivial. Even the seemingly most powerful 'individuals' of our age, like Hitler or Stalin, are seen as products of social and political forces. Predictably, the progressive theatre of our time has de-individualized its figures to an extent unknown since the Renaissance, putting on stage representative types reminiscent of Ancient Greek and medieval theatre.

The impact of technological and political change was particularly strong in Germany: within half a century its economic structure, which had developed little since the late Middle Ages, was transformed into that of a modern industrial nation, and politically it grew from a collection of disparate and often tiny states into a world power. As we have seen, the German intellectuals felt alienated by this process and – unlike the conservative elements who looked backwards in the hope of restoring ancient values to society – the Expressionists looked for new answers to their predicament.

This search led them into a contradiction. As alienated members of society they understandably championed their own individuality, since this alone set them off from a society they despised. On the other hand, their sense of alienation remained acute and they tried to overcome it by submerging their individuality in cosmic notions of a brotherhood of regenerated humanity. This contradiction is summed up in one sentence by the Millionaire's Son in Kaiser's *Gas I*. Having, as an isolated individual, devised a plan for the renewal of humanity, he meets with rejection and incomprehension from everyone about him. As he lies bleeding after being stoned by rioting workers, his daughter comes to him and asks him if he is alone. He answers: 'Ultimately alone, like all who tried to become one with all men!'[1] It is not the individual who has failed humanity, but the reverse: mankind has betrayed itself.

It is the desire for cosmic union that lies at the root of the abstractionist impulse in Expressionist theatre. Here the protagonist is an Everyman figure in a generalized situation, surrounded by types and stereotypes. The more abstract the theatre, however, the further removed it was from what is central to the theatrical experience: the living presence of the actor. Significantly, abstractionist experimentation was pursued most consistently in ballets, as in Picasso's designs for Satie's *Parade* in 1917 or Oskar Schlemmer's *Triadic Ballet* of 1922. Freed from language, as is for the most part the first piece of truly abstract theatre, Kandinsky's *Der gelbe Klang* of 1912, these ballets could exploit the more abstract arts of music and dance.

The most successful attempt to create a theatre of abstraction that embraces language has been made by Samuel Beckett. Like the Expressionists, even if in a more sophisticated manner, he is acutely aware of his isolation and is obsessed with the search for the meaning of existence. He too must remain alone: Godot will never come, the universe has failed him as well.

It is known that Beckett developed a considerable interest in German Expressionism after seeing the plays performed by the Dramik theatre group in Dublin and in his conversations with a former stage designer during the war years in France.[2] Beckett's dramatic figures are usually abstract beings without a past or individual psychology, and it is interesting to observe, as Günther Rühle points out,[3] that it was the actors trained by Jessner, namely Fritz Kortner, Walter Franck and Bernhard Minetti, who in our own time have coped best with portraying Beckett's characters on the German stage.

Apart from his superb poetry, one aspect of Beckett's success in establishing a theatre of abstraction is his choice of a strong central image for his pieces. Instead of abandoning reality to create a world of abstraction, he employs components of reality in a manner that de-individualizes his figures. By giving many of his characters 'costumes' that conceal their physicality, he has discovered a solution to a perennial problem of abstractionist theatre; how to create abstract figures from living actors. In *Endgame* Nagg and Nell appear from dustbins; the man and two women of *Play* are in urns, their faces 'so lost to age and aspect as to seem almost part of the urns';[4] in the second half of *Happy Days* Winnie is buried up to the neck in sand. These figures all become talking heads, abstractions of the human situation. For all its realism, *Krapp's Last Tape* contains an ingenious piece of abstraction: the younger Krapp makes his appearance as a tape-recording – the actor reduced to a voice in a machine. Similarly, *Footfalls* concentrates the light on the actress's feet, and *Not I* reduces the actress to a mouth hovering in space. Without recourse to the elaborate and fanciful designs of Picasso and Schlemmer, Beckett has discovered a viable form of abstraction on stage. And he has done this, paradoxically, not by selecting abstract images, but by creating concrete if improbable situations: Winnie in her mound brushes her teeth, perspires, and lives in a manner not so remote from everyday existence. The abstract theme of the agony of isolation is rendered theatrically tangible.

The other strain in Expressionism, the assertive individuality of the alienated intellectual, is an important element in the impulse towards primitivism. Rejecting the civilization that had corrupted society into its present state, the primitivist sought within his own instinctual impulses the basis for renewal. The spontaneous and ecstatic performances to which primitivism gave rise are the progenitors of Artaud's Theatre of Cruelty. Anaïs Nin's description of Artaud's own 'performance' at his notorious lecture on 'The theatre and the plague' at the Sorbonne on 6 April 1933 could easily be mistaken for a report on the acting of Ernst Deutsch or Kortner a decade and a half earlier:[5]

His face was contorted with anguish, one could see the perspiration dam-
pening his hair. His eyes dilated, his muscles became cramped, his fingers
struggled to retain their flexibility. He made one feel the parched and
burning throat, the pain, the fever, the fire in the guts. He was in agony.
He was screaming. He was delirious. He was enacting his own death, his
own crucifixion.

The same total self-commitment of the actor, admittedly with insistence on greater discipline and with a more developed awareness of the social responsibility of theatre, reappears in the work of Grotowski. Again, the following statement from his work *Towards a Poor Theatre* might have come from an Expressionist manifesto:[6]

We do not want to teach the actor a predetermined set of skills or give him
a 'bag of tricks'. Ours is not a deductive method of collecting skills. Here
everything is concentrated on the 'ripening' of the actor which is expressed
by a tension towards the extreme, by a complete stripping down, by the
laying bear [sic] of one's own intimity – all this without the least trace of
egotism or self-enjoyment. The actor makes a total gift of himself. This is a
technique of the 'trance' and of the integration of all the actor's psychic
and bodily powers which emerge from the most intimate layers of his being
and his instinct, springing forth in a sort of 'translumination'.

The Expressionists did not have to wait for Beckett to demonstrate the bankruptcy of individualism. The political events of the 1920s and the early 1930s showed only too clearly the limited efficacy of individual striving. Some Expressionists, like Hasenclever, abandoned their agonized search and began to write comedies (a tendency later to be pursued by Dürrenmatt); others joined forces with the political movements of the day, both of the right and of the left. Predictably, most playwrights of nationalism attempted to resuscitate the heroic idiom of the past, and the progressive political theatre was that of socialism.

Piscator ultimately failed because, while he recognized the need for the theatre to develop a collective consciousness, his remedies were usually superficial. He introduced the generalizing elements of film and back-projections without radically rethinking the function of theatre, without above all questioning the individualistic style of his actors.

It was Brecht who saw the need for a more fundamental change: as he had said: 'If you hit a car with a coachman's whip, it won't get it going'.[7] His experiments, many of them deriving from the abstractionist theatre of Kaiser and Jessner, led him, if not into blind alleys, at least into very narrow tunnels. His 'Lehrstücke', for instance, are a very complete answer to the search for a collectivist role for theatre; but his *Massnahme (The Measures Taken)* was not originally intended for performance but as an educative experience for the participants. For all its radical reassessment of the theatre, it could not point the way forward for a theatre of performance. It was later, in his years of exile, that Brecht in his major plays succeeded in reconciling a generalized political awareness with the strong individuals which are the life-blood of theatre.

In 1922 Alfred Polgar had drawn up the balance sheet on Expressionist theatrical style:[8]

> Stage design, stage action, the performance, the delivery and posture of actors are all intended to reveal the essence of the play, its central idea, its inner law of form. The advantages of such a directing style are: clarity; hardness; precision of all theatrical lines and their concision into a few sharp angles that determine the form; transparency; a saving of time and resources. The losses are: the full, colourful roundedness of the actor; warmth, colour, the delightful ebb and flow of organic life; all the magic of ordinary theatre; all the higher and semi-tones of the dramatic melody.

It was ultimately Brecht who in characters like Galileo and Mother Courage combined clarity with colour and precision with warmth.

Just as Beckett has achieved a high point in the theatre of abstraction, so Brecht has to date created the most successful political theatre. And while both have abandoned individual psychology to portray representative types, both have succeeded by remaining essentially theatrical, by starting from a clear and concrete situation, whether it derives from absurdist philosophy or

Marxist analysis. For some time to come no doubt the theatre will continue to draw on the divergent inspiration of Beckett and Brecht, as it will on the theatre of Artaud and Grotowski. But it should be remembered how much in turn these four major figures of twentieth-century theatre owe to an inspiration that is all but forgotten: the revolution in German theatre, 1900–33.

Chronology 1900–33

This table lists the 200 most significant productions on German-language stages for this period, together with information on the historical and cultural background. After a summary of major events for each year the following information is given:

1 Author and title of work performed. An asterisk indicates a private performance, usually to avoid censorship. An exact date indicates that the production was a premiere or at least the first public performance in Germany. A date in brackets after the title is the date of composition, where this is significantly earlier than the date of the first performance. Long titles have been abbreviated. Titles of all non-German pieces are rendered into English.
2 Theatre(s) where performed
3 Director
4 Designer | given only in significant cases
5 Lead actors/actresses |

The following abbreviations are used:

Bln – Berlin; Bn – Bühne(n); Dt – Deutsch(es); Ddf – Düsseldorf; Fft – Frankfurt/Main; Gr – Grosses; Hbg – Hamburg; Kgl – Königliches; Ksp – Kammerspiel(e); Lpzg – Leipzig; Nbg – Nüremberg; Schsph – Schauspielhaus; Sdamm – Schiffbauerdamm; Th – Theater.

1900

Science/technology: First Zeppelin flight. Publications: Freud: *Die Traumdeutung*; George: *Der Teppich des Lebens*. Theatre: Reinhardt directs for the first time. Premiere of Strindberg's *To Damascus* in Stockholm.

3.10 Hartleben: *Rosenmontag*	Dt Th Bln	Brahm	Reinhardt
21.12 Hauptmann: *Michael Kramer*	Dt Th Bln	Brahm	Reinhardt

1901

Politics: Failure of negotiations towards Anglo-German alliance. Publications: Thomas Mann: *Buddenbrooks*. Theatre: Founding of Schall und Rauch cabaret in Bln (Reinhardt) and Elf Scharfrichter in Munich (Wedekind and Falckenberg); Prinzregententh Munich opened. Premiere of Chekhov's *Three Sisters* in Moscow, Strindberg's *Dance of Death* in Stockholm.

11.10 Wedekind: *Marquis von Keith*	Residenzth Bln	Sickel	

1902

Arts: 22 paintings of Munch exhibited at Secession in Berlin. Theatre: Kleines Th Bln opened; Hülsen becomes Chief Director of Kgl Schsph Bln. Premiere of Gorky's *Lower Depths* in Moscow.

5.1 Büchner: *Dantons Tod* (1835)	Belle-Alliance-Th Bln (Volksbn)	Moest/ Halen	
22.2 Wedekind: *König Nicolo*	Schsph Munich	Stollberg	
* Wilde: *Salome*	Kleines Th Bln	Reinhardt	Eysoldt
Wedekind: *Erdgeist*	Kleines Th Bln	Oberländer	Eysoldt

1903

Science/technology: First flight by 'heavier than air machine'. Publications: Otto Weininger: *Geschlecht und Charakter*. Theatre: Th des Westens opened in Bln; Reinhardt leaves Brahm's Dt Th Bln to become Director of Kleines Th Bln and also leases Neues Th (am Sdamm) Bln.

23.1 Gorky: *Lower Depths*	Kleines Th Bln	Reinhardt	Reinhardt
30.10 Hofmannsthal: *Elektra*	Kleines Th Bln	Reinhardt	Eysoldt
31.10 Hauptmann: *Rose Bernd*	Dt Th Bln	Brahm	Lehmann, Bassermann
Maeterlinck: *Pelleas and Melisande*	Neues Th Bln	Reinhardt	Impekoven

1904

Politics: Anglo-French Entente Cordiale; Russo-Japanese War. Arts: Isadora Duncan founds dance school in Bln; Cézanne, Van Gogh and Gauguin exhibit in Munich; Kirchner 'discovers' negro art. Theatre: Brahm becomes Director of Lessingth Bln and commissions designs from Craig; death of Chekhov.

* 1.2 Wedekind: *Büchse der Pandora*	Intimes Th Nbg	Messthaler	

1905

Politics: 'Bloody Sunday' in St Petersburg; First Moroccan Crisis. Science/technology: Einstein's Theory of Relativity. Arts: fauvisme exhibition in Paris; Die Brücke formed in Dresden. Theatre: Meyerhold's first experiments; Craig: *The Art of the Theatre* published in England and Germany; drama schools open in Bln, Cologne and Ddf; first use of revolving stage as integral part of performance (Reinhardt); Jacobsohn founds periodical *Die Schaubühne*; Ddf Schsph opened; Reinhardt becomes Director of Dt Th Bln; Barnowsky becomes Director of Kleines Th Bln.

18.2 Wedekind: *Hidalla*	Schsph Munich	Stollberg		Wedekind
* 2.5 Wedekind: *Totentanz*	Intimes Th Nbg	Messthaler		
Shakespeare: *Midsummer Night's Dream*	Neues Th Bln	Reinhardt	Knina	Eysoldt

1906

Politics: Conference of Algeciras resolves Moroccan Crisis. Science/technology: Max Planck's Theory of Radiation. Theatre: Guest-performance by Stanislavsky's Moscow Art Th at Berlinerth; Reinhardt, now owner of Dt Th Bln, opens Ksp there and begins collaboration with designer Ernst Stern; death of Ibsen.

19.1 Hauptmann: *Und Pippa tanzt*	Lessingth Bln	Brahm		
20.11 Wedekind: *Frühlings Erwachen* (1891)	Dt Th Ksp Bln	Reinhardt	Walser	Moissi, Wedekind
Ibsen: *Ghosts*	Dt Th Ksp Bln	Reinhardt	Munch	Moissi

1907

Politics: Anglo-Russian Entente. Arts: Picasso: *Demoiselles d'Avignon*. Theatre: Schillerth Bln opened; Krolloper Bln first theatre to instal sky-dome. Premiere of Strindberg's *Dream Play* in Stockholm.

27.5 Grabbe: *Scherz, Satire ...* (1822)	Munich			
Wedekind: *Marquis von Keith*	Dt Th Ksp Bln	Wedekind		Wedekind
* Kokoschka: *Sphinx und Strohmann*	Kunstgewerbeschule Vienna	Kokoschka		

1908

Politics: 'Daily Telegraph Affair'. Arts: Schönberg's first atonal compositions; Worringer: *Abstraktion und Einfühlung* published. Theatre: Craig founds periodical *The Mask*; playwrights' union formed in Bln; Künstlerth Munich, designed by Littmann, opened under direction of Georg Fuchs. Premiere of Strindberg's *Ghost Sonata* in Stockholm.

Schiller: *Die Räuber*	Dt Th Bln	Reinhardt	Moissi, Wegener

1909

Science/technology: Blériot flies the Channel. Arts: Marinetti's Futurist Manifesto.

29.3 Kokoschka: *Sphinx und Strohmann*	Fledermaus Cabaret Vienna	Kokoschka	
4.7 Kokoschka: *Mörder, Hoffnung …*	Gartenth der Kunstschau Vienna	Kokoschka	
Hofmannsthal/Strauss: *Elektra*	Hofoper Vienna	Mahler	Roller

1910

Arts: First consciously abstract painting in history of art by Kandinsky; periodical *Der Sturm* founded.

25.9 Sophocles/ Hofmannsthal: *Oedipus*	Munich Exhibition Hall Zirkus Schumann Bln	Reinhardt	Roller	Moissi, Wegener, Durieux

1911

Politics: Second Moroccan Crisis. Philosophy: First theories of Heidegger. Arts: Der blaue Reiter group formed in Munich; Marinetti's Futurist Manifesto published in Germany; Dalcroze Institute founded in Hellerau near Dresden; Laban founds dance school in Munich; Craig publishes *On the Art of the Theatre* (expanded version of 1905 text); periodicals *Die Aktion* and *Die Szene* founded; Stravinsky: *Petroushka*. Theatre: Neues Th opened in Fft.

14.1 Hauptmann: *Die Ratten*	Lessingth Bln	Brahm		Lehmann
26.1 Hofmannsthal/ Strauss: *Rosenkavalier*	Hofoper Dresden	Reinhardt	Roller	

25.2 Sternheim: *Die Hose*	Dt Th Bln	Reinhardt		
24.11 Sternheim: *Die Kassette*	Dt Th Bln	Hollaender		Bassermann
1.12 Hofmannsthal: *Jedermann*	Zirkus Schumann Bln	Reinhardt	Roller	
15.12 Unruh: *Offiziere*	Dt Th Bln	Reinhardt		
Aeschylus: *Oresteia*	Musikfesthalle Munich	Reinhardt	Roller	Moissi

1912

Politics: First Balkan War. Publications: C. G. Jung: *Wandlungen und Symbole der Libido*. Arts: Kandinsky publishes *Der gelbe Klang* and *Über das Geistige in der Kunst*; Schlemmer's first work on the *Triadic Ballet*; Gerhart Hauptmann receives Nobel Prize for Literature; Sorge receives Kleist Prize for *Der Bettler*. Theatre: Appia goes to Dalcroze Institute in Hellerau; Barnowsky takes over Lessingth Bln on death of Brahm; Reinhardt tours *King Oedipus* in Poland, Russia and Scandinavia, and tours ballet in USA; death of Strindberg. Annual Wedekind season at Dt Th Bln, directed by Wedekind, until 1914.

24.10 Hofmannsthal/ Strauss: *Ariadne*	Hofth Stuttgart	Reinhardt	Stern	
Strindberg: *Dance of Death*	Dt Th Bln	Reinhardt		Eysoldt, Wegener

1913

Politics: Second Balkan War. Publications: Husserl: *Phenomenology*; Thomas Mann: *Der Tod in Venedig*; Kafka: *Das Urteil*; Trakl: *Gedichte*. Arts: Stravinsky: *The Rite of Spring*. Theatre: Foundation of Deutsche Arbeiter Theater Bund; Appia designs Gluck opera for Dalcroze at Hellerau.

5.3 Sternheim: *Bürger Schippel*	Dt Th Ksp Bln	Reinhardt	Knina	
8.11 Büchner: *Woyzeck* (1836/7)	Residenzth Munich	Kilian	Roller	Steinrück
Büchner: *Woyzeck*	Lessingth Bln	Barnowsky		

1914

Politics: Outbreak of First World War in August. Science/technology: First radio broadcast of a drama. Arts: 'Expressionism' first used to refer to literature; Joyce begins *Ulysses*; Kaiser publishes *Die Bürger von Calais*; Hasenclever gives public reading of *Der Sohn*. Theatre: Dresden Hoftheater (later Schsph) opened; Neue Freie Volksbn opened in Bln; Hartung goes to Schsph Fft.

2.2	Sternheim: *Der Snob*	Dt Th Ksp Bln	Reinhardt		Bassermann
	Claudel: *Tidings Brought to Mary*	Hellerau	Dalcroze	Appia	
	Strindberg: *To Damascus*	Lessingth Bln	Barnowsky		

1915

Politics: German army's advance halted in the west; use of poison gas; sinking of the *Lusitania*; bread-rationing introduced. Arts: Tours by Italian Futurists in support of War; Stramm killed in action. Theatre: Munich Ksp opened; Reinhardt becomes Director of Volksbn Bln; Jessner goes to Neues Schsph Königsberg; K. H. Martin goes to Schsph Fft.

| 1.5 | Strindberg: *Ghost Sonata* | Ksp Munich | Falckenberg | |
| | Schiller: *Die Räuber* | Volksbn Bln | Reinhardt | Wegener |

1916

Politics: Verdun offensive; naval battle of Jutland; Battle of the Somme; formation of the Spartacus League; meat-rationing introduced. Arts: Dada founded in Zurich; Sorge and Marc killed in action. Theatre: Sturmbn founded in Bln.

17.3	Strindberg: *A Dream Play*	Th in der Königgratzerstr Bln	Bernauer		
22.4	Werfel: *Die Troerinnen*	Lessingth Bln			
20.9	Hasenclever: *Der Sohn* (1913)	Dt Landesth Prague	Demetz		Fricke
* 8.10	Hasenclever: *Der Sohn*	Albertth Dresden	Licho	Gliese	Deutsch
	Büchner: *Dantons Tod*	Dt Th Bln	Reinhardt	Stern	Moissi, Krauss
	Schiller: *Kabale und Liebe*	Dt Th Bln	Reinhardt		
	Strindberg: *Ghost Sonata*	Dt Th Ksp Bln	Reinhardt		

1917

Politics: With introduction of unrestricted submarine warfare army leaders in charge of state; USA declares war; formation of Independent Socialist Party (USPD); October Revolution in Russia; Treaty of Brest-Litovsk negotiated. Arts: Hasenclever receives Kleist Prize for his *Antigone*. Theatre: Ksp Hbg opened; Reinhardt hands over direction of Volksbn Bln to Friedrich Kayssler; Falckenberg becomes Director of Ksp Munich; Reinhardt initiates 'Junges Deutschland' season of modern plays at DT Th Bln, opening with Sorge's *Der Bettler*.

| 29.1 | Kaiser: *Bürger von Calais* (1913) | Neues Th Fft | Hellmer | Klöpfer |

28.4 Kaiser: *Von morgens bis mitternachts* (1912)	Ksp Munich	Falckenberg	Pasetti	Kalser
3.6 Kokoschka: *Mörder* (1909), *Hiob* and *Der brennende Dornbusch* (1911)	Albertth Dresden	George	Kokoschka	Richter, Deutsch
27.10 Kaiser: *Die Koralle*	Neues Th Fft	Hellmer		Klöpfer
27.10 Kaiser: *Die Koralle*	Ksp Munich	Falckenberg	Pasetti	
2.11 Johst: *Der Einsame*	Schsph Ddf	Lindemann		
17.11 Wedekind: *Schloss Wetterstein* (1910)	Pfauenth Zurich	Reucker		Wedekind, Bergner
8.12 Kornfeld: *Die Verführung* (1913)	Schsph Fft	Hartung	Delavilla	Feldhammer
* 15.12 Hasenclever: *Antigone*	Stadtth Lpzg			
* 23.12 Sorge: *Der Bettler* (1912)	Dt Th Bln	Reinhardt	Stern	Deutsch, Wegener, Eysoldt, Thimig

1918

Politics: Failure of Spring Offensive; strikes in opposition to War; sailors mutiny in Kiel; revolution in Bln; Kaiser abdicates; Armistice; German Communist Party (KPD) formed. Arts: Heinrich Mann: *Der Untertan*; Brecht: 'Legende vom toten Soldaten'; Spengler: *Der Untergang des Abendlandes*; death of Wedekind; Tristan Tzara's Dada manifesto. Theatre: End of censorship; Fehling goes to Volksbn Bln; Engel becomes Director of Ksp Hbg; Viertel becomes Director of Staatsth Dresden.

* 10.2 Goering: *Seeschlacht*	Kgl Schsph Dresden	Lewinger/ Linnebach	Büttner	
* 16.6 Unruh: *Ein Geschlecht*	Schsph Fft	Hartung	Babberger	Müller
* 15.10 Stramm: *Sancta Susanna*	Sturmbn Bln	Schreyer		
16.11 Kaiser: *Brand im Opernhaus*	Ksp Hbg	Ziegel		Kortner, Horwitz
28.11 Kaiser: *Gas I*	Neues Th Fft	Hellmer	Neppach	Ebert
28.11 Kaiser: *Gas I*	Schsph Ddf	Lindemann		
Hasenclever: *Der Sohn*	Nationalth Mannheim	Weichert	Sievert	Odemar
* Hasenclever: *Der Sohn*	Dt Th Bln	Hollaender	Stern	Deutsch, Wegener
* Goering: *Seeschlacht*	Dt Th Bln	Reinhardt	Stern	Jannings, Krauss
Unruh: *Ein Geschlecht*	Dt Th Bln	Herald	Stern	Bertens
Kokoschka: *Mörder* and *Hiob*	Neues Th Fft	George	Kokoschka	George, Müller
Kaiser: *Die Koralle*	Dt Th Ksp Bln	Hollaender	Knina	Wegener, Krauss, Deutsch

1919

Politics: Spartacist uprising; Karl Liebknecht and Rosa Luxemburg shot; elections for National Assembly of Weimar Republic; Ebert President; Treaty of Versailles; short-lived Räterepublik in Munich; Toller imprisoned; January rate for dollar = 8.50 Marks (1913: 1 dollar = 4.20 Marks). Arts: Bauhaus founded in Weimar; Kurt Schwitters's MERZ manifesto. Theatre: Court theatres become state theatres; Tairov publishes *Notes of a Director* in Russia; Zirkus Schumann converted by Poelzig into Reinhardt's Gr Schsph Bln, opens with *Oresteia*; Tribüne opens in Bln under direction of K. H. Martin, who then co-founds first Proletarian Theatre, which soon fails; Jessner becomes Director of Staatsth Bln; Kortner goes to Staatsth Bln; Piscator opens Das Tribunal in Königsberg; Brecht's first theatre reviews in Augsburg and first published play, *Trommeln in der Nacht*.

23.1 Sternheim: *1913* (1914)	Schsph Fft	Hartung	Delavilla	Faber, George
20.2 Hasenclever: *Antigone*	Schsph Fft	Weichert	Sievert	Müller, George
13.3 Johst: *Der junge Mensch*	Thaliath Hbg			
20.3 Barlach: *Der arme Vetter*	Ksp Hbg			
27.4 Lasker-Schüler: *Die Wupper* (1909)	Dt Th Bln	Herald	Stern	
30.9 Toller: *Die Wandlung*	Tribüne Bln	Martin	Neppach	Kortner
22.11 Barlach: *Der tote Tag* (1907)	Schsph Lpzg			
5.12 Kaiser: *Hölle Weg Erde*	Neues Th Fft	Hellmer	Delavilla	
* Kokoschka: *Hiob* and *Der brennender Dornbusch*	Dt Th Bln	Kokoschka	Stern	
Kaiser: *Von morgens bis mitternachts*	Dt Th Bln	Hollaender	Stern	Pallenberg
Kaiser: *Gas I*	Volksbn Bln	Legband	Hirsch	Stahl-Nachbaur
Schiller: *Wilhelm Tell*	Staatsth Bln	Jessner	Pirchan	Bassermann, Kortner

1920

Politics: Unsuccessful right-wing Kapp putsch in Bln; first devaluation of the Mark. Arts: Publication of *Menschheitsdämmerung*, anthology of Expressionist verse, and of Werfel's short story *Nicht der Mörder, der Ermordete ist schuldig*; Robert Wiene's film *Das Kabinett des Dr Caligari* (starring Werner Krauss); Mary Wigman opens dance school in Dresden. Theatre: Salzburg Festival opens with *Jedermann*; Reinhardt hands over direction of Bln theatres to Hollaender and works now mainly in Austria (esp. Th in der Josefstadt, Vienna); K. H. Martin directs at Dt Th and Gr Schsph Bln; Weichert leaves Mannheim to become Director of Staatsth Fft; Hartung goes to Landesth Darmstadt; Laban goes to Nationalth Mannheim; Brecht goes to Munich; Piscator joins Proletarisches Theater in Bln. Premiere of Kaiser's *From Morning till Midnight* in London.

21.4 Kornfeld: *Himmel und Hölle*	Dt Th Bln	Berger	Bamberger	Straub, Krauss

15.5 Hasenclever: *Die Menschen* (1918)	Dt Landesth Ksp Prague	Demetz		
3.6 Unruh: *Platz*	Schsph Fft	Hartung	Babberger	George
29.10 Kaiser: *Gas II*	Vereinigte Dt Th in Brünn			
5.11 Kaiser: *Europa* (1914)	Gr Schsph Bln	Martin		George, Bahn
* 15.11 Toller: *Masse Mensch*	Stadtth Nbg	Neubauer		
23.12 Schnitzler: *Reigen* (1897)	Kleines Schsph Bln			
Hasenclever: *Antigone*	Gr Schsph Bln	Martin	Stern	Jannings, Eysoldt
Kaiser: *Gas II*	Neues Th Fft	Hellmer		
Kokoschka: *Hiob* and *Mörder*	Neues Th Fft	George	Babberger	
Wedekind: *Marquis von Keith*	Staatsth Bln	Jessner	Pirchan	Kortner, Müthel
Kaiser: *Gas I*	Ksp Hbg	Engel	Schröder	
Rolland: *Danton*	Gr Schsph Bln	Reinhardt	Stern	Wegener
Shakespeare: *Richard III*	Staatsth Bln	Jessner	Pirchan	Kortner

1921

Politics: Heavy reparation demands on Germany; political unrest; Allied troops occupy Rhineland; by November 1 dollar = 200Marks. Arts: Schlemmer goes to the Bauhaus; Kaiser on trial for misappropriating landlord's property. Theatre: Th am Kurfürstendamm opened in Bln; Anton Wildgans becomes Director of Burgth Vienna; Piscator's Proletarisches Th closed by police; guest-performance of Stanislavsky's Moscow Art Th in Bln. Premiere of Pirandello's *Six Characters in Search of an Author* in Rome.

23.3 Barlach: *Die echten Sedemunds*	Ksp Hbg	Engel		
12.4 Stramm: *Kräfte* (1914)	Dt Th Ksp Bln	Reinhardt	Dworsky	Straub, Klöpfer
14.5 Stramm: *Erwachen* and *Haidebraut*	Staatsth Dresden	Viertel		Ponto
29.9 Toller: *Masse Mensch*	Volksbn Bln	Fehling	Strohbach	Dietrich
15.10 Werfel: *Der Spiegelmensch*	Altes Th Lpzg	Kronacher	Barnowsky	
7.11 Hofmannsthal: *Der Schwierige*	Residenzth Munich	Stieler		
Kaiser: *Von morgens bis mitternachts*	Lessingth Bln	Barnowsky	Klein	Granach
Büchner: *Woyzeck*	Dt Th Bln	Reinhardt	Heartfield	Klöpfer
Schiller: *Die Verschwörung des Fiesco*	Staatsth Bln	Jessner	Pirchan	Deutsch, Kortner

Schiller: *Die Räuber*	Gr Schsph Bln	Martin	Richter	Krauss
Strindberg: *A Dream Play*	Dt Th Bln	Reinhardt		Thimig
Shakespeare: *Othello*	Staatsth Bln	Jessner	Pirchan	Kortner, Steinrück

1922

Politics: Russo-German treaty of Rapallo; Italian fascists march on Rome; assassination of Rathenau; increasing inflation (July: 1 dollar = 550 Marks; December: 1 dollar = 7,500 Marks). Arts: Brecht receives Kleist Prize for *Trommeln in der Nacht*; Schlemmer's *Triadic Ballet* performed in Stuttgart; Hauptmann's sixtieth birthday widely celebrated; James Joyce's *Ulysses* published in Paris; first successful sound film. Theatre: Schsph Ddf forced to close; actors' strike at end of year in all private theatres in Bln; Theodor Tagger (i.e. Ferdinand Bruckner) opens Renaissanceth in Bln; Moriz Seeler founds 'Junge Bühne' at Dt Th Bln; Viertel leaves Dresden for Bln, opens Junge Bühne with Bronnen's *Vatermord*; Fehling goes to Staatsth Bln; Piscator and Rehfisch open Proletarische Volksbühne in Centralth Bln; Helene Weigel comes to Staatsth Bln from Fft; Jessner negotiates formation of film company; New York premiere of Kaiser's *From Morning till Midnight*.

5.2 Jahnn: *Krönung Richards III*	Schsph Lpzg	Rothe		
22.4 Bronnen: *Vatermord* (1915)	Schsph Fft	Hoffmann-Harnisch		
30.6 Toller: *Die Maschinenstürmer*	Gr Schsph Bln	Martin	Heartfield	Dieterle, Granach
12.8 Hofmannsthal: *Salzburger Gr Weltth*	Kollegienkirche Salzburg	Reinhardt		
29.9 Brecht: *Trommeln in der Nacht*	Ksp Munich	Falckenberg	Reigbert	Faber
* Bronnen: *Vatermord*	Dt Th Bln	Viertel	Dworsky	Straub, Granach
Kaiser: *Von morgens bis mitternachts*	Schsph Dresden	Viertel	Mahnke	Ponto
Brecht: *Trommeln in der Nacht*	Dt Th Bln	Falckenberg	Pilartz	Granach, George
Schiller: *Don Carlos*	Staatsth Bln	Jessner	Strnad	Müthel, Deutsch
Grabbe: *Napoleon*	Staatsth Bln	Jessner	Klein	Hartau
Grabbe: *Scherz, Satire, Ironie*	Staatsth Munich/ Dt Th Bln	Engel		Faber
Hebbel: *Judith*	Dt Th Bln/Gr Schsph Bln	Viertel	Schütte	Straub, George

1923

Politics: French and Belgian troops occupy Ruhr; Stresemann becomes Chancellor; unsuccessful Nazi putsch in Munich; Nazi and Communist parties temporarily banned; soaring inflation (August: 1 dollar = 1m. Marks; November: 1 dollar 1 = 2,500 billion Marks). Publications: Rilke: *Duineser*

Elegien and *Sonette an Orpheus*. Theatre: Guest-performances of Tairov in Bln; Tairov's *Notes of a Director* published in Germany; Gr Schsph Bln now performs only operettas and revues; Piscator and Rehfisch take over Centralth Bln; Jessner takes over Schillerth Bln as second theatre; Viertel founds short-lived 'Die Truppe' in Bln; George founds 'Actors' Theatre' in Bln; Kortner leaves Staatsth to work for Reinhardt; Zuckmayer becomes Dramaturg at Schsph Munich; Hollaender leaves Reinhardt to become critic; Engel directs in Bln for first time; British premiere of Kaiser's *Gas I* in Birmingham.

9.5 Brecht: *Im Dickicht*	Residenzth Munich	Engel	Neher	Faber
23.8 Jahnn: *Pastor Ephraim Magnus*	Das Theater Bln	Bronnen		
19.9 Toller: *Hinkemann*	Altes Th Lpzg	Wiecke		
3.11 Kaiser: *Nebeneinander*	Truppe Bln	Viertel	Grosz	Forster, Steckel
8.12 Brecht: *Baal* (1918)	Altes Th Lpzg	Kronacher	Thiersch	Körner
Brecht: *Trommeln in der Nacht*	Schsph Fft	Weichert	Sievert	
Barlach: *Der arme Vetter*	Staatsth Bln	Fehling		
Goethe: *Faust I*	Staatsth Bln	Jessner	Klein	Ebert, Klöpfer
Marlowe: *Edward II*	Schauspielerth Bln	Martin		George
Shakespeare: *Merchant of Venice*	Truppe Bln	Viertel		Kortner

1924

Politics: Dawes Plan on reparations; introduction of the Reichsmark; new economic stability; Toller released after serving full prison sentence; Hitler released after serving one fifth of his sentence. Arts: Ernst Barlach receives Kleist Prize; Thomas Mann: *Der Zauberberg*; Kafka: *Der Hungerkünstler*; Kurt Jooss founds Neue Tanzbühne in Münster. Theatre: Ddf Schsph reopens; Reinhardt resumes direction of Bln theatres and acquires Komödie Bln; Barnowsky hands over Lessingth Bln to Rotter Brothers who also take over Piscator's Centralth Bln; Piscator goes to Volksbn Bln; Brecht directs for first time, then goes with Zuckmayer as Dramaturg to Dt Th Bln; Hartung goes to Cologne; Krauss goes to Staatsth Bln; death of Duse.

17.1 O'Neill: *Emperor Jones*	Truppe Bln	Viertel		Homolka, Hilpert
27.1 Stramm: *Rudimentär* (1914)	Volksbn Bln	Vogt		
18.3 Marlowe/Brecht: *Leben Eduards II*	Ksp Munich	Brecht	Neher	Faber, Homolka
27.3 Kaiser: *Kolportage*	Lessingth Bln	Lind		
6.4 Bronnen: *Anarchie in Sillian*	Dt Th Bln	Hilpert		Franck
26.5 Paquet: *Fahnen*	Volksbn Bln	Piscator	Suhr	
13.10 Goll: *Methusalem*	Dramatisches Th Bln	Dieterle		
14.10 Shaw: *St Joan*	Dt Th Bln	Reinhardt		Bergner
30.12 Pirandello: *Six Characters*	Komödie Bln	Reinhardt	Krehan	

Brecht: *Leben Eduards II*	Staatsth Bln	Fehling	Gliese	Faber, Krauss
Brecht: *Im Dickicht der Städte*	Dt Th Bln	Engel	Neher	Kortner, Franck
Toller: *Hinkemann*	Residenzth Bln	Lind		George
Barlach: *Der tote Tag*	Ksp Munich	Falckenberg	Reigbert	
Büchner: *Dantons Tod*	Dt Th Bln	Engel		Kortner

1925

Politics: Hindenburg elected President; Allies withdraw from Ruhr; Treaty of Locarno; Hitler refounds Nazi Party, forms SS and publishes first volume of *Mein Kampf*. Arts: 'Neue Sachlichkeit' exhibition in Mannheim; André Breton's surrealist manifesto; Kafka: *Der Prozess*; Bauhaus moves to Dessau, where it has its own stage; premiere of Berg's *Wozzeck* in Bln; Krenek composes first jazz opera, *Jonny spielt auf*; death of Kafka. Theatre: Brecht's first theoretical writings.

3.1 Klabund: *Der Kreidekreis*	Schsph Fft	Weichert		
* 7.6 Bronnen: *Die Exzesse*	Lessingth Bln	Hilpert		Müller, Franck
22.12 Zuckmayer: *Der fröhliche Weinberg*	Th am Sdamm Bln	Bruck		
Klabund: *Der Kreidekreis*	Dt Th Bln	Reinhardt	Neher	Bergner, Klöpfer
Barlach: *Die Sündflut*	Staatsth Bln	Fehling		
Shakespeare: *Coriolanus*	Dt Th in Lessingth Bln	Engel	Neher	Kortner, Straub

1926

Politics: Allies withdraw from area around Cologne; Germany joins League of Nations; Russo-German treaty of neutrality; founding of Hitler Youth. Arts: Kafka: *Das Schloss*; Eisenstein's *Battleship Potemkin* widely seen in Germany; Fritz Lang's *Metropolis*; deaths of Rilke and critic Siegfried Jacobsohn. Theatre: Moves to introduce stricter legislation against obscenity; first international conference of actors in Bln; wide celebration of Reinhardt's twenty-fifth year of directing in Bln; Engel and Kortner go to Staatsth Bln; Stanislavsky publishes *My Life in Art*.

29.1 Bronnen: *Ostpolzug*	Staatsth Bln	Jessner		Kortner
20.2 Paquet: *Sturmflut*	Volksbn Bln	Piscator	Suhr	
4.5 Jahnn: *Medea*	Staatsth Bln	Fehling	Gliese	Straub, Faber
21.5 Zech: *Das trunkene Schiff*	Volksbn Bln	Piscator	Suhr, Grosz	
25.9 Brecht: *Mann ist Mann*	Landesth Darmstadt	Geis	Neher	Legal
12.10 Barlach: *Der blaue Boll*	Landesth Stuttgart	Brandenburg		

17.10 Bruckner: *Krankheit der Jugend*	Ksp Hbg	Horwitz		
Brecht: *Baal*	Dt Th Bln	Brecht/ Homolka	Neher	Homolka
Schiller: *Die Räuber*	Staatsth Bln	Piscator	Müller	Ebert, Faber
Gorky: *The Lower Depths*	Volksbn Bln	Piscator	Suhr	
Shakespeare: *Hamlet*	Staatsth Bln	Jessner	Neher	Kortner

1927

Politics: Growing prosperity; unemployment sinks as low as 300,000; Nationalist Party represented in new government. Publications: Heidegger: *Sein und Zeit*; Hesse: *Der Steppenwolf*; Brecht *Die Hauspostille*; T. S. Eliot: *Sweeney Agonistes*. Arts: First German Dance Congress in Magdeburg (Schlemmer, Laban, Pavlova); first edition of periodical *Der Tanz*; first sound film. Theatre: Magdeburg Theatre Exhibition; Reinhardt tours USA and delivers 'Rede über den Schauspieler'; Piscator leaves Volksbn Bln and opens first Piscatorbn (Th am Nollendorfplatz) Bln; Nazis found 'Grossdeutsche Theatergemeinschaft' in Bln in opposition to Volksbn; Hartung becomes Director of Renaissanceth Bln.

23.3 Welk: *Gewitter über Gottland*	Volksbn Bln	Piscator	Müller	George, Granach
17.7 Brecht/Weill: *Kleines Mahagonny*	Stadtth Baden-Baden	Brecht	Neher	Lenya
1.9 Toller: *Hoppla, wir leben!*	Ksp Hbg	Lotz		Gründgens
3.9 Toller: *Hoppla, wir leben!*	Piscatorbn Bln	Piscator	Müller/ Heartfield	Granach, Steckel
14.10 Zuckmayer: *Schinderhannes*	Lessingth Bln	Bruck		
10.11 Tolstoi *et al*: *Rasputin*	Piscatorbn Bln	Piscator	Müller	Wegener, Granach

1928

Politics: Two million unemployed; SPD and KPD gain 40 per cent of seats in Reichstag elections. Arts: First Mickey Mouse cartoon. Theatre: Piscator takes over Lessingth Bln and has to give up Piscatorbn; continuing right-wing attempts to remove Jessner from Staatsth Bln; death of Appia.

23.1 Hašek/Brod: *Schwejk*	Piscatorbn Bln	Piscator	Grosz	Pallenberg
4.2 Hofmannsthal: *Der Turm* (1925)	Prinzregententh Munich	Stieler		
10.4 Lania: *Konjunktur*	Piscatorbn Bln	Piscator	Müller	
31.8 Brecht/Weill: *Dreigroschenoper*	Th am Sdamm Bln	Engel	Neher	Ponto, Lenya
16.10 Weisenborn: *U-Boot S4*	Volksbn Bln	Reuss		George, Straub

23.10 Bruckner: *Die Verbrecher*	Dt Th Bln	Hilpert	Gliese	
2.12 Lampel: *Revolte im Erziehungshaus*	Thaliath Bln	Deppe	Böttcher	
21.12 Zuckmayer: *Katharina Knie*	Lessingth Bln	Martin		
Brecht: *Mann ist Mann*	Volksbn Bln	Engel	Neher	George, Weigel
Kaiser: *Gas I*	Staatsth Bln	Jessner	Pirchan	Franck, Müthel

1929

Politics: Growing unemployment; Young Plan on reparations provides for repayments until 1988; polarization and violence in political life; Stresemann dies; Wall Street crash. Science/technology: First television transmission in Bln. Arts: Thomas Mann receives Nobel Prize for Literature; Döblin: *Alexanderplatz*; death of Hofmannsthal. Theatre: Police raids on theatres effectively restore censorship; actors protest against their economic situation; many studio-theatres opened; Piscator publishes *Das politische Theater* and opens second Piscatorbn am Nollendorfplatz Bln, but it too soon fails; Brecht publishes first theories on theatre and begins writing 'Lehrstücke'; K. H. Martin goes to Volksbn; Weichert goes to Bln.

30.3 Fleisser: *Pioniere in Ingolstadt*	Th am Sdamm Bln	Geis		
31.8 Lane/Hauptmann/ Brecht: *Happy End*	Th am Sdamm Bln	Engel/ Brecht	Neher	Homolka
6.9 Wolf: *Cyankali*	Lessingth Bln	Hinrich		
6.9 Mehring: *Der Kaufmann von Berlin*	Piscatorbn Bln	Piscator	Moholy-Nagy	
Sophocles: *Oedipus*	Staatsth Bln	Jessner	Poelzig	Kortner

1930

Politics: Young Plan on reparations finally adopted by Reichstag; final evacuation of Rhineland by Allies; Communist and Nazi gains in elections; four million unemployed. Arts: Musil: *Der Mann ohne Eigenschaften*; premiere of Berg's opera *Lulu*. Theatre: Guest-performances of Kabuki theatre and Meyerhold in Bln; Jessner resigns as Director of Staatsth Bln; Brecht publishes his *Versuche*; Piscator reopens at Wallnerth Bln; Reinhardt, Barnowsky and Eugen Roberts associate in 'Reibaro' season-ticket cartel.

16.2 Goering: *Südpolexpedition des Scott*	Staatsth Bln	Jessner	Neher	Franck
9.3 Brecht/Weill: *Mahagonny*	Opernhaus Lpzg	Brugmann	Neher	
13.5 Unruh: *Phaea*	Dt Th Bln	Reinhardt		George
23.6 Brecht: *Der Jasager*	Zentralinstitut für Erziehung und Unterricht Bln	Brecht/ Weill		

31.8 Toller: *Feuer aus den Kesseln*	Th am Sdamm Bln	Hinrich	Neher	Lorre, Lingen
1.11 Bruckner: *Elisabeth von England*	Dt Th Bln	Hilpert	Schütte	Straub, Krauss
13.12 Brecht: *Die Massnahme*	Philharmonie Bln	Dudow		
Barlach: *Der blaue Boll*	Staatsth Bln	Fehling	Gliese	George

1931

Politics: Plans for customs union between Germany and Austria fail; reparations suspended for one year (Hoover Moratorium); five and a half million unemployed; banks close temporarily; Nationalists walk out of Reichstag; left-wing form 'Eiserne Front'; increasing street violence. Arts: Pabst's film version of *Dreigroschenoper*; Fritz Lang's *M*; Gründgens achieves success as opera director. Theatre: Krolloper Bln forced to close; unemployed actors form own troupes; agitprop groups particularly active until their banning in March; Piscator leaves Bln for Soviet Union; death of Hollaender.

15.1 Wolf: *Tai Yang erwacht*	Wallnerth Bln	Piscator	Heartfield	
5.3 Zuckmayer: *Hauptmann von Köpenick*	Dt Th Bln	Hilpert		Krauss
2.11 Horváth: *Wienerwald*	Dt Th Bln	Hilpert		Neher, Lorre
Brecht: *Mann ist Mann*	Staatsth Bln	Brecht	Neher	Lorre, Weigel

1932

Politics: Disarmament talks in Geneva fail; six million unemployed; Hitler narrowly outvoted as President; Nazis gain almost 40 per cent of votes for Reichstag. Arts: Brecht co-writes film-script for *Kuhle Wampe*; Brecht's *Heilige Johanna der Schlachthöfe* broadcast by Radio Bln; Bauhaus in Dessau forced to close by Nazis; celebration of centenary of Goethe's death; celebration of Hauptmann's seventieth birthday. Theatre: Artaud publishes first manifesto of Theatre of Cruelty; Rotter Brothers close all nine theatres in Bln; Hilpert becomes Director of Volksbn Bln; K. H. Martin becomes Director of Dt Th Bln with Rudolf Beer; Gründgens goes to Staatsth Bln.

15.1 Gorky/Brecht: *Die Mutter*	Komödienhaus Bln	Brecht/ Burri	Neher	
16.2 Hauptmann: *Vor Sonnenuntergang*	Dt Th Bln	Reinhardt		Krauss, Thimig
Goethe: *Faust I*	Staatsth Bln	Müthel		Wegener, Gründgens

1933

Politics: Hitler appointed Chancellor; Reichstag fire; Nazis achieve control of Germany. Arts: Black-lists of authors and works published in press; five hundred tons of books impounded in Bln alone; Nazis stage exhibition of 'Cultural Bolshevism'. Theatre: The following emigrate from Germany in this and subsequent years: Reinhardt, Brecht, Jessner, Kaiser, Kortner, Deutsch, Grosz, Heartfield, Kandinsky, Kokoschka, Bassermann, Barnowsky, Kerr, Granach.

Goethe: *Faust II*   Staatsth Bln   Lindemann

Notes

Introduction

1 E. Starkie, *From Gautier to Eliot: The Influence of France on English Literature 1851–1939*, London, 1969, p. 209.
2 See *Magdeburg Theater-Ausstellung*, Amtlicher Katalog, Mitteldeutsche Ausstellungs-Gesellschaft, Magdeburg, 1927, exhibit nos 1074–97, pp. 208–9.
3 J. M. Ritchie, *German Expressionist Drama*, Twayne, Boston, 1976, p. 169; cf. H. Schwerte, 'Anfang des expressionistischen Dramas: Oskar Kokoschka', *Zeitschrift für deutsche Philologie*, vol. 83, no. 2, 1964, pp. 171–91.
4 For example, in the ninety pages devoted to Expressionist drama in the standard work by Albert Soergel and Curt Hohoff, *Dichtung und Dichter der Zeit*, Düsseldorf, 1961–3, less than one deals with the practice of the Expressionist theatre.

Chapter 1   Origins of the revolution

1 K. Pinthus, 'Versuch eines zukünftigen Dramas', reprinted in *Literatur-Revolution 1910–1925*, ed. P. Pörtner, Luchterhand, Darmstadt, 1969, vol. 1, p. 343.
2 Cit. G. Rühle, *Zeit und Theater: Vom Kaiserreich zur Republik, 1913–1925*, Propyläen Verlag, Berlin, n.d. (1973), vol. 1, pp. 11–12.
3 R. Pascal, *From Naturalism to Expressionism*, Weidenfeld & Nicolson, London, 1973, p. 11.
4 Cit. M. Pasley, 'Modern German literature', *Germany: A Companion to German Studies*, Methuen, London, 1972, p. 577.
5 M. Hamburger, *From Prophecy to Exorcism*, Longmans, London, 1965, p. 6.
6 Cit. E. Eyck, *A History of the Weimar Republic*, Oxford University Press, 1962, vol. 1, p. 36.
7 A. Schopenhauer, *The World as Will and Idea*, trans. R. B. Haldane and J. Kemp, London, 1883, vol. 1, p. 231.
8 A. Schopenhauer, 'Zur idealistischen Grundansicht', *The Intellectual Tradition of Modern Germany*, ed. R. Taylor, G. Bell, London, 1973, vol. 1, p. 192.

9 W. H. Sokel, *The Writer in Extremis*, Stanford University Press, 1959, p. 102.
10 F. Nietzsche, *Zur Genealogie der Moral*, I, section 7, *Werke*, ed. G. Colli and M. Montinari, Gruyter, Berlin, vol. 6:2, 1968, p. 281.
11 Ibid., I, section 10, p. 285.
12 Nietzsche, *Also sprach Zarathustra*, section 3, *Werke*, vol. 6:1, p. 8.
13 Nietzsche, *Werke in drei Bänden*, ed. K. Schlechta, Hanser, Munich, 1956, p. 422.
14 G. Benn, Introduction to *Lyrik des expressionistischen Jahrzehnts*, 1955, cit. W. Steffens, *Expressionistische Dramatik*, Friedrich, Velber bei Hannover, 1971, p. 18.
15 W. Kandinsky, *Über das Geistige in der Kunst*, Piper, Munich, 1912, p. 23.
16 Sokel, op. cit., p. 116.
17 W. Hasenclever, *Gedichte Dramen Prosa*, ed. K. Pinthus, Rowohlt, Reinbek bei Hamburg, 1963, p. 103.
18 K. Otten, 'Thronerhebung des Herzens', *Der rote Hahn*, vol. 4, 1918, p. 13.
19 B. Brecht, Notebook, 17 June 1921, *Schriften zum Theater*, ed. W. Hecht, Suhrkamp, Frankfurt/Main, 1963, vol. 2, p. 27.
20 H. K. Moderwell, *The Theatre of To-day*, John Lane, New York, 1914, cit. W. R. Fuerst and S. J. Hume, *Twentieth-Century Stage Decoration*, Dover Publications Reprint, New York, 1967, vol. 1, p. 4.
21 B. Diebold, *Anarchie im Drama*, Frankfurter Verlags-Anstalt, Frankfurt/Main, 1921, pp. 28–9.
22 *Vossische Zeitung*, Berlin, 15 June 1913.
23 E. v. Winterstein, *Mein Leben und meine Zeit*, Berlin, 1947, p. 303.
24 For a fuller account see: C. W. Davies, 'The Volksbühne: a descriptive chronology', *Theatre Quarterly*, vol. 2, no. 5, January–March 1972, pp. 57–64.
25 For further details see: Susanne Jährig-Ostertag, 'Das dramatische Werk: seine künstlerische und kommerzielle Verwertung', Dr Phil. dissertation, Cologne, 1971.
26 Hasenclever, op. cit., p. 502.
27 F. Emmel, *Das ekstatische Theater*, Kampmann & Schnabel, Prien, 1924, p. 117.
28 K. Pinthus, 'Die Zukunft des Theaters?', in M. Krell, *Das deutsche Theater der Gegenwart*, Rösl, Munich, 1923, p. 247.
29 B. Viertel, 'Wege zur Truppe', in Krell, op. cit., p. 253.
30 *Düsseldorfer Nachrichten*, 28 October 1925.
31 Cit. H. Kindermann, *Theatergeschichte Europas*, Otto Müller, Salzburg, vol. 8, 1968, p. 125.
32 K. Frenzel, *Nationalzeitung*, 21 October 1889.
33 O. Koplowitz, *Otto Brahm als Theaterkritiker*, Zürich, 1936, p. 133.
34 H. Ihering, 'Der Volksbühnenverrat', cit. E. Piscator, *Schriften*, Henschelverlag, Berlin, 1968, vol. 1, p. 50.
35 Cit. L. M. Fiedler, *Max Reinhardt in Selbstzeugnissen und Bilddokumenten*, Rowohlt, Reinbek bei Hamburg, 1975, p. 42.
36 Ibid., p. 44.
37 E. Stern, *Bühnenbildner bei Max Reinhardt*, Berlin, 1955, p. 38.

38 H. Ihering, *Regie*, Hans von Hugo Verlag, Berlin, 1943, p. 12.
39 K. Kraus, 'Die Handschrift des Magiers', *Die Fackel*, nos 912–15, August 1935, p. 45.
40 G. Adler, *Max Reinhardt: Sein Leben*, Salzburg, 1964, p. 42.
41 Ibid., p. 43.
42 S. Jacobsohn, 'Danton', *Die Weltbühne*, no. 9, 1920, p. 274.
43 Cf. G. C. Izenour, *Theatre Design*, McGraw-Hill, New York, 1977, pp. 292–3.
44 Cit. G. Rühle, *Theater für die Republik 1917–1933 im Spiegel der Kritik*, S. Fischer, Frankfurt/Main, 1967, p. 304.
45 J. Rühle, *Theater und Revolution*, Deutscher Taschenbuch Verlag, Munich, 1963, p. 130.
46 H. Ihering, 'Das neue Theater', *Die neue Rundschau*, vol. 32, no. 1, 1921, pp. 423–4.
47 *Illustrated Sporting and Dramatic News*, 11 May 1882, cit. J. Stokes, *Resistible Theatres*, Paul Elek, London, 1972, p. 71.
48 N. Hern, 'Expressionism', *The German Theatre*, ed. R. Hayman, Oswald Wolff, London, 1975, p. 116.
49 P. Fechter, *Das europäische Drama*, Bibliographisches Institut, Mannheim, 1957, vol. 2, p. 421.
50 E. G. Craig, *On the Art of the Theatre*, Heinemann, London, 1911, caption to plate facing p. xiv.
51 E. G. Craig, *Index to the Story of My Days*, London, 1957, p. 290.
52 Craig, *On the Art of the Theatre*, p. 287.
53 R. Frank, *Das neue Theater*, Berlin, 1928, p. 32, cit. R. Samuel and R. Hinton Thomas, *Expressionism in German Life, Literature and the Theatre (1910–1924)*, Heffer, Cambridge, 1939, p. 66.
54 Craig, *On the Art of the Theatre*, p. 58.
55 Ibid., p. 81.
56 Ibid., p. 61.
57 Ibid., pp. 84–5.
58 H. Bahr, *Kritiken*, ed. H. Kindermann, Vienna, 1963, pp. 236–7.
59 A. Strindberg, *The Plays*, trans. M. Meyer, Secker & Warburg, London, 1975, vol. 2, p. 553.
60 R. Schickele, *Die Aktion*, 1912, p. 104.
61 R. Kayser, 'Das neue Drama', *Das junge Deutschland*, Deutsches Theater, Berlin, 1918, p. 139.
62 K. Edschmid, 'Schauspielkunst', in Krell, op. cit., p. 118.
63 H. Ball, *Phöbus*, vol. 1, no. 3, Munich, 1914, pp. 105–8, reprinted in Pörtner, op. cit., p. 339.
64 L. Schreyer, *Expressionistisches Theater*, Toth, Hamburg, 1948, p. 37.
65 A. Ehrenstein, 'Junges Drama', *Die neue Rundschau*, 1916, p. 1711.
66 O. Kokoschka, *My Life*, Thames & Hudson, London, 1974, pp. 28–9. For a fuller account of this performance see: D. Pam, 'Murderer, the Women's Hope', *Drama Review*, New York, vol. 19, no. 3 (T-67), September 1975, pp. 5–12.
67 Craig, *On the Art of the Theatre*, p. 144.

68 *Seven Expressionist Plays*, translated J. M. Ritchie and H. F. Garten, Calder & Boyars, London, 1968, p. 32.
69 [W.] Kandinsky, 'On stage composition', *The Blaue Reiter Almanac*, Thames & Hudson, London, 1974, p. 201.
70 Cf. [W.] Kandinsky, *Über das Geistige in der Kunst*, 3rd edn, Piper, Munich, 1912, p. 65.
71 Kandinsky, 'On stage composition', p. 191.
72 Kandinsky, *The Yellow Sound*, in *The Blaue Reiter Almanac*, p. 225.
73 Ibid., p. 214.
74 1956 in Paris, directed by Jacques Polieri and Richard Mortensen; 1978: free adaptation by Zone Theatre of Boston in Guggenheim Museum, New York.
75 Music by Barbara Winrow, choreography by Michael Huxley; for full details see J. Davies, 'Der gelbe Klang: a pre-Expressionist experiment in multi-media theatre', unpublished MA dissertation, Leeds University, 1977.
76 B. Balázs, *Der Geist des Films*, Halle, 1930, pp. 127–8, cit. G. M. Vajda, 'Outline of the philosophic backgrounds of Expressionism', *Expressionism as an International Literary Phenomenon*, ed. U. Weisstein, Didier, Paris, 1973, p. 48.

Chapter 2   The theory of Expressionist theatre

1 W. Worringer, *Abstraktion und Einfühlung*, 3rd edn, Piper, Munich, 1916, pp. 19–20.
2 Ibid., p. 19.
3 P. Klee, *Tagebücher 1898–1918*, ed. F. Klee, Du Mont Schauberg, Cologne, 1957, entry no. 951, p. 323.
4 Ibid., entry no. 951, p. 323.
5 F. Marc, *Briefe, Aufzeichnungen und Aphorismen*, Berlin, 1920, cit. W. Grohmann, *Bildende Kunst und Architektur zwischen den beiden Kriegen*, Frankfurt/Main, 1953, p. 411.
6 Cit. M. Pasley, 'Modern German literature', *Germany: A Companion to German Studies*, Methuen, London, 1972, p. 574.
7 P. Kornfeld, 'Kunst, Theater und anderes', in P. Pörtner, *Literatur-Revolution 1910–1925*, Luchterhand, Darmstadt, 1960, vol. 1, p. 365.
8 B. Brecht, *Augsburger Volkswille*, 14 December 1920, reprinted in *Schriften zum Theater*, ed. W. Hecht, Suhrkamp, Frankfurt/Main, 1963, vol. 1, pp. 49–50.
9 W. Hasenclever, 'Das Theater von morgen', *Die Schaubühne*, no. 12, 1916, pp. 476–7, reprinted in Pörtner, op. cit., pp. 352–3.
10 W. Hasenclever, *Gedichte Dramen Prosa*, ed. K. Pinthus, Rowohlt, Reinbek bei Hamburg, 1963, p. 102.
11 A. Wildgans, *Liebe*, Leipzig, 1916, p. 119.
12 G. Kaiser, *Die Erneuerung*, in *Schrei und Bekenntnis: Expressionistisches Theater*, ed. K. Otten, Luchterhand, Darmstadt, 1959, p. 53.
13 W. H. Sokel, *The Writer in Extremis*, Stanford University Press, 1959, p. 41.

14 R. Sorge, *Der Bettler*, in *Zeit und Theater*, ed. G. Rühle, Propyläen Verlag, Berlin, 1973, vol. 1, p. 114.

15 H. Herald, 'Notiz zur Bettler-Aufführung', *Das junge Deutschland*, Deutsches Theater, Berlin, vol. 1, no. 1, 1918, p. 30.

16 Hasenclever, *Gedichte Dramen Prosa*, p. 215.

17 B. Diebold, *Anarchie im Drama*, Frankfurter Verlags-Anstalt, Frankfurt/Main, 1921, p. 269.

18 Ibid., p. 319.

19 G. Kaiser, 'Vision und Figur', *Stücke Erzählungen Aufsätze Gedichte*, ed. W. Huder, Kiepenheuer & Witsch, Cologne, 1966, p. 666.

20 A. Stramm, *Das Werk*, Limes Verlag, Wiesbaden, n.d. (1963), p. 230.

21 E. Toller, *Masse Mensch*, Kiepenheuer, Potsdam, 1924, p. 10.

22 Ibid., p. 50.

23 Ibid., p. 52.

24 Ibid., p. 58.

25 Ibid., p. 68.

26 R. Weichert, *Die Szene*, May–June 1918, cit. L. Richard, *Phaidon Encyclopaedia of Expressionism*, Phaidon, Oxford, 1978, p. 190.

27 E. Toller, *Die Wandlung*, in *Zeit und Theater*, ed. G. Rühle, Propyläen Verlag, Berlin, 1973, vol. 1, p. 558.

28 H. Johst, *Der junge Mensch*, Munich, 1924, p. 15.

Chapter 3   Abstractionist theatre

1 G. Kaiser, *From Morning till Midnight*, trans. J. M. Ritchie: *Five Plays*, Calder & Boyars, London, 1971, p. 19. All quotations are from this translation, based on Kaiser's published text, which underwent minor revision in 1931.

2 S. Jacobsohn, 'Kaiser und Toller', *Die Weltbühne*, no. 42, 1919, p. 453.

3 G. Kaiser, 'Der Mensch im Tunnel', *Das Kunstblatt*, vol. 6, no. 1, Weimar, 1922, p. 516, reprinted in P. Pörtner, *Literatur-Revolution 1910–1925*, Luchterhand, Darmstadt, 1960, vol. 1, p. 389.

4 B. Diebold, *Anarchie im Drama*, Frankfurter Verlags-Anstalt, Frankfurt/Main, 1921, p. 27.

5 S. Grossmann, *Das Theater*, cit. G. Rühle, *Theater für die Republik 1917–1933 im Spiegel der Kritik*, S. Fischer, Frankfurt/Main, 1967, p. 106.

6 Kaiser, *From Morning till Midnight*, p. 30.

7 G. Kaiser, radio conversation with H. Kasack (1928), reprinted in *Die Literatur*, vol. 4, 1929–30.

8 P.W. [(= Paul Wiegler), *BZ*, February 1919?], Georg-Kaiser-Archive, Akademie der Künste, West Berlin.

9 J.A.B., [February 1919], Georg-Kaiser-Archive.

10 Dr W. Schmits, [1919], Georg-Kaiser-Archive.

11 *From Morning till Midnight*, p. 55.

12 P.W. [(= Paul Wiegler), *BZ*, February 1919?], Georg-Kaiser-Archive.

13 H. Ihering, *Regisseure und Bühnenmaler*, Bibliophiler Verlag, Berlin-Wilmersdorf, 1921, p. 22.

14 H. G. Scheffauer, *The New Vision in the German Arts*, Benn, London, 1924, p. 54.

15 H. Ihering, *Der Tag*, Berlin, 22 January 1920; reprinted in G. Rühle, op. cit., pp. 187–8.

16 *From Morning till Midnight*, p. 37.

17 O. Kokoschka, *Schriften 1907–1955*, Munich, 1956, p. 189.

18 *From Morning till Midnight*, p. 73.

19 Ibid., p. 54.

20 Diebold, op. cit., pp. 26–7.

21 G. Grosz, *Ein kleines Ja und ein grosses Nein*, Hamburg, 1955, p. 129.

22 I. Goll, 'Das Überdrama', *Die Unsterblichen*, Kiepenheuer, Potsdam, 1920, pp. 5–7, reprinted in Pörtner, op. cit., vol. 1, pp. 380–1.

23 See W. R. Fuerst and S. J. Hume, *Twentieth-Century Stage Decoration*, Dover Publications, New York, 1967, vol. 2, plates 337–40.

24 A. Winds, *Die Technik der Schauspielkunst*, Verlag Heinrich Minden, Dresden, 1904, pp. 34–5.

25 See p. 33.

26 F. Emmel, *Das ekstatische Theater*, Kampmann & Schnabel, Prien, 1924, p. 24.

27 Cit. A. Winds, *Geschichte der Regie*, Deutsche Verlags-Anstalt, Stuttgart, 1925, p. 136.

28 See pp. 37–8.

29 *From Morning till Midnight*, p. 63.

30 B. Kellermann, 'Japanische Schauspielkunst', *Theater-Kalender auf das Jahr 1912*, ed. Dr H. Landsberg and Dr A. Rundt, Oesterheld, Berlin, 1912, p. 45.

31 K. H. Martin, 'Bühne und Expressionismus', *Neue Hamburger Zeitung*, no. 230, 1918.

32 W. Turszinsky, 'Tilla Durieux', *Bühne und Welt*, vol. 12, 1910, p. 609.

33 Ibid., p. 606.

34 S. Jacobsohn, *Max Reinhardt*, Erich Reiss, Berlin, 1910, pp. 77–8.

35 S. Jacobsohn, 'Wegeners Othello', *Die Schaubühne*, no. 8, 1917, p. 182.

36 W. Hasenclever, 'Über das Tragische', *Menschen*, Dresden, 1921, vol. 4, no. 2, p. 18, reprinted in Pörtner, op. cit., vol. 1, p. 383.

37 W. H. Sokel, *The Writer in Extremis*, Stanford University Press, 1959, p. 39.

38 P. Kornfeld, *Die Verführung*, reprinted in *Zeit und Theater*, ed. G. Rühle, Propyläen Verlag, Berlin, n.d. (1973), vol. 1, p. 258.

39 P. Kornfeld, 'Nachwort an den Schauspieler', *Die Verführung*, Berlin, 1916, pp. 202–4, reprinted in Pörtner, op. cit., vol. 1, pp. 350–2.

40 B. Diebold, *Frankfurter Zeitung*, 10 December 1917, reprinted in G. Rühle, *Theater für die Republik*, pp. 93–4.

41 K. Edschmid, *Vossische Zeitung*, Berlin, 12 December 1917, reprinted in Rühle, *Theater für die Republik*, p. 95.

42 E. Faktor, *Berliner Börsen-Courier*, 4 March 1918, reprinted in Rühle, *Theater für die Republik*, p. 115.

43 Cf., e.g., M. Gordon, 'German Expressionist acting', *Drama Review*, New York, vol. 19, no. 3 (T-67), 1975, p. 46.

44 *From Morning till Midnight*, p. 36.

45 Ibid., p. 38.
46 H. Ihering, *Die zwanziger Jahre*, Berlin, 1948, p. 29.
47 *Josef-Kainz-Gedenkbuch*, ed. Benno Deutsch, Vienna, 1924, p. 52.
48 F. Sebrecht, *Die neue Schaubühne*, Berlin, 1919, no. 1, cit. M. Gordon, op. cit., pp. 36–7.
49 Walter von Hollander, 'Expressionismus des Schauspielers', *Die neue Rundschau*, vol. 28, 1917, no. 1, pp. 575–6.
50 Emmel, op. cit., p. 41.
51 Diebold, *Anarchie im Drama*, p. 27.
52 Ihering, *Die zwanziger Jahre*, p. 38.
53 H. Ihering, *Regie*, Hans von Hugo Verlag, Berlin, 1943, pp. 31–2.
54 *From Morning till Midnight*, pp. 41–2.
55 Ibid., p. 42.
56 Cit. W. Petzet, *Die Münchner Kammerspiele 1911–1972*, Verlag Kurt Desch, Munich, 1973, p. 130.
57 F. Engel, [*Berliner Tageblatt*, February 1919], Georg-Kaiser-Archive.
58 E. Faktor, [*Berliner Börsen-Courier*, February 1919], Georg-Kaiser-Archive.
59 A. Polgar, *Max Pallenberg*, Berlin, n.d., p. 22.
60 Anon., [February 1919], Georg-Kaiser-Archive.
61 S. Jacobsohn, 'Hölle Weg Erde', *Die Weltbühne*, no. 5, 1920, p. 150.
62 Ihering, *Regisseure und Bühnenmaler*, p. 19.
63 V. Barnowsky, 'Herr Stefan Grossmann', *Die Weltbühne*, no. 8, 1920, pp. 248–9.
64 J. Bab, *Schauspieler und Schauspielkunst*, Berlin, 1926, p. 190.
65 A. Klaar, [*Vossische Zeitung*, Berlin, April 1921], cit. G. Rühle, *Theater für die Republik*, p. 58.
66 F.S.-s.[(= Franz Servaes), *Lokal-Anzeiger*, Berlin, April 1921?], Georg-Kaiser-Archive.
67 E. Faktor, [*Berliner Börsen-Courier*, April 1921], Georg-Kaiser-Archive.
68 F. E. Schmidt, [Dresden, April 1922], Georg-Kaiser-Archive.
69 F. Mack, *Leipziger Neueste Nachrichten*, 6 October 1924.
70 H. Kubsch, *Deutsche Tageszeitung*, Berlin, 4 February 1925.
71 Anon., [February 1925], Georg-Kaiser-Archive.
72 S. Jacobsohn, 'Von morgens bis mitternachts', *Die Weltbühne*, no. 6, 1925, p. 208.
73 C. Hoffmann, [Dresden, October 1916], cit. G. Rühle, *Theater für die Republik*, p. 106.
74 F. Engel, *Berliner Tageblatt*, 24 December 1917, reprinted in Rühle, *Theater für die Republik*, p. 101.
75 Bab, op. cit., pp. 173–4.
76 Cit. G. Rühle, *Theater in unserer Zeit*, Suhrkamp, Frankfurt/Main, 1976, p. 62.
77 Cit. L. Richard, *Phaidon Encyclopaedia of Expressionism*, Phaidon, Oxford, 1978, p. 195.
78 L. Jessner, notes to his unpublished 'Theaterbuch', cit. H. Müllenmeister, 'Leopold Jessner: Geschichte eines Regiestils', Dr Phil. dissertation, Cologne, 1958, p. 40.

79 S. Jacobsohn, *Das Jahr der Bühne*, Berlin, 1919–20, p. 60.
80 N. Falk, *BZ am Mittag*, Berlin, 13 December 1919, reprinted in G. Rühle, *Theater für die Republik*, p. 197.
81 F. Servaes, *Lokal-Anzeiger*, Berlin, 13 March 1920.
82 K. T. Bluth, *Leopold Jessner*, Berlin, 1928, cit. G. Rühle, *Theater in unserer Zeit*, p. 62.
83 L. Jessner, 'Das Theater, ein Vortrag', *Die Szene*, Berlin, March 1928, p. 70.
84 See L. Müthel, 'Meine Zusammenarbeit mit Leopold Jessner', *Die Szene*, Berlin, 1928, p. 74.
85 Emmel, op. cit., p. 73.
86 Scheffauer, op. cit., p. 212.
87 L. Jessner, 'Heutige Bühnenmusik', *Die Szene*, 1925, p. 41.
88 A. Polgar, 'Shakespeare, Jessner und Kortner', *Die Weltbühne*, no. 3, 1922, p. 70.
89 H. Ihering, *Aktuelle Dramaturgie*, Verlag die Schmiede, Berlin, 1924, p. 61.
90 Polgar, op. cit., p. 71.
91 Jessner, 'Das Theater, ein Vortrag', p. 70.
92 Polgar, op. cit., p. 70.
93 Jessner, 'Das Theater, ein Vortrag', cit., p. 70.
94 Cit. G. Rühle, *Theater in unserer Zeit*, p. 62.

Chapter 4   Primitivist theatre

1 This incident is recounted almost verbatim in Act 2, Scene 1 of Toller's *Hoppla, wir leben!*
2 E. Toller, *Die Wandlung*, reprinted in G. Rühle, *Zeit und Theater*, Propyläen Verlag, Berlin, n.d. (1973), vol. 1, p. 525.
3 Ibid., p. 527.
4 E. Toller, *Quer durch Reisebilder und Reden*, Berlin, 1930, p. 280.
5 E. Toller, *Die literarische Welt*, no. 16, 1929, cit. G. Rühle, op. cit., p. 912.
6 K. H. Martin, cit. J. Bab, *Das Theater der Gegenwart*, Leipzig, 1928, p. 178.
7 K. H. Martin, Tribüne programme, September 1919, cit. W.-J. Schorlies, 'Karl Heinz Martin', Dr Phil. dissertation, Cologne, 1971, p. 77.
8 K. H. Martin, 'Die Bühne und ich', *Die vierte Wand*, Organ der deutschen Theaterausstellung, Magdeburg, 1927, nos 14–15 (Martin's italics).
9 *Die Wandlung*, p. 531.
10 Diebold, *Frankfurter Zeitung*, 29 November 1918, reprinted in G. Rühle, *Theater für die Republik*, S. Fischer, Frankfurt/Main, 1967, p. 127. Neppach is here mistakenly referred to as Reppach.
11 E. L. Stahl, *Neue Badische Landeszeitung*, Mannheim, 19 January 1918, reprinted in G. Rühle, *Theater für die Republik*, p. 109.
12 K. MacGowan and R. E. Jones, *Continental Stagecraft*, Harcourt, Brace, New York, 1922, p. 167.
13 W. R. Fuerst and S. J. Hume, *Twentieth-Century Stage Decoration*, Dover Publications, New York, 1967, vol. 1, p. 111.
14 A. Kerr, *Die Welt im Drama*, Cologne, 1954, p. 158.

15 S. Grossmann, *Vossische Zeitung*, Berlin, 1 October 1919.
16 Ibid.
17 E. Faktor, *Berliner Börsen-Courier*, 1 October 1919.
18 H. Ihering, *Der Tag*, Berlin, 2 October 1919.
19 K. Tucholsky, *Die Weltbühne*, no. 15, 1919, pp. 635f.
20 Faktor, op. cit.
21 E. Toller, *Die literarische Welt*, no. 16, 1929, cit. G. Rühle, *Zeit und Theater*, p. 912.
22 H. Ihering, *Die zwanziger Jahre*, Berlin, 1948, p. 48.
23 F. Kortner, *Aller Tage Abend*, Kindler, Munich, 1959, cit. G. Rühle, *Zeit und Theater*, pp. 910–11.
24 H. Ihering, *Der Tag*, Berlin, 2 October 1919.
25 H. Ihering, *Regisseure und Bühnenmaler*, Bibliophiler Verlag, Berlin-Wilmersdorf, 1921, p. 50.
26 H. Grosse, 'Die szenische Entwicklung in Beispielen', *Theater in der Weimarer Republik*, Kunstamt Kreuzberg und Institut für Theaterwissenschaft der Universität Köln, Berlin, 1977, p. 717.
27 MacGowan and Jones, op. cit., p. 148.
28 H. G. Scheffauer, *The New Vision in the German Arts*, Benn, London, 1924, p. 236.
29 This was the case with two Kaiser productions emanating from the Workshop Theatre of Leeds University. *Gas I* was described as 'profuse yet restrained, simple but spellbinding' (J. Peter, *Sunday Times*, 11 April 1976); for Alec Baron writing in the *Yorkshire Arts Bulletin*, April 1978, *From Morning till Midnight* produced 'one of the most exciting theatrical evenings in years'.

Chapter 5 Piscator's theatre

1 E. Piscator, *Das politische Theater* (1929), *Schriften*, Henschelverlag, Berlin, 1968, vol. 1, pp. 14–15.
2 L. Jessner, 'Das Theater, ein Vortrag', *Die Szene*, Berlin, March 1928, p. 66.
3 G. Rühle, *Theater in unserer Zeit*, Suhrkamp, Frankfurt/Main, 1976, p. 72.
4 Cit. Piscator, op.cit., p. 33.
5 Ibid., p. 24.
6 L. Schreyer, *Expressionistisches Theater*, Toth, Hamburg, 1948, p. 125.
7 Piscator, op. cit., p. 36.
8 Ibid., p. 52.
9 J. Rühle, *Theater und Revolution*, Deutscher Taschenbuch Verlag, Munich, 1963, p. 132.
10 Piscator, op. cit., p. 40.
11 Cit. Rühle, op. cit., p. 132.
12 Piscator, op. cit., p. 124.
13 *Rote Fahne*, 17 October 1920, in Piscator, op. cit., p. 43.
14 Piscator, op. cit., p. 71.
15 See pp. 26–7.

16 Statement by the management of the Volksbühne, March 1927, in Piscator, op. cit., p. 102.
17 F. Pfemfert, *Die Aktion*, cit. Piscator, op. cit., p. 120.
18 E. Piscator, 'Rechenschaft (1)', *Schriften*, vol. 2, p. 55.
19 Piscator, *Das politische Theater*, p. 245.
20 See p. 9.
21 See C. D. Innes, *Erwin Piscator's Political Theatre*, Cambridge University Press, 1972, pp. 16–18.
22 Piscator, *Das politische Theater*, p. 60.
23 Piscator, 'Über Grundlagen und Aufgaben des Proletarischen Theaters', *Schriften*, vol. 2, p. 12.
24 Cit. G. Rühle, op. cit., p. 167.
25 For a full account of this production see H. Rorrison, 'Piscator directs Schiller's *Die Räuber* at the Staatliches Schauspielhaus, Berlin', *Regie in Dokumentation, Forschung und Lehre*, ed. M. Dietrich, Otto Müller, Salzburg, 1975, pp. 168–75.
26 *Berliner Börsen-Courier*, 25 December 1926, cit. Piscator, *Das politische Theater*, p. 90.
27 Piscator, *Das politische Theater*, p. 85.
28 Ibid., p. 140.
29 Cf. ibid., p. 128.
30 Ibid., p. 40.
31 Ibid., p. 65.
32 B. Diebold, *Das Piscator-Drama*, cit. ibid., p. 173.
33 Piscator, *Das politische Theater*, p. 66.
34 Piscator, *Schriften*, vol. 2, p. 15.
35 F. Gasbarra, *Die Welt am Abend*, Berlin, January 1928, cit. Piscator, *Das politische Theater*, p. 191.
36 *Schriften*, vol. 2, p. 59.
37 *Das politische Theater*, p. 82.
38 Ibid., p. 83.
39 *Schriften*, vol. 2, p. 24.
40 Ibid., p. 29.
41 Ibid., p. 12.
42 *Das politische Theater*, p. 83.
43 Ibid., p. 84.
44 E. Piscator, 'Objective acting', *Actors on Acting*, ed. T. Cole and H. K. Chinoy, Crown Publishing, New York, 1949, p. 289.
45 H. Reimann, *Mein blaues Wunder*, Munich, 1959, pp. 401f.
46 S. Priacel, 'Meyerhold à Paris', *Monde*, ed. H. Barbusse, Paris, 7 July 1928.
47 Cf. F. Sternberg, *Der Dichter und die Ratio*, Sachse & Pohl, Göttingen, p. 33, cit. J. Willett, *The Theatre of Erwin Piscator*, Methuen, London, 1978, p. 120.
48 Piscator, *Das politische Theater*, p. 198.
49 E. Piscator, 'Tai Yang erwacht', *Blätter der Piscatorbühne*, 15 January 1931, reprinted in *Schriften*, vol. 2, p. 81.
50 *Das politische Theater*, pp. 69–70.

51 *Das politische Theater*, revised edn., Rowohlt, Reinbek bei Hamburg, 1963, pp. 48–9.
52 See pp. 159–60.
53 *Das politische Theater*, p. 272.
54 *Schriften*, vol. 2, p. 15.
55 *Das politische Theater*, p. 24.
56 Ibid., p. 147.
57 E. Toller, *Quer durch*, Kiepenheuer, Potsdam, 1939, p. 292.
58 *Das politische Theater*, pp. 148–9.
59 E. Toller, *Hoppla, wir leben!*, reprinted in G. Rühle, *Zeit und Theater*, Propyläen Verlag, Berlin, n.d. (1973), vol. 2, pp. 162–3.
60 Ibid., p. 186.
61 Ibid., p. 163. Cf. P. Weiss, *Marat/Sade*, Suhrkamp, Frankfurt/Main, 1964, pp. 85f.
62 E. Piscator, 'Regiebuch zu Tollers *Hoppla, wir leben!*', unpublished MS; original in Akademie der Künste, East Berlin; photocopy here referred to in Akademie der Künste, West Berlin.
63 *Das politische Theater*, p. 148.
64 Cf. H. Rorrison, op. cit., pp. 173f.
65 W. Kuhlke, 'Introduction to Alexander Tairov, *Notes of a Director*', University of Miami Press, 1969, p. 36.
66 R. F. Müller, 'Die neue russische Bühne', *Katalog Programm Almanach*, ed. F. Kiesler, Internationale Ausstellung neuer Theatertechnik, Theaterfest der Stadt Wien, 1924, pp. 68–80.
67 E. Piscator, 'Was ich will', *Berliner Tageblatt*, 6 April 1927; reprinted in *Schriften*, vol. 2, p. 24.
68 *Das politische Theater*, pp. 149–50 (Piscator's italics).
69 R. Grimm, 'Zwischen Expressionismus und Faschismus', *Die sogenannten zwanziger Jahre*, ed. R. Grimm and J. Hermand, Gehlen, Bad Homburg, 1970, pp. 35–6.
70 *Das politische Theater*, p. 151.
71 Anon., *Das Theater*, vol. 8, no. 18, September 1927, p. 441.
72 *Das politische Theater*, pp. 68–9.
73 P. Fechter, *Deutsche Allgemeine Zeitung*, Berlin, 6 September 1927, reprinted in G. Rühle, *Theater für die Republik*, S. Fischer, Frankfurt/Main, 1967, p. 797.
74 B. Brecht, *Exstrabladet*, Copenhagen, 20 March 1934, cit. J. Willett, *Brecht on Theatre*, Methuen, London, 1964, p. 66.
75 First programme of the Proletarisches Theater, October 1920; reprinted in *Das politische Theater*, p. 34.
76 Cit. J. Rühle, op. cit., p. 157.
77 E. Schumacher, *Die dramatischen Versuche Bertolt Brechts 1918–1933*, Rütten & Loening, Berlin, 1955, p. 136.
78 Cf. G. Rühle, *Theater für die Republik*, S. Fischer, Frankfurt/Main, 1967, p. 1063.
79 Personal communication by Professor Huder, October 1978.

Chapter 6   Brecht's epic theatre

1   B. Brecht, *Augsburger Volkswille*, 14 December 1920; reprinted in *Schriften zum Theater*, ed. W. Hecht, Suhrkamp, Frankfurt/Main, vol. 1, 1963, pp. 49–50 (hereafter abbreviated to ST, followed by volume and page numbers). All translations are my own and are Copyright © Stefan S. Brecht 1981.

2   B. Brecht, *Stücke*, Aufbau Verlag, Berlin, vol. 1, 1955, p. 203.

3   B. Brecht, 'Über den Expressionismus', notebook, [1920]; ST 2;9.

4   K. Edschmid, 'Über den dichterischen Expressionismus', *Frühe Manifeste*, Luchterhand, Darmstadt, 1960, p. 33.

5   'Über den Expressionismus'; ST 2;9.

6   'Dem fünfzigjährigen Georg Kaiser', *Berliner Börsen-Courier*, 24 November 1928; ST 1;128.

7   *Augsburger Volkswille*, 26 March 1920; ST 1;14–15.

8   Notebook, 17 June 1921; ST 2;26–7.

9   'Über den Expressionismus'; ST 2;9.

10   'Schminken'; ST 4;37–8.

11   Cf., e.g., R. Hayman, 'Brecht in the English theatre', *The German Theatre*, ed. R. Hayman, Wolff, London, 1975, pp. 202f.

12   'Das Theater als sportliche Anstalt', notebook, [1920]; ST 2;14.

13   *Berliner Börsen-Courier*, 6 February 1926; ST 1;62.

14   The first full statement, and probably the clearest, of Brecht's conception of epic theatre was set down in 1930 as notes to *Mahagonny*; see ST 2;109–26. Translated by J. Willett as 'The modern theatre is epic theatre', *Brecht on Theatre*, Methuen, London, 1964, pp. 33–42.

15   Notebook, 1 September 1920; ST 2;18–19.

16   'Die Beleuchtung'; ST 5;265.

17   ST 1;204–5.

18   Lenin, *On Culture and the Cultural Revolution*, Moscow, 1970, pp. 147–9.

19   See 'Über reimlose Lyrik mit unregelmässigen Rhythmen', *Das Wort*, Moscow, 1939, no. 3; cf. J. Willett, op. cit., pp. 119–20.

20   'Der Anlass neuer Bewegungen'; ST 3;125.

21   'Die Übernahme des bürgerlichen Theaters'; ST 3;121.

22   See pp. 49–50.

23   'Realistisches Theater und Illusion'; ST 3;37.

24   E. Bond, 'On Brecht: a letter to Peter Holland', *Theatre Quarterly*, vol. 8, no. 30, Summer 1978, p. 34.

25   B. Brecht, *Man equals Man*, trans. G. Nellhaus; in Bertolt Brecht, *Collected Plays*, ed. J. Willett and R. Mannheim, Methuen, London, vol. 2, part 1, 1979, p. 11. All quotations are taken from this translation.

26   'Vorrede zu *Mann ist Mann*', April 1927; ST 2;85.

27   *Man equals Man*, p. 76.

28   Bertolt-Brecht-Archive 1340/95.

29   John Willett and Ralph Mannheim are incorrect in their assertion that the last two scenes had already been omitted in the 1928 production (Introduction to *Man equals Man*, p. xii). Cf. Brecht's own statement on p. 108 of this edition and also Herbert Ihering's review of the 1928 production, *Berliner Börsen-*

Courier, 5 January 1928, reprinted in G. Rühle, *Theater für die Republik*, S. Fischer, Frankfurt/Main, 1967, p. 1070. For a detailed analysis of Brecht's repeated revisions of the play see *Man equals Man*, pp. 109–38.

30 *Man equals Man*, p. 38.
31 'Anmerkungen zur Oper *Aufstieg und Fall der Stadt Mahagonny*', [1930]; ST 2;117.
32 *Man equals Man*, pp. 42 and 44.
33 Ibid., p. 40.
34 Ibid., p. 52.
35 Ibid., p. 53.
36 Ibid., p. 58.
37 Ibid., p. 60.
38 'Die Gesänge'; ST 5;266.
39 'Über experimentelles Theater', [4 May 1939]; ST 3;101.
40 'Kurze Beschreibung einer neuen Technik der Schauspielkunst, die einen Verfremdungseffekt hervorbringt', [1940]; ST 3;155–6.
41 J. Geis, 'Meine Inszenierung von Bertolt Brechts *Mann ist Mann*', *Die Szene*, Berlin, vol. 16, 1926, pp. 300–1.
42 H. Ihering, *Regie*, Hans von Hugo Verlag, Berlin, 1943, p. 59.
43 *Arnolt Bronnen gibt zu Protokoll*, Hamburg, 1954, p. 98; cit. J. Willett, *The Theatre of Bertolt Brecht*, Methuen, London, 1959, p. 154.
44 Cf. Bertolt-Brecht-Archive 936/14.
45 P. Szondi, *Theorie des modernen Dramas*, Suhrkamp, Frankfurt/Main, 1966, p. 16.
46 'Die Vorhänge'; ST 5;264–5.
47 *Man equals Man*, p. 71.
48 Bertolt-Brecht-Archive 2219/1–69.
49 'Das Nötigste ist genug'; ST 3;240.
50 Bertolt-Brecht-Archive 2219/2.
51 ST 3;242.
52 ST 3;242–3.
53 Bertolt-Brecht-Archive 1089.
54 See *Man equals Man*, pp. 120–1.
55 'Anmerkungen zum Lustspiel *Mann ist Mann*', [1931]; ST 2;72–3. I have used the translation given in *Man equals Man*, p. 103.
56 'Über die Kargheit'; ST 3;239.
57 H. Ihering, *Berliner Börsen-Courier*, 5 January 1928, reprinted in G. Rühle, *Theater für die Republik*, p. 1070.
58 A. Kuckhoff, *Die Volksbühne*, Berlin, 13 January 1928.
59 Bertolt-Brecht-Archive 331/01.
60 For the text of the 1931 ending of the play, see *Man equals Man*, p. 133.
61 B. Diebold, *Frankfurter Zeitung*, 11 February 1931.
62 *Man equals Man*, p. 106.
63 Ibid., p. 53.
64 B. Diebold, *Frankfurter Zeitung*, 27 September 1926; reprinted in G. Rühle, *Theater für die Republik*, p. 731.
65 See 'Die Sichtbarkeit der Lichtquellen'; ST 3;241.

66 See pp. 101–2.
67 In the programme of this production, after it had transferred to the Theater am Bülowplatz, Berlin, Hiobja is described as Begbick's sister, but this is probably a typographical error. See Bertolt-Brecht-Archive 1383/07.
68 'Kunst als Veranstaltung', Bertolt-Brecht-Archive 158/15.
69 R. Fernau, *Uraufführung von Bert Brecht 'Baal' am 8. Dezember 1923 im alten Leipziger Stadttheater*, Friedenauer Presse, Berlin, 1971, pp. 5–6.
70 Ibid., pp. 23–4.
71 P. Kornfeld, 'Nachwort an den Schauspieler', *Die Verführung*, Berlin, 1916, pp. 202–4; reprinted in P. Pörtner, *Literatur-Revolution 1910–1925*, Luchterhand, Darmstadt, 1960, vol. 1, p. 352.
72 'Die Strassenszene', [1938]; ST 5;72.
73 Ibid., 5;78–9.
74 Cf., e.g., ST 3;102ff.
75 'Anweisungen an die Schauspieler'; ST 4;33.
76 See ST 3;168.
77 ST 4;50.
78 *Man equals Man*, p. 3.
79 Ibid., p. 4.
80 Ibid., p. 8.
81 Ibid., p. 14.
82 Ibid., p. 22.
83 'Kurze Beschreibung einer neuen Technik der Schauspielkunst', [1940]; ST 3;161.
84 *Man equals Man*, p. 4.
85 'Mehr guten Sport!'; ST 1;64.
86 ST 4;8.
87 W. Wauer, 'Der Schauspieler', *Katalog Programm Almanach*, ed. F. Kiesler, Internationale Ausstellung neuer Theatertechnik, Theaterfest der Stadt Wien, 1924, p. 20.
88 'Über rationellen und emotionellen Standpunkt'; ST 3;26.
89 'Was arbeiten Sie?', interview, 30 July 1926; ST 2;269.
90 'Betrachtungen über die Schwierigkeiten des epischen Theaters', *Frankfurter Zeitung*, 27 November 1927; ST 1;186.
91 'Über rationellen und emotionellen Standpunkt'; ST 3;25.
92 'Anmerkungen zur *Mutter*'; ST 2;185.
93 'Über experimentelles Theater', [1939]; ST 3;99.
94 Cf. ST 3;117 and 3;157.
95 'Kleine Liste der beliebtesten, landläufigsten und banalsten Irrtümer über das epische Theater'; ST 3;70.
96 'Kleines Privatissimum für meinen Freund Max Gorelik', [June 1944]; ST 3;263.
97 'Dialog über Schauspielkunst', *Berliner Börsen-Courier*, 17 February 1929; ST 1;214.
98 See 'Beziehung des Schauspielers zu seinem Publikum'; ST 4;30.
99 *Man equals Man*, p. 5.
100 Ibid., p. 52.

101 Ibid., p. 54.
102 'Über experimentelles Theater' [1939]; ST 3;97–8.
103 'Anmerkungen zu *Mahagonny*' [1930]; ST 2;116.
104 'Anmerkungen zur *Dreigroschenoper*' [1931]; ST 2;96–7.
105 'Kurze Beschreibung einer neuen Technik der Schauspielkunst', [1940]; ST 3;167–8.
106 'Über die Verwendung von Musik für ein episches Theater'; ST 3;270–1.
107 See J. Willett, *Brecht on Theatre*, p. 42.
108 ST 4;31.
109 See G. E. Lessing, *Hamburgische Dramaturgie*, 12 May 1767.
110 'Kurze Beschreibung einer neuen Technik der Schauspielkunst'; ST 3;157–8.
111 'Anweisungen an die Schauspieler'; ST 4;32.
112 Cf., e.g., M. Argyle, *The Psychology of Interpersonal Behaviour*, Penguin Books, Harmondsworth, 1967; D. Morris, *Manwatching: A Field Guide to Human Behaviour*, Triad Panther, London, n.d.
113 Anon., 'Berliner Theaterwinter 1930/31', *Die literarische Welt*, Berlin, no. 24, 1931; Bertolt-Brecht-Archive 463/74–8.
114 A. Kerr, *Berliner Tageblatt*, 7 February 1931, reprinted G. Rühle, *Theater für die Republik*, p. 1076.
115 B.W., review of 7 February 1931; reprinted Rühle, *Theater für die Republik*, p. 1072.
116 H. Ihering, *Berliner Börsen-Courier*, 7 February 1931, reprinted Rühle, *Theater für die Republik*, p. 1074.
117 *Man equals Man*, p. 104.
118 Bertolt-Brecht-Archive 331/01.
119 *Man equals Man*, p. 105.
120 Ibid., p. 105.
121 'Anweisungen an die Schauspieler'; ST 4;34.
122 *Man equals Man*, p. 107.
123 E. Burri, 'Anmerkungen zu den Proben von *Mann ist Mann*', programme of *Mann ist Mann*, Staatliches Schauspielhaus, Berlin, 6 February 1931; Bertolt-Brecht-Archive 1089.

Conclusion

1 G. Kaiser, *Five Plays*, trans. B. J. Kenworthy, R. Last and J. M. Ritchie, Calder & Boyars, London, 1971, p. 240.
2 See D. Bair, *Samuel Beckett*, Jonathan Cape, London, 1978, pp. 236 and 332.
3 G. Rühle, *Theater in unserer Zeit*, Suhrkamp, Frankfurt/Main, 1976, p. 81.
4 S. Beckett, *Comédie et actes divers*, Editions de Minuit, Paris, 1966, p. 9.
5 Cit. R. Hayman, *Artaud and After*, Oxford University Press, 1977, p. 89.
6 J. Grotowski, *Towards a Poor Theatre*, Methuen, London, 1969, p. 16.
7 B. Brecht, 'Die Not des Theaters', 1928; *Schriften zum Theater*, Suhrkamp, Frankfurt/Main, vol. 1, 1963, p. 116.
8 A. Polgar, 'Shakespeare, Jessner und Kortner', *Die Weltbühne*, no. 3, 1922, p. 69.

Select bibliography

Bablet, Denis, *Les Révolutions scéniques du vingtième siècle*, Internationale d'Art Vingtième Siècle, Paris, 1975.

Brecht, Bertolt, *Schriften zum Theater*, ed. W. Hecht, Suhrkamp, Frankfurt/Main, 7 vols, 1963–4.

Brecht, Bertolt, *Brecht on Theatre*, trans. and ed. John Willett, Methuen, London, 1964.

Brecht, Bertolt, *Collected Plays*, ed. J. Willett and R. Mannheim, Methuen, London (vols 1, 2 and 7 published; remainder in preparation).

Calandra, Denis, 'Georg Kaiser's *From Morn to Midnight*: the nature of Expressionist performance', *Theatre Quarterly*, vol. 6, no. 21, spring 1976, pp. 45–54.

Diebold, Bernhard, *Anarchie im Drama*, Frankfurter Verlags-Anstalt, Frankfurt/Main, 1921.

Emmel, Felix, *Das ekstatische Theater*, Kampmann & Schnabel, Prien, 1924.

Fuerst, Walter René, and Samuel J. Hume, *Twentieth-Century Stage Decoration*, Dover Publications, New York, 2 vols, 1967.

Gordon, Mel, 'German Expressionist acting', *Drama Review*, New York, vol. 19, no. 3 (T-67), September 1975, pp. 34–50.

Hern, Nicholas, 'The theatre of Ernst Toller', *Theatre Quarterly*, vol. 2, no. 5, January–March 1972, pp. 72–92.

Hern, Nicholas, 'Expressionism', *The German Theatre*, ed. R. Hayman, Oswald Wolff, London, 1975.

Innes, C. D., *Erwin Piscator's Political Theatre*, Cambridge University Press, 1972.

Kaiser, Georg, *Five Plays*, trans. B. J. Kenworthy, Rex Last and J. M. Ritchie, Calder & Boyars, London, 1971.

Kane, Martin, 'Erwin Piscator's 1927 production of *Hoppla, We're Alive!*', *Performance and Politics in Popular Drama*, ed. D. Bradby, L. James and B. Sharratt, Cambridge University Press, 1980.

Knellessen, Friedrich Wolfgang, *Agitation auf der Bühne: Das politische Theater der Weimarer Republik*, Lechte, Emsdetten, 1970.

MacGowan, Kenneth and Robert Edmond Jones, *Continental Stagecraft*, Harcourt, Brace, New York, 1922.

Pascal, Roy, *From Naturalism to Expressionism: German Literature and Society 1880–1918*, Weidenfeld & Nicolson, London, 1973.

Pasley, Malcolm (ed.), *Germany: A Companion to German Studies*, Methuen, London, 1972.

Piscator, Erwin, *Schriften*, Henschelverlag, Berlin, 2 vols, 1968.

Piscator, Erwin, *The Political Theatre*, trans. Hugh Rorrison, Eyre Methuen, London, 1980.

Pörtner, Paul (ed.), *Literatur-Revolution 1910–1925*, Luchterhand, Darmstadt, 2 vols, 1960.

Raabe, Paul (ed.), and J. M. Ritchie (trans.), *The Era of German Expressionism*, Calder & Boyars, London, 1974.

Richard, Lionel (ed.), *Phaidon Encyclopaedia of Expressionism*, Phaidon, Oxford, 1978.

Ritchie, J. M., *German Expressionist Drama*, Twayne Publishers, Boston, 1976.

Ritchie, J. M., and H. F. Garten (trans.), *Seven Expressionist Plays*, Calder & Boyars, London, 1968.

Ritchie, J. M., and R. W. Last, 'Expressionist drama in English: a bibliography', *New German Studies*, vol. 6, no. 1, spring 1978, pp. 59–70.

Ritchie, J. M. and J. D. Stowell (trans.), *Vision and Aftermath: Four Expressionist War Plays*, Calder & Boyars, London, 1969.

Rorrison, Hugh, 'Piscator's production of *Hoppla, wir leben!*', *Theatre Quarterly*, vol. 10, no. 37, spring 1980, pp. 30–41.

Rühle, Günther, *Theater in unserer Zeit*, Suhrkamp, Frankfurt/Main, 1976.

Rühle, Günther (ed.), *Theater für die Republik 1917–1933 im Spiegel der Kritik*, S. Fischer, Frankfurt/Main, 1967.

Rühle, Günther, *Zeit und Theater: Vom Kaiserreich zur Republik, 1913–1925*, Propyläen Verlag, Berlin, 2 vols, n.d. (1973).

Scheffauer, Herman George, *The New Vision in the German Arts*, Benn, London, 1924.

Schumacher, Ernst, *Die dramatischen Versuche Bertolt Brechts 1918–1933*, Rütten & Loening, Berlin, 1955.

Schürer, Ernst (ed.), *Von morgens bis mitternachts: Erläuterungen und Dokumente*, Reclam, Stuttgart, 1975.

Sokel, Walter H., *The Writer in Extremis: Expressionism in Twentieth-Century German Literature*, Stanford University Press, 1959.

Sokel, Walter H. (ed.), *An Anthology of German Expressionist Drama: A Prelude to the Absurd*, Anchor Books, New York, 1963.

Theater in der Weimarer Republik, Kunstamt Kreuzberg und Institut für Theaterwissenschaft der Universität Köln, Berlin, 1977.

Toller, Ernst, *Seven Plays*, trans. Edward Crankshaw and others, John Lane, London, 1935.

Völker, Klaus, *Brecht Chronicle*, Seabury Press, New York, 1975.

Willett, John, *The Theatre of Bertolt Brecht: A Study from Eight Aspects*, Methuen, London, 1959.

Willett, John, *Expressionism*, Weidenfeld & Nicolson, London, 1970.

Willett, John, *The New Sobriety 1917–1933: Art and Politics in the Weimar Period*, Thames & Hudson, London, 1978.

Willett, John, *The Theatre of Erwin Piscator*, Methuen, London, 1978.

Wyss, Monika (ed.), *Brecht in der Kritik*, Kindler, Munich, 1977.

Index

The Revolution in German Theatre
1900–1933

Theatre Production Studies

Editor
John Russell Brown
School of English and American Studies,
University of Sussex